To my beloved teachers

&

my family

Language Form, Meaning
and the Language Learner

Language Form, Meaning and the Language Learner

语言的形式、意义与语言学习者

常新萍◎著

中山大學出版社
SUN YAT-SEN UNIVERSITY PRESS
·广州·

图书在版编目（CIP）数据

语言的形式、意义与语言学习者 = Language Form, Meaning and the Language Learner：英文/常新萍著. —广州：中山大学出版社，2014. 7

ISBN 978 -7 -306 -04927 -8

Ⅰ. ①语…　Ⅱ. ①常…　Ⅲ. ①第二语言—研究—英文　Ⅳ. ①H003

中国版本图书馆 CIP 数据核字（2014）第 115145 号

出 版 人：徐　劲
策划编辑：熊锡源
责任编辑：熊锡源
封面设计：林绵华
责任校对：林彩云
责任技编：何雅涛
出版发行：中山大学出版社
电　　话：编辑部 020 -84111996，84113349，84111997，84110779
　　　　　发行部 020 -84111998，84111981，84111160
地　　址：广州市新港西路 135 号
邮　　编：510275　　　　传　真：020 -84036565
网　　址：http：//www. zsup. com. cn　E-mail：zdcbs@ mail. sysu. edu. cn
印 刷 者：虎彩印艺股份有限公司
规　　格：880mm ×1230mm　1/32　　11. 375 印张　　377 千字
版次印次：2014 年 7 月第 1 版　　2014 年 7 月第 1 次印刷
印　　数：1 ～ 1000 册　　定　　价：35. 00 元

前　言

第二语言发展过程涉及的因素纷繁复杂，且各因素内部或自成体系，或与其他因素交织互动，形成更具影响力的动态系统，并以不同方式影响着第二语言习得的过程和效果。应用语言学家 Diane Larsen-Freeman (1997) 曾经把第二语言习得研究与基于自然科学研究的复杂性理论（complexity theory）和混沌理论 (chaos theory) 联系在一起来尝试解读第二语言习得过程中的非线性特征。由此我们看到，虽然世界上千千万万的人在学习和研究第二语言发展过程，然而至今，它对于学习者和研究者而言仍然是一个难解之谜。本书正是针对这个谜团所做的一个尝试性探索。

本研究从十多年前就逐渐开展，其主题和内容融合了我个人感兴趣的多个话题。作为外语学习者和研究者，一直以来我最为着迷的问题就是：同样是语言，为什么我们学习第二语言的时候就会显得那么困难？为什么不同的语言符号会带给我们那么大的交际障碍？第二语言学习过程到底有什么因素在起作用？语言的表现形式与它的意义的关系在学习过程中是如何体现出来的？各种影响学习的因素又是如何互相交织影响到学习过程的？作为学习过程主体的学习者在这个过程中扮演的是怎样的角色？等等。这类问题长期凝结不散，推动着一代又一代的研究工作者步步深入。本研究也是对这类基础问题探讨的一种尝试。

本书所谈到的语言的形式指的是语言的外在表现，如语言的发音、拼写、单项词汇和句子结构等。如英语中“It is cold today.”这个句子，如果我们纯粹从形式上看，看到的是四个单词组成的简单句子，听到的是/it iz 'kəuld tə'dei/的发音。但是，这个句子的意义在使用中却会带来不同的效果，因为除了符号本身的意义，它还有在使用中的具体语境的意义，即语用意义。语言的意义产生于语言符号与语境在使用中的互动过程。由此，我们这里谈到的意义是语言使用者结合具体语境选择形式和概念进行组织而构成的结构在使用中产生的意义。除此之外，无论我们对语言如何精细地研究，然而，当我们把语言学理论用于解读第二语言发展时就会发现，没有对学习者作为完整的人的理解和关注，就很难真正理解第二语言的学习过程，因为学习者才是整个学习过程的主体参加者。因此，第二语言学习过程研究如果没有对语言学习者相关因素的关注，就会感觉与我们的实际语言学习过程有很远的距离。正是基于此种想法才引出了本书的标题。

本书的主要读者对象是对第二语言学习过程感兴趣的研究工作者、教师和学生。写作角度尝试把第二语言习得领域中的基础问题诸如隐性学习与明晰学习、以规则为基础的学习与以意义为基础的学习等过程与应用语言学中长期关注的能力、知识等概念，通过实际研究概念框架结合起来讨论，以期对第二语言发展过程中的各种因素交织关系和影响有一定的解读，从而启发和推进中国环境下的外语教学课堂干预模式探讨。

本书以报告一个研究项目为切入点展开讨论，共涵盖八章内容。虽然整本书内部内容联系紧密，但读者若对不同方面感兴趣，也可以单独分章阅读。第一章主要是对本书基本主题和主要概念及布局的介绍。第二章主要围绕着语言能力内容的演变展开讨论，从语言学和应用语言学的不同角度详细探讨了第二语言学习过程中所追求的语言能力的本质。第三章则注重从第二语言习得过程出发，分析了基于不同角度对第二语言习得过程的各种解释以及这个过程所涉及到的各种因素，并结合本书所汇报的研究中涉及的主要因素进行了讨论。第四章是在第二、三章讨论的基础上提出了一个指导本书汇报的一项研究的理论框架。该框架以图示方式勾勒了影响第二语言学习过程中内外各种主要因素之间的关系以及不同互动方式产生的不同结果，同时也可以作为今后课堂语言实践中的课堂干预理论指导框架。第五、六章重点汇报了基于这个理论框架而开展的一项具体实证研究的设计和发现。该研究是在理论指导下的一项涉及面较广的针对中国青少年英语学习者的课堂学习过程和效果的深层调查分析研究。第七章针对这项研究所提出的具体问题、假设以及研究发现展开理论讨论。本书的最后一章第八章一方面对本书的研究内容和发现进行了归纳和总结，另一方面，讨论了本研究成果对英语课堂干预方式及对第二语言习得过程理解方面带来的启发，并在此基础上提出了可行性操作建议。该章还对全书主题进行了总结。

本书的写作过程由于各种繁杂工作而不得不反复中断，推延至今。但是，凡事都有利弊。可能正是由于没有速成，才使得我有机会对一些问题反复思考、研读，从而使得自己的一些想法更趋成熟。不求完美，但求进步。本书在成稿过程中得到了来自多方面的启发和帮助。感谢书中所引文献的作者所给予的各种启迪。由衷感激曾经培养过和帮助过我的许许多多师长们，他们的教诲已经融入此书的字里行间。感谢曾经给予我无私帮助的同学和朋友们，许多感激已经在鸣谢（Acknowledgements）部分一一列出，此处不再赘述。同时，感谢同事廖海青教授对此书出版所给予的支持。除此之外，非常感谢出版社的责任编辑熊锡源先生以及编排人员为本书的出版所付出的努力。本书虽几经修改，但限于水平，舛误之处、言未尽意之处在所难免，敬请读者批评指正。

写作作为语言产生的过程之一实际上是一个不断探索、发现、自我修正和学习提升的过程。直到这一刻，我依然对自己的作品不甚满意，但是也不得不强行暂停于某一个思维点上，靠读者的理解和智慧来补充了。

常新萍
2014年4月22日
于中山大学康乐园

Acknowledgements

This book grew out of my Ph. D. thesis (Chang, 1996), which was completed at Guangdong University of Foreign Studies, Guangzhou. An enormous debt is owed to my supervisor, Professor Li Xiaoju (李筱菊), for her enlightening instruction, wisdom, encouragement, stimulating and critical comments, and prompt help and care in my Ph. D. years. Her enduring insights about language and language learning have profoundly influenced this work in innumerable ways.

My deep gratitude also goes to Professor Gui Shichun (桂诗春) who leads me into the applied linguistics field, instills in me a deep respect for the complexities of linguistic data patterns and research methodology, and shares his deep insights through his enlightening instruction with incredible generosity. I am also grateful for his spearheading the empirical research orientation of applied linguistics in China which has inspired interest in and research on second language acquisition on which this work is based.

Thanks are extended to Professor He Ziran (何自然) for his enthusiasm in leading us to the readings of linguistic philosophy in the 20th century; to Professor Xu Luomai (许罗迈) for his instruction and training in my computer programming, Professor Li Shaoshan (李绍山), Dr. Chen Siqing (陈思清), Professor Li Wei (李崴) for their instruction in statistics; to Professor Ning Chunyan (宁春岩) and Professor Wang Chuming (王初明) for their valuable suggestions in the research process. Special thanks go to Professor Wu Xudong (吴旭东) for his generous help and valuable advice in the statistical analyses.

I would also like to record here their names and express my

special thanks here to the panel committee for my Ph. D. dissertation whose gracious encouragement, valuable comments and suggestions have been encouraging me ever since to keep on working on this field and finally lead me to the decision of turning what I have done into a monograph. They are: Professor Gui Shichun (桂诗春), Professor Qin Xiubai (秦秀白), Professor Xiao Huiyun (肖惠云), Professor Xiao Jiewen (肖洁文), and Professor Ning Chunyan (宁春岩). Their questions, comments and suggestions have been inspiring me to move further ever since.

I was fortunate enough to have very intelligent and kind classmates and friends whose generous help I have been always grateful for. I am grateful to Zeng Yongqiang (曾用强) and Du Jinbang (杜金榜) for their critical advice, to Wen Bingli (温宾利) for his help in contacting the related personnel in the City Education Bureau, to Yao Nan (姚楠) and Hu Xiaoqong (胡晓琼) for their generous help with the scoring procedures in the experiment, and to Ms. Julia Ponsford for her advice in my devising of the writing tasks in the experiment.

I would also like to express my deep and sincere thanks to Mr. Lu Zonggan (鲁宗干) and Mr. Huang Zicheng (黄子诚) of the City Education Bureau and the teachers and students at the schools, i. e. School No. 2, School No. 28, and School No. 11, where the experiment and the investigation were carried out. Without their cooperation, this research would have been surely impossible.

Finally, my deepest gratitude also goes to my parents, my parents-in-law and my own family, who managed to take pride and pleasure in my work even though it has meant time away from them. I have been fortunate beyond words to have enjoyed the love, support, encouragement, wisdom, and laughter of my mother, my husband, my little son, and my other family members.

Preface

Second language acquisition (SLA) has been a discipline of deep mystery and enchantment ever since its inception. Although much has been learned about it, a clear understanding of this "complex, dynamic non-linear process" (Larsen-Freeman, 1997) is still far from us. The complexity of SLA process can be perceived from the proposed factors such as the source language, the target language, the amount and type of input, the amount and type of interaction, the amount and type of feedback, the cognitive styles of the learner, age, motivations, learning strategies, interests, the instructor factors, the social and cultural contexts, etc. and various ways of interactions among them. It is just because of this complexity that renders this field so much enduring appeal.

This book is an exploration of the interrelationship among some of the identified factors and how the different interactions among the factors work to facilitate or inhibit EFL learners' acquisition of the targeted language system on the basis of an empirical study of a group of Chinese EFL learners in Guangzhou. The focus of the discussion in this book is centered around the nature of the latent knowledge that the learners under study have constructed and how different types of input together with other factors exert their impact on the learners' final attainment.

The research reported in the book was motivated by the following considerations. Firstly, second language acquisition research is in want of a better understanding of whether, when and how learning takes place among different groups of learners' learning processes and the role the EFL learners' attained knowledge plays in their pragmatic use. An investigation into the nature of Chinese EFL learners' English language attainment can provide further evidence to assist our understanding in this regard and help us pinpoint the problems of different sources involved in the learning process. Secondly, it was motivated by the paucity of studies on EFL learning in Chinese secondary schools (*Henceforth* CSS) and by the urgent need to determine the status quo of the teaching and learning in CSS so as to propose constructive suggestions for classroom practice in CSS.

The data employed in this book come from two parts in the research, i.e. an experiment which aims to examine the learners' performance in contextualized tasks and decontextualized tasks, and a follow-up investigation into the learning experiences of the same group of participants. The research was conducted based on a working conceptual framework which hypothesizes the possible relationships among different types of learning process, performance and possible factors undergirding the learning processes. The framework assumes that learners' differences in their language performance are brought about by the different types of knowledge represented in their minds which result from the different interacting factors in the learning process.

This book aims at sketching a rough picture of the secondary school EFL learning in China, diagnosing some of the problems in these schools, and exploring how the factors under study work together to manipulate the trajectory of the learners' second language development. It is hoped that the findings of the study and the discussion carried out in the book can spark further research and more thinking around Chinese EFL teaching and learning at different levels.

Contents

List of Figures

List of Tables

LIST OF ABBREVIATIONS

ADJRCG:	recognition of the forms of comparative and superlative degrees of adjectives and adverbs
ADJRCL:	recalling of the forms of comparative and superlative degrees of adjectives and adverbs
Aexp:	expect to learn English well
Affect1:	talking with others about one's own feeling in learning
Affect2:	constantly encouraging oneself in learning English
Alike:	like English
Aprepr:	always prepare for English class
ATITD:	total scores for attitude variables
CA:	the Communicative Approach
CAC:	Cognitive and affective capacity
CC:	Communicative Competence
CCP:	CC-based performance
Cogn1:	training mental processes by summarizing ideas in reading
Cogn2:	training mental processes by attempting to understand materials directly in English
Comspt1:	compensating with gestures when failing to converse
Compst2:	compensating by guessing when failing to understand
DC:	Discourse Competence
E1:	exposure in listening
E2:	exposure in reading
E3:	exposure in speaking
E4:	exposure in writing
EFL:	English as a Foreign Language
ELK:	Explicit Linguistic Knowledge
ESP:	English for Specific Purposes
EXPTL:	total scores for outside classroom language exposure
FLL:	Foreign Language Learning

GC: Grammatical Competence
GCP: GC-based Performance
GL: the grammatical forms and lexical items needed to encode the essential ideas contained in the WT
ILK: Implicit Linguistic Knowledge
KT: Knowledge Task (i.e. the decontextualized task)
KTCONT: the basic grammatical concepts in the KT
KTFCT: the function words in the KT
KTMPH: the morphological forms in the KT
KTPRON: the pronouns in the KT
KTRCGTL: the total scores for the recognition of the morphological forms in the KT
KTRCLTL: the total scores for the recalling of the morphological forms in the KT
KTTOTL: the students' total attainment in the KT
KTVFS: the verb forms in sentences in the KT
KTVOC: the vocabulary in the KT
LAD: Language Acquisition Device
LS: Learning Strategies
MC: Multiple Choice
Mem1: memorizing words by means of association with sounds
Mem2: memorizing words by associating the old with the new
MET: the Matriculation English Test
Metacog1: trying to arrange more time to learn English
Metacog2: always paying attention to one's own progress
M1: memorize words and learn grammar after class
M2: read textbooks after class
M3: do exercises after class
M4: review lesson notes after class
M5: listen to tapes after class
M6: write compositions or diaries after class
M7: practise speaking with classmates after class
Minst1: learning English helps one find a good job
Minst2: learning English helps one raise his social status
Minst3: learning English helps one pass the MET to universities and colleges
Mintg1: learning English helps one understand the people and

	their life in other countries
Mintg2:	learning English helps one contact with different people and talk with them
Mintg3:	learning English helps one think and behave like foreigners
NEE:	the National Entrance Examinations to universities and colleges
NMET:	the National Metriculation English Test
NPLRCG:	recognition of noun plurals
NPLRCL:	recalling of noun plurals
QL:	Questionnaire for Learners
QT:	Questionnaire for Teachers
SA:	the Structuralist Approach
SC:	Strategic Competence
SLA:	Second Language Acquisition
SLC:	Sociolinguistic Competence
SLL:	Second Language Learning
SLLner:	Second Language Learners
Social1:	often attempting to speak with others in English
Social2:	often learning with others and asking questions in English
TA:	the Traditional Approach
UG:	the Universal Grammar
VCRCG:	recognition of verb conjugations
VCRCL:	recalling of verb conjugations
WT:	Writing Task (i.e. the contextualized task)
WTK:	the grammatical forms and lexical items generated by the learners for their accomplishment of the WT
WTKVOC:	the vocabulary produced correctly by the students in the WT
WTKMPH:	the morphological forms produced correctly by the students in the WT
WTKFCT:	the function words produced correctly by the students in the WT
WTKPRON:	the pronouns produced correctly by the students in the WT
WTKCONT:	the basic grammatical concepts produced correctly by

the students in the WT

WTKVFS: the verb forms in sentences produced correctly by the students in the WT

WTKTOTL: the students' total scores for their correct production of the WTK in the WT

WTTOTL: the students' total scores based on holistic scoring methods

Chapter 1
Introduction

Human beings learn languages as they are growing up, and they learn through languages. As Halliday (1993) points out in the last century, "the ontogenesis of language is at the same time the ontogenesis of learning" (p. 93). Language learning, hence, is part of the learner's growing process. Second language learning (SLL), however, accompanies some learners' growing-up process, while being absent for some time to other groups of learners. For those who are unable to be immersed in a second language speaking environment, difficulties almost always occur in their learning process. Even for those who are able to be immersed in second language sociocultural milieux, difficulties for the final attainment of the second language form and its meaning are also daunting. Questions, thus, arise. What are the internal and external mechanisms that make some learners successful and fail among others? What kinds of knowledge have those successful learners gained and what type of knowledge have those learners who are still struggling gained? Are there any other factors also working underneath their learning processes? Questions of such type have been puzzling generations of second language acquisition (SLA) researchers. This book is an exploration into such questions, too, but by means of discussing the relationships among language form, meaning, the language learner and the nature of the knowledge that work underneath the learner.

1.1 Issues and themes: two stances in linguistics and SLA studies

Second language acquisition field has seen vast publications during the last 40 years or so. Reading through most of the literature, we can easily find two basic streams flowing toward the shared goal—an adequate description and explanation of the second language learning process. One of the streams can be named as the *rule-oriented research*, well-nurtured by the constant progress of formalism in linguistics, targeting its goal at finding the universal rules of the language acquisition process, whereas the other stream can be named as the *usage-oriented research*, enlightened by the increasing number of new discoveries rooted in cognitive functionalism in linguistics and a sociocultural orientation in applied linguistics and L. S. Vygotsky's historical sociocultural psychological theory, aiming at finding the systematic interaction of different factors working beneath the language learning process. The latter is becoming more and more accepted especially among the applied linguists.

Influenced and undergirded by these two streams in linguistics are the two orientations in second language acquisition field, which are reflected in the hot debate between the effectiveness of form-based learning and meaning-based learning or explicit learning versus implicit learning. Form-based learning itself also arouses debate around focus-on-form and focus-on-forms in second language instruction (Long, 1991; Long & Robinson, 1998), whereas implicit learning initiates further exploration into a pure unconscious learning or a kind of unconscious learning with some consciousness-raising of forms at certain point in certain context. Research and debates around these crucial topics in second language acquisition have furthered our understanding of the L2 acquisition process from a wide scale.

However, this book does not attempt to provide a complete coverage of the whole field. Rather, it aims to argue very narrowly for particular viewpoints around the nature of L2 learners' attainment and how it affects learners' meaning-oriented products among a group of learners in a foreign language learning context. In that respect, it attempts to redress what I see as misplaced emphases in EFL (English as a Foreign Language) teaching and learning in China, thus helping to facilitate understanding of the relationship between the nature of input and intake and how this relationship affects L2 learners' production.

Stating briefly the problems will help to clarify the issues:

(1) Form and meaning relationship used to be discussed separately in our field, and has not been given sufficient attention in the field of SLA.

(2) Different understandings of explicit learning and implicit learning processes cause a lot of confusions among actual practices.

(3) Learner factors have been given some stress in SLA field, but a different orientation is emphasized, whereas learners' cognitive and affective factors have not been discussed in depth.

1.1.1 Form and Meaning in Second Language Learning

The paucity of discussions around form-meaning connection in EFL studies, the first theme of this book, has been blocking us from a good understanding of the nature of different groups of learners' success or failure. As one of the key issues in SLA, the nature of the knowledge acquired by learners plays a crucial role in the determination of learners' choice of language in communicative tasks. But it has been accepted by default in SLL field that linguistics is the parent discipline for second language learning and teaching. Therefore, different orientations in linguistics heavily influence the research and practice orientations in the applied linguistics field. Hence, when structural linguistics is popular, linguistic form is of main concern. When Transformational Generative Linguistics is welcomed, rules are of particular interest. When Functional Grammar comes to the front, meaning is the most welcomed. I am not arguing that linguistic theories do not play a role in explaining second language acquisition, because anyway, what a second language learner learns is language, and linguistic theories do help SLA researchers understand better the nature of language. What I am concerned here is that researchers and practitioners easily fall into a habit of keeping up with the Joneses by following linguists rather than taking into consideration learners' problems from a practical perspective while probing into the nature of second language development.

What concerns SLLners is what type of knowledge they are supposed to master to help them communicate freely at their disposal. It is in this sense that this book picks up the topic of form-meaning relationship from a SLA perspective, although this has also been discussed by such linguists or applied linguists as N. Chomsky, M. A. K. Halliday, D. Hymes, L. Bachman, E. Tarone, W. Labov, B. VanPatten, F. Newmeyer, R. Ellis, N. Ellis, etc., who have explicated this type of knowledge from different perspectives. This book will, however, discuss this type of knowledge from a cognitive-functional perspective, in which language is regarded as an inherent part of the human conceptual system and language learning is taken as a dynamic meaning-making process which involves an active effort of constructing relationships between linguistic forms and their meanings. A cognitive-functional view of language and language learning (also called Usage-Based view) has been emerging these years (Tomasello, 2003), although not given sufficient attention, as has been complained in Skehan (1998). This line of inquiry into the nature of language and language learning is actually not new, as can be obviously perceived from the insights drawn from such people's works as Skehan (1998), Langacker (1991), Goldberg (1995), N. Ellis (2004), and Givón (1995), Bybee & Scheibman (1999), Bybee & Thompson (2000), etc. The key assumption in this theory is that language is conceived as "a structured inventory of symbolic units", each with its own structure and function (Langacker, 1987). According to Tomasello (2003), abstract constructions are also an important part of the inventory of symbolic resources that language users control, but they are best seen as just one form that linguistic constructions may take. Individuals do not hear abstract constructions, but only individual utterances. Language learners must find patterns from what they hear to create abstract constructions. Hence, second language learning in this view is the learning of constructions that relate form and meaning (N. Ellis, 2004).

By form in this book, we refer to the linguistic units of language, including both lexical and grammatical units. All linguistic forms and expressions are surface manifestations of a language user's internal representations both phonologically and semantically.

Meaning in this book refers to the semantic structure of a surface manifestation or a symbolic unit, which is usually referred to as conceptualization in cognitive linguistic term. The acquisition of meaning involves the acquisition of meanings of English words, sentence structure, tense, aspect, discourse structure, etc. Aspects involved in this book are mainly the meanings that are related to the analysed forms, which, although limited in its scope, also cover the basic elements of meanings in language learning.

What should learners aim at in learning? Form or meaning? An obvious answer seems to be: both. Nonetheless, in our real language learning practice, practitioners and researchers seem to favor one or the other as claimed to be constrained by energy and desire for practical urgency and rapidity. " Few people start learning an L2 for the exotic sounds or for the elegant sentence structure that they detect in it. Meaning is what we are all after." (Slabakova, 2010, p. 249). However, exams, sometimes as the guiding baton, force learners to turn to exercises focusing on discrete linguistic units or single rules, although frustrations and embarrassment have been constantly noticed or heard about in real communication. When examining what has been tested and taught in classrooms, one cannot help throwing doubt on today's classroom practice and textbooks in China.

1.1.2 Two processes in SLA: Explicit learning and implicit learning

One subarea in SLA is instructed classroom learning. Does instruction make a difference in SLL? This question has been asked constantly since Long (1983). What people actually concern is whether explicit learning facilitates L2 learning process. Most SLA researchers in the past 40 years hold the view that real language learning can only take place in implicit learning situations (Krashen, 1985). However, other researchers (R. Ellis, 1984; VanPatten, Williams, Rott & Overstreet, 2004) believe that instructed learning does make a difference especially when the input is manipulated well to match the state of the learners. Questions then arise: What kind of learning process can really facilitate the happening of intake? A cognitive-functional view of language learning assumes that simply concluding the decisive role of either one of the processes is misleading, because it depends on the manipulation of the nature of the two processes, and whether the process is facilitative in helping learners construct the form-meaning relations. Explicit or form-based learning gives more attention to language forms, i.e. the learning of declarative facts about language while implicit learning targets its attention to the construction of a holistic, integrated and systematic knowledge system. If meaning is created in the process of interacting different participants in contexts, then learners' acquisition of meaning needs to be developed in those contexts.

In SLL, what learners need to do in their comprehension and production involves at least three things: first, they must be able to identify the linguistic items; second, they must be able to identify the corresponding meanings, and thirdly, they must be able to establish the relationships between the forms and meanings. Learners, either through explicit learning or implicit learning, should finally aim at establishing the relationships between forms and meanings, so as to eventually enable themselves to retrieve this relationship automatically within limited time in communication.

Hence, the focus of learning should be channeled to the mastery of implicit knowledge while not ignoring some of the roles played by explicit knowledge in language learning and use, and trying to create favorable conditions for the transfer from explicit knowledge to implicit knowledge to occur.

Influenced by the dichotomous thinking of always favoring one or the other, SLA research in the past 40 years or so also argues around which process is the better one to explain successful learners or failed learners. Implicit learning is still considered to play a key role in facilitating the acquisition process although recent research also indicates the relative role played by explicit learning. This warns us of hasty conclusions about the complex nature of second language acquisition process. More inquiry is still necessary.

1.1.3 Learner factors

Attention to learner factors is a typical new orientation in SLA since the 1970s. However, learner factors used to be considered as peripheral rather than internal when linguistic forms are given prominence, especially when learners' cognitive and affective factors are concerned.

Language learner should be in an emic position rather than an etic position. By an emic position, we mean that learning is actually the learner's business rather than others' business. With this understanding in mind, when language learning is the subject of study, we cannot just concentrate on the study of language, teaching techniques, or approaches. Rather, we need to shift our attention to the learner, to the understanding of what learners are doing, how they are doing and what they have learnt after so many years' schooling and effort.

Learner factors covered here in this book are not dealt with in an inclusive sense, but only include the following aspects: *learning strategies*, *cognitive and affective factors*, *motivations* and *attitudes*,

The above three issues - the form-meaning relationship, the explicit and implicit learning processes and the learner factors are the key issues this book is trying to explore by means of an empirical investigation into the language performance of a group of Chinese secondary school EFL learners' language performance both in contextualized situations and decontextualized situations and factors involved in their learning processes. The examination of their language performance is targeted at exploring the nature of the learners' knowledge of English. The knowledge here refers to both explicit knowledge which is mainly declarative and discrete in nature, and implicit knowledge which is procedualized, integrative and a reflection of an established relationship between form and meaning. The study of the processes here include an investigation into the possible factors behind this group of learners' learning and an exploration of how these factors conspired to channel learners' learning to a certain state. To make later chapters easy to follow, this chapter will also contribute to the basic explanations of the terms involved in this study and a brief panorama of the whole book.

1.2 Definition of relevant terms

To make the following chapters easier to follow, the working definitions for some of the concepts adopted for this book are provided here first.

Second Language Acquisition (henceforth SLA): This term is used here in a broad sense in accordance with the definition provided by Larsen-Freeman & Long (1991). It refers to a field covering any study of the acquisition or learning of a second language besides a mother tongue. The term is extended by the addition of the research on bilingual acquisition and third or fourth language learning or even dialects. The research on FLL (see the following) in this book belongs to the field of SLA. "Acquisition" in the term "SLA" has lost its original sense when it is used to refer to the whole discipline. However, the original sense of "acquisition" always causes confusion and reminds one of L1 acquisition. Therefore, in this book, with the broader sense of SLA in mind, for clarity and to show the particularity of EFL learning in the Chinese situation, the term ***FLL*** or ***SLL*** is more frequently used which emphasizes more the learner's role and the learning of a second language in instructed situations.

Foreign Language Learning (henceforth FLL): It is still controversial whether there exists a difference between SLA and FLL or not. As far as the research on English learning in China is concerned, the term "foreign language learning" is preferred although it is still subsumed under SLA. English learning in China is characterized by the following features: (1) it has been accepted that China is mainly a monolingual country, in which there is no steady English speaking communities; (2) English learning in China occurs mainly in classrooms where instruction is the major means for English learning; and (3) learners have few opportunities to expose themselves to English after class. English in China is a compulsory course both in secondary schools and in universities. It is taught in classrooms through the medium of a native language in most cases in underdeveloped areas. Thus, English learning in China is often called ***EFL*** learning. However, English learning can also be considered as a second language apart from the learners' mother tongue, hence, in this book, ***SLL*** is also used.

Communicative Competence (hereafter CC): This term has been popularly used in the field of SLA since Hymes' introduction (Hymes, 1972). However, researchers have not come to an agreement as to the connotations and denotations of this term. Adequate discussions about different views of CC will be presented in Chapter II. A brief account will be given here. Abstractly, from its nature, in this research, CC refers to the acquired internalized language system including the ability for use which operates or directs actual performance. Concretely, the elaborated understanding of CC supplied by Canale and Swain (1980), Canale (1983) and Li (1987, 1990a, etc.) is adopted here in this book, which consists of at least three components including linguistic competence (grammatical competence (GC) in Canale and Swain's term), pragmatic competence (i. e. sociolinguistic competence (SLC), discourse competence (DC) and strategic competence (STC) in Canale and Swain's terms) and cognitive and affective capacity (CAC) (In Li (1987)'s term). In terms of target language development in SLA, CC is that kind of knowledge which is dynamic in nature, meaning that this type of knowledge is constantly updated, reviewed, improved and perfected in the constructing process with the development of the learner's linguistic system. So far as its nature is concerned, it is often associated with the implicit knowledge posited in line with the cognitive-psycholinguistic-oriented perspective of SLA inquiry.

Decontextualised Language Task (the Knowledge Task, abbreviated as KT in this book): This refers to the task devised in the experiment which consists of word or sentence level linguistic forms (i. e. lexis and grammar) for recognition, recalling and simple judgment. The linguistic forms "tested" in this task are sorted out from the two minimally passable model versions for the two writing tasks which are regarded as tasks with contexts, and are then called ***contextualised language task*** (the Writing Task, abbreviated as WT). Learners' performance on the same linguistic forms in the two kinds of tasks was elicited for comparison.

Attitude: In this research, it is not used in a broad sense. It refers to states of emotions and thought relating to the learning of English. The emotions relating to the culture of English speaking peoples are not included in this research.

Motivation: This term is employed here to refer to the emotions and needs that constitute the source of drive to expend effort required to learn a second or foreign language. In this study, two aspects in relation to the orientations of motivations were investigated, i. e. the instrumental orientation and the integrative orientation (terms adopted from Gardner and Lambert, 1972). The ***instrumental orientation*** of motivations refers to the force that comes from the learner's needs which might be from within the learner himself or from the force that comes from outside the learner. The ***integrative orientation*** of motivations refers to the force that comes from the learner's emotions relating to the language he is learning, e.g. the learner's interest in the culture of the group that speaks the language.

Learning Strategy: This term can be defined both from macro and micro views. Holistically speaking, it can refer to the general approaches to language study. A learner's general approach to language study is determined by how he sees language. He may see it as a habit formation process or the process of discovering a language rule system. Specifically speaking, it can refer to the techniques or habits in language learning. The choice of the techniques or habits is affected by his adoption of the approach, e.g. it might be inferencing or memorization of sentences or rules. In this study, learners' learning techniques and habits were investigated and final inference of their approaches was drawn from the investigation. The strategies listed in the investigation are mainly those that have been widely discussed in SLA.

Outside Class Language Exposure: This term refers to the total contact with the target language by learners after instructed learning in class. It was investigated on the following four skills:

listening, speaking, reading and writing. It is hypothesized that there is always little exposure after class in FLL context. This investigation could provide some evidence for this hypothesis.

1.3 Motivations for this research

The present research was initiated on the basis of the observation of the phenomenon that a great number of EFL learners in China can pass a variety of tests of grammar, vocabulary, and so on, yet exhibit disproportionate low ability to accomplish tasks of a communicative nature. Particularly, this research was motivated by the following reasons.

1.3.1 Practical needs

EFL education in China experienced ups and downs in the long history of China for some complicated reasons. Detailed descriptions of the history of EFL teaching may be found in the book ***The History of English Language Teaching in China*** by Li Liangyou, Zhang Risheng and Liu Li in 1988. For the present research, the author was primarily motivated by some practical problems.

(1) Little is known about situations in secondary schools and what secondary school EFL learners have attained. There was a large-scale investigation about the situations of EFL teaching and learning in secondary (both junior and senior) schools in China conducted by the government during 1985—1986, when schools from 15 provinces and cities were involved. The results provided a general picture of the secondary school EFL education at that time and indicated that most of the secondary school EFL learners under investigation generally failed in either listening (both sentence level and discourse level) or reading comprehension (discourse level) but scored highly in discrete language knowledge. It was also interesting to find out that learners were intelligent in understanding but failed to grasp the main ideas of the given texts which were limited in vocabulary and content. A conclusion was finally drawn that the investigated learners had the ability to master English, but teachers ignored

the training of the skills required (For details, see Li Liangyou et al. 1988). As the investigation was targeted toward sketching a general picture of the situations in secondary school EFL education in China at that time, it could not tell us theoretically why the learners failed in the use of the target language. But it did point out one important problem in secondary school EFL teaching and learning, i.e. most learners failed to achieve the expected level. But what might be the case after so many years? Little is known.

(2) Few questions have been asked about what secondary school EFL teachers and learners are thinking and doing, about the nature of those teachers' instruction, about how the nature of the instruction influences the learners' final attainment, and about what the secondary school EFL learners are able to do in the target language after their time and effort has been spent. What is taking place in schools seems to be taken for granted, which is fatal for the EFL teaching and learning and even for educational policy-making. The term of "reform" is prevailing but what should be "reformed" is still unclear. What is enlightening to us now is the work that has been done by the explorers in this field in China since 1980s. In addition to the introductory work at the preliminary stage, experimental and practical efforts have been made since the late 1980s (e. g. Gui, 1987, 1988, 1990, 1992; Li, 1984, 1987, 1990a, 1990b, 1992, 1993). Reforms around the National Matriculation English Test (NMET) in the National Entrance Examinations (NEE) to universities and colleges have been introduced and the effect of this effort has shown its strong power (Li, 1990b). Nonetheless, the effect of a test is limited, and in-depth research on the teaching and learning processes in secondary schools should follow up. Otherwise, even this achievement might be quickly worn down without strong theoretical research work as its basis.

1.3.2 Theoretical needs

This research, theoretically, is intended to contribute to the field of SLA, to be exact, the subarea of FLL.

The research on second language acquisition has up to now a

history of almost 40 years, which has been acknowledged by Larsen-Freeman and Long (1991) to have passed infancy and adolescence and come to the youth period, during which a kind of sobriety has been observed in the research of this field. However, it does not indicate that the research in the youth period is adequate for sufficient understanding of second language acquisition. The research in the youth period implies more problems waiting to be solved, more supporting evidence required, much broader views of the field, and more specific research needed. Research in the field of SLA has touched upon a large area of topics by means of interweaving the field of SLA with other disciplines such as psycholinguistics, cognitive science, sociolinguistics, linguistics, neurolinguistics, and so on. However, they develop too fast to be carefully chewed and digested. They explore some interesting topics, but stop where they start and turn quickly for new pursuit. Thus, if the field is a "youth", it is still a restless "youth". Looking through the research in the past 40 years, the following characteristics can be summarized.

(1) Acquisition-centered study

The research methodology in SLA is very much influenced by the research on children's L1 acquisition. Many studies in this field have been carried out to compare the acquisition process of a second language and that of a first one. Both similarities and differences have been found which are inspiring for subsequent studies. However, most of the research is concerned with the learning of a second language in naturalistic or mixed classroom situations, where learners have many opportunities to be in contact with the target language in realistic communicative situations.

(2) Learner-centered study

Another characteristic of studies in SLA is learner-centered study. Studies of learners are mainly concerned with the contribution of learners' individual factors to second language learning. These factors include learners' aptitude, intelligence, motivation, attitude, learning strategy, etc. However, the influence of teachers and the nature of input are more or less put aside while learners are given some attention. The nature of input in

FLL context, which might be of crucial importance, is seldom questioned and researched.

(3) Variety of models

Research in SLA is characterized by increasing varieties of SLA models. However, no models have ever been sufficiently testified.

(4) Learners other than adolescents are studied.

In addition to the interest in children learning a second language, adult learners are of much concern. However, secondary school learners are seldom touched upon, although some studies on high school students have been conducted (Felix, 1981; Chandrasegaran, 1981; etc.).

Since SLA focuses its attention on learning process, learner factors, and the comparison of L2 learning with L1 learning, the other aspect — the teaching process is not widely discussed. This phenomenon can be easily seen from the lack of literature on FLL. Only recent classroom studies show researchers' increasing interest in the effect of instruction on FLL. Another problem is that the increase of SLA models leaves no time for researchers to calm down to verify or digest the theories put forward. Different kinds of factors influencing SLA have been researched, but few studies have attempted to consider how different kinds of factors influence FLL as a whole when they are put together.

Specifically, with regard to Chinese secondary school EFL learning and teaching, the following problems have been found.

(1) Discontinuity in research on EFL teaching and learning. Although situations were getting better since the foundation of new China, research, however, were suspended several times. It so happened that when there were favorable attitudes towards EFL teaching and learning, magazines and journals on EFL teaching and learning appeared in turn. Associations of EFL teaching and learning were established, and studies on EFL teaching and learning were advocated. Instances of this can be found in the 1950s, the early 1960s and the present time. But research of this kind was often suspended when there were opposite opinions. This discontinuity in EFL research in China brings about a series of problems for the EFL education development. One of the

problems is the paucity of systematic research on EFL teaching and learning, which leads to another problem, i.e. the lack of firm bases for later research and EFL teaching practices. Thus it causes a third problem, i.e. waste of time and personnel in EFL teaching and learning. The paucity of fundamental research in EFL teaching and learning makes it hard for the study of specific problems.

(2) The phenomenon of following others blindly in the choice of EFL teaching methodology in practice. Tracing the history of EFL teaching in China, it can be seen that there exists a tendency to follow others blindly in the choice of teaching methodologies. The case is more obviously seen from the upsurge of the application of the *Audiolingual Method* in the 1970s. The follow-up action of buying sets of language-lab equipment proves the existence of this phenomenon. The sudden liking for the *Communicative Approach* recently cannot put our hearts at ease, since this approach might have the fate similar to the previous ones if corresponding theoretical research cannot come up in time. The psychology of following the general trend can easily make teachers pour out the bath water together with the baby if they lack the knowledge of the principles underlying these prevailing teaching approaches. This is also a problem caused by the lack of theoretical research. Misapprehensions and confusions about basic concepts such as teaching methods, techniques and approaches exist widely among EFL teachers in universities and secondary schools. There is an urgent need for specific research concerning EFL teaching and learning in the Chinese context as has been pointed out by Gui (Gui, 1988), although there has been some introductory work and preliminary research work on university EFL teaching and learning.

(3) The negligence of learners in teaching. The discontinuity in research on EFL teaching and learning makes it hard for teachers to adopt new ideas. SLA theories in the West have prevailed for as long as over 40 years. In China, however, it was only after the 1980s that researchers started introducing the new research methods and perspectives in EFL teaching and learning. Traditional EFL teaching in class is always teacher-centered.

Since teachers lack the knowledge in Applied Linguistics, learner factors have never been taken seriously. Learners' contribution to EFL learning is still not widely accepted yet. This indicates that there is a need to go into classrooms to conduct more studies.

(4) One other point that merits attention is about the materials and syllabuses in Chinese secondary schools. Syllabuses are in fact the instruction system for schools. They are mainly about what, why and how to teach and learn. Reading through the EFL teaching syllabuses for secondary schools of recent years, one can find a gradual change to a more communicative thought. This is the effect of the research that has been carried out since 1977. But it appears that what the syllabuses state and what teachers and learners actually do are two different things. The syllabuses gradually call for the fostering of communicative competence, and have listed possible functional expressions together with grammatical rules and limited vocabulary. What teachers and learners do is not much different from what they did in the past. There are many reasons for this. The rooted belief in teachers and learners' minds is one. Another reason is the separation of ideas in textbooks from syllabuses. The change of thinking about language teaching and learning reflected in the syllabuses cannot find its soil to root itself. This makes the syllabuses unable to come into force as they were expected.

With regard to the topic in this study, i.e. the nature of the knowledge attained by secondary school EFL learners, few questions have been asked before. Most researchers give much attention to the study of acquisition process and even rate of learning affected by instruction, but little attention has been paid to the nature of learners' attainment. In this respect, this study is intended to contribute to the study of FLL based on an in-depth investigation into the learners. There already exist some models attempting to explain learners' internalized knowledge system, yet few empirical studies have been done to testify those theories and the internal system is still left "internal". With reference to different groups of learners in China, research concerning university EFL learners has been seen recently (Wu Xudong, 1999, 2006; Wen, 1995; Wu & Liu, 1993; Wang Chuming, 1997;

Wang Qiang, 2002; Gui & Yang, 2003; etc.). Wu Xudong's study, a longitudinal study of the development of a group of university EFL learners' oral production, demonstrates that those learners' lack of oral practice both in and out of the classroom resulted in a great gap between a highly analytical knowledge about the target language and an under-developed procedural knowledge. Besides, the form-oriented instruction made those learners adopt the type of learning strategies which enabled them to extend only knowledge about the target language (Wu Xudong, 1999). Then, what about the nature of secondary school EFL learners' final attainment and the possible underlying factors in their learning process? What has been discussed above as a whole sketches such a basic problem that there exists a misty understanding of EFL competence, the learning purpose, and learning process, which motivates the author to delve into the present topic. As Wexler and Culicover (1980, p. 486) pointed out, "Without a precise characteristic of what is to be learnt, the question of whether it can be learned is virtually meaningless" (Saleemi, 1989, p. 179).

1.4 Research questions and delimitation

1.4.1 Methods used

Basically, according to Nunan (1992), two paradigms are widely accepted in this field (Nunan, 1992): qualitative paradigm and quantitative paradigm, which embodies different ways of thinking behind. Each has its advantages and disadvantages. For this study, it is empirical research in which both qualitative and quantitative methods are employed. The research is quantitative because it involves testifying hypotheses by collecting data from an experiment, and it is qualitative because the ways dealing with the problems under study also involve the researcher's interptetations and qualitative analysis within a framework. Thus, this study aims at pinpointing problems, exploring potential factors and making an attempt at giving an objective account of the present secondary school English learning in China.

1.4.2 Justification of the research

As mentioned above, although there have been some studies about EFL learning in China, little attention is given to EFL learning in secondary school learning and learners. Besides, research on classroom instruction, the acquisition of communicative competence, and second language learning process are mainly carried out in English-speaking countries and the subjects are mainly English-speaking students of French or Spanish or other languages. The series of studies carried out in Canada, Germany, Australia, such as the experiment of the Immersion Program, the ZISA Project, etc. (see Felix, 1981; Pica, 1983, 1985; Pienemann, 1984, 1987, 1989; Swain, 1981; etc.) have resulted in some important conclusions. Yet as Chandrasegaran (1981) pointed out in his study of Malaysian secondary school EFL learners, "It must be pointed out that the importance of French to the English-speaking students of North America is not quite equal to the importance of English to students in Malaysia or any other Southeast Asian country" (p. 4). It is also possible that the attitudes, motivations and learning strategies of English-speaking students of other countries are not the same as those of the Chinese learners.

It is therefore necessary both theoretically and empirically to probe into this area which can assist our understanding of the nature of the learner's attained knowledge system and what it means to know a language. It can also help us interpret the role of many extralinguistic factors involved in teaching and learning processes.

1.4.3 The delimitation of this research

This research was delimited to the exploration of the nature of the knowledge mastered by Chinese secondary school EFL learners and the investigation of these learners' learning process. The writing skill and the possible relevant linguistic devices involved in the designed tasks were chosen for observation. The factors under study were limited to five factors mainly: *motivation, attitude, outside class language exposure, learning strategy and classroom instruction*. Even for these factors, they were also further limited to some aspects only. Therefore, this study was not to provide answers for all the questions of FLL in China, rather an attempt in this area for the questions concerned.

1.4.4 Research questions

This research seeks to probe into two problems pertaining to FLL. First, it seeks to explore the nature of the knowledge mastered by the Chinese secondary school English learners after their hard work for at least over 800 hours in the classrooms. Second, it aims to explore the nature and the extent of the relationship between the learners' attained knowledge and the factors under investigation, i.e. *attitude*, *motivation*, *outside class exposure*, *learning strategy*, and *classroom instruction*. With the above goals in mind, the following broad questions arise: (1) What are the possible factors that hinder effective English learning? (2) What factors could contribute to successful English learning? These two big problems were approached within a working conceptual framework which hypothesized the possible relationships between the factors under study and learners' final attainment. The framework served as a theoretical basis both for the conducting of the experiment, the investigation and for the interpretations of the results obtained. As the title of this book indicates, although the study is delimited within a certain scope, it is a means to help us approach the relationship between language form, its meaning and the language learner. As we move on, a glimpse of the complicated relationship among these factors will be perceived bit by bit, and thus we invite you to experience this complexity through the reading of the following chapters.

1.5 An outline of the book

The organization of the book is outlined as below. Eight chapters are covered in this book. With Chapter 1 as such as the introduction, Chapters 2 and 3 present a review of relevant theories and studies concerning the nature of the targeted knowledge which SLLners are supposed to acquire and the processes involved in SL learning. Those who are interested in tracing the discussions around the concepts of communicative competence, explicit and implicit knowledge can refer to Chapter 2 independently, while those who are interested in the discussions of theories around how different factors conspire to affect SLA can refer to Chapter 3 independetly. Chapter 4 serves as the theoretical basis for the followed study by presenting a working conceptual framework for the research proposed by the author. Chapter 5 introduces the design of the study in detail and presents the specific questions and hypotheses involved in the study while Chapter 6 displays the investigation results according to the research questions. On the basis of the findings in the study, Chapter 7 gives an in-depth discussion around the results in the study in relation to the conceptual framework presented in Chapter 4. Finally, Chapter 8 presents the conclusion by means of a discussion of the implications of this study on the basis of the findings. Pedagogical suggestions are proposed in terms of practical EFL instruction in Chinese situations.

Chapter 2
Pursuing an Understanding of the Underlying System

What knowledge do we need to comprehend others and produce what we want to mean? This inquiry has been responded in different ways by researchers in different disciplines. In SLA field, terms that have been most frequently mentioned are such ones as *communicative competence*, *mental representations*, *form-meaning connections*, etc., each of which stands for a different perspective into the nature of the knowledge underpinning language users' behavior in practice. This chapter will review two strands of research around the discussion of communicative competence and form-meaning relationship.

2. 1 The competence-performance issue

The discussion of the nature of the internalized language system is in fact to answer the question of what constitutes knowledge of language as a language bearer, which is a moot point in modern linguistics and hereupon in other fields in which language is involved, such as in anthropology, cognitive psychology, psycholinguistics, applied linguistics, and so on. Different answers to the above question rouse various and endless arguments among linguists, sociologists, psychologists, language practitioners and researchers of many other disciplines. The following part will present a review of the theories of some of the most representative figures in linguistics and sociolinguistics around this topic.

2. 1. 1 The Competence-performance distinction

Since late 1950s, Chomsky's theory of language and his related terms in studying language cause a lasting stir in the field of linguistics and applied linguistics. In constructing his theory of transformational-generative grammar, he challenged the basic principles of structural linguistics and behavioural psychology by making a number of assumptions among which making a distinction between *competence* and *performance* was one of them. This distinction was first introduced in the following well-quoted paragraph in the initial pages of his book *Aspects of the Theory of Syntax.*

> We thus make a fundamental distinction between *competence* (the speaker-hearer's knowledge of his language) and *performance* (the actual use of language in concrete situations) ...In actual fact, it [performance] obviously could not directly reflect competence. A record of natural speech will show numerous false starts, deviations from rules, changes of plan in mid-course, and so on. (Chomsky, 1965, p. 4, *his emphasis*).

The distinction, in principle, resembles Saussure's (1964 [1916]) distinction between *langue* and *parole,* which points to a dichotomous orientation of linguistic study. Based on this distinction, Chomsky then gives the following statement of a linguistic theory he is concerned with:

> Linguistic theory is primarily concerned with an ideal speaker-listener, in a completely homogeneous speech community who knows its language perfectly and is unaffected by such grammatically irrelevant conditions as memory limitations, distractions, shifts of attention and interest, and errors (random or characteristic) in applying his knowledge of the language in actual performance (Chomsky, 1965, p. 3).

By giving the above statement, he delimits his interest of linguistic study to the ideal speaker-listener and presents the concept of *competence* as opposed to *performance.* Language, through this distinction, is considered as a rule-governed system which is not affected by social and situational variation (Lyons,

1996, p. 18). Although Chomsky's distinction has its ontological significance to his orientation of linguistic study in a certain way, it basically puts *rules* and *the ability for use* at different ends at the same time. Hence, his redefining of the term *competence* as the knowledge of an ideal speaker-listener was soon criticized by researchers who took a more sociolinguistic approach. In responding to the challenges around whether *the ability for use* should be included, Chomsky made an explicit response that his definition excluded *the ability for use.* Obviously, "competence" in Chomsky mainly refers to the mental state, a static, descriptive and a technical concept. He equates "competence" with "knowledge" and excludes any idea of dynamic use of that knowledge. In answering the question of "What does it mean to know a language?", Chomsky wrote in his *Rules and Representations* (1980):

> To know a language, I am assuming, is to be in a certain mental state, which persists as a relatively steady component of transitory mental state. What kind of mental state? I assume further that to be in such a mental state is to have a certain mental structure consisting of a system of rules and principles that generate and relate mental representations of various types (Chomsky, 1980, p. 48).

It is clear that Chomsky's idea of "competence" is restricted to the mental state of grammatical structure. What intrigues Chomsky is mainly the syntax part of language. Thus *the ability for the use* of the internalized knowledge system is left out of the "competence" concept in his theory.

Another aspect that is worthy of attention concerning Chomsky's use of competence is that his theory is confined mainly to monolingual native individual speakers only. The application of Chomsky's use of the term "competence" to the fields of non-native speakers or second language learners without much thinking is fraught with problems. The "competence" which characterizes these individuals in Chomsky's theory has an absolute quality. It is biologically based, as Chomsky states that

"Ultimately the study of language is a part of human biology" (Chomsky, 1980, p. 226). Many of the discussions about competence in SLA, however, seem to depart from Chomsky's idea of linguistic competence. Chomsky defines the terms "competence" and "performance" in a technical sense and uses it as a device in his study. It is important to clearly understand the original idea of "competence" as has been pointed out by many researchers with respect to this issue (Spolsky 1989; Taylor 1988; Widdowson, 1983, 1989). Thus, for Chomsky, what linguists should do is to give adequate explanations to competence (mainly syntax), while performance should be left to the others to study. Just as Spolsky pointed out,

> ... it is a mistake to confuse the Chomskyan notion of competence with the general notion of ability. Furthermore, Chomsky proposed to confine his attention to the rules of the language needed for a generative grammar, with a general restriction to sentence-length utterances and the exclusion of variation, however interesting these matters might have appeared to other linguists (Spolsky, 1989, p. 138).

However, the deliberate exclusion of other aspects of language such as rules of use or the *ability for use* in linguistic studies causes a lot of confusion among researchers who try to apply his theory to the explanation of second language learning and some other applied fields. For instance, when applying this theory to SLA – a field which bases its research mainly on tracing learners' learning process and their performance, although it might not be appropriate, researchers cannot come to agreement, since in SLA, learners' difficulties in learning and use of the second language cannot be satisfactorily explained with Chomsky's concept of "competence", and it is still unknown as to whether the LAD also works for SLA or whether there is some other device operating it. These conundrums cause researchers to consider other factors that might operate. Therefore, re-explanations of competence and new terms in different perspectives appear in turn, which might be a side effect of the influence of Chomsky's competence-performance distinction.

2.1.2 Hymes' s introduction of communicative competence

The discussion of the nature of competence in the linguistic field is confronted with disagreement among researchers from other fields. The core dispute is around the confinement of research on competence to the syntax part of language in linguistic field by Chomsky. Viewing language in the perspective of anthropology and sociology, researchers such as D. H. Hymes (1972) believe that it is a great drawback not to consider the human factors and the social context in which language is used when language competence is discussed. According to Hymes (1972), the underlying competence of the language user does not only contain the syntax part, it should also include factors that are necessary for communication. Believing that there is a gap left by Chomsky when defining competence, Hymes states as follows:

> We have then to account for the fact that a normal child acquires knowledge of sentences not only as grammatical but also as appropriate. He or she acquires competence as to when to speak, when not, and as to what to talk about with whom, when, where, in what manner. In short, a child becomes able to accomplish a repertoire of speech acts, to take part in speech events, and to evaluate their accomplishment by others ... (Hymes, 1972, pp. 277-8).

Having examined Chomsky's statements about the nature of *competence*, Hymes found that there was "a major gap in not dealing with the issue of appropriacy: the knowledge not that a sentence is well-formed but that it is appropriately used in a specific context" (cited from Spolsky, 1989, p. 39).

> There are rules of use without which the rules of grammar would be useless. Just as rules of syntax can control aspects of phonology, and just as rules of semantics perhaps control aspects of syntax, so rules of speech acts enter as a controlling factor for linguistic form as a whole (Hymes, 1972, p. 278).

Here, Hymes is introducing the idea of *ability for use* as part of competence, which is his starting point. Therefore, according to Hymes, an individual's competence cannot rule out the *ability for use.* "The acquisition of competence for use, indeed, can be stated in the same terms as acquisition of competence for grammar" (Hymes, 1972, p. 279). Now that Chomsky's term of competence cannot include the meaning he wants to express, Hymes, therefore, introduces another term *communicative competence* (henceforth CC), which includes four sectors, of which the grammatical is one. He explains that "there is behavior, and underlying it, there are several systems of rules reflected in the judgments and abilities of those whose messages the behavior manifests" (ibid). Thus the core of the Communicative Competence theory is:

> If an adequate theory of language users and language use is to be developed, it seems that judgments must be recognized to be in fact not of two kinds but of four. And if linguistic theory is to be integrated with theory of communication and culture, this fourfold distinction must be stated in a sufficiently generalized way. I would suggest, then, that for language and for other forms of communication (culture), four questions arise: 1. Whether (and to what degree) something is formally *possible*; 2. Whether (and to what degree) something is *feasible* in virtue of the means of implementation available; 3. Whether (and to what degree) something is *appropriate* (adequate, happy, successful) in relation to a context in which it is used and evaluated; 4. Whether (and to what degree) something is in fact done, actually *performed*, and what its doing entails (Hymes, 1972, p. 281).

He further explains and illustrates the sectors as follows:

> A linguistic illustration: a sentence may be grammatical, awkward, tactful and rare. (One might think of the four as successive subsets; more likely they should be pictured as overlapping circles.) (Hymes, 1972, p. 281).

Here, competence is defined as "the capabilities of a person", and it is "dependent upon both (tacit) *knowledge* and (ability for) *use*" (Hymes, 1972, p. 282). For the parallel parenthesis, he later explains that they point to things underlying (Hymes, 1989, p. 247). Thus, for Hymes, competence has two aspects, as Widdowson later on pointed out (Widdowson, 1989), i.e. knowledge on the one hand and ability on the other hand. According to Hymes,

> Knowledge also is to be understood as subtending all four parameters of communication just noted. There is knowledge of each. *Ability for use* also may relate to all four parameters. Certainly it may be the case that individuals differ with regard to ability to use knowledge of each: to interpret, differentiate, etc. The specification of *ability for use* as part of competence allows for the role of noncognitive factors, such as motivation, as partly determining competence (Hymes, 1972, pp. 282-3).

What Hymes insisted on is that Chomsky equates the theory of performance with the theory of use under the "catch-all term" of performance, and that some aspects of what Chomsky lumps together under performance are systematic, can hence be described in the form of rules, and can thus be seen as a form of competence (Taylor, 1988).

As far as "competence" is concerned, the above quoted paragraph indicates that in Hymes's theory of *Communicative Competence*, there are at least two parts: *knowledge* and *ability*. But in Chomsky, competence is taken as "the knowledge of something much more abstract than language: it is a knowledge of systems of rules, of parameters or principles, configurations in the mind for which language simply serves as evidence" (Widdowson, 1989, p. 129). Thus, we can conclude that Chomsky and Hymes are considering different things. If we look at these theories from the point of cognitive science as a whole, Chomsky's theory and Hymes's are complementary to each other. Chomsky (1980)'s interest is in the whole knowledge system of which "language is a derivative" (p. 90), i. e. the abstract part of language, whereas Hymes concerns himself with language in human society, i.e. the language in use in a dynamic sense. Just as Hornberger (1989,

p. 217) pointed out, "Since competence was limited to knowledge of the grammar of the language, performance was the only place left for much that had to be considered a kind of knowledge, namely, knowledge of when, where, how, and with whom any particular language use should occur. And that was not satisfactory either since performance was given such a depreciated connotation ... ". For this criticism, Chomsky later on acknowledges it and elaborates his idea as follows:

> For purposes of enquiry and exposition, we may proceed to distinguish "grammatical competence" from "pragmatic competence", restricting the first to the knowledge of form and meaning and the second to knowledge of conditions and manner of appropriate use, in conformity with various purposes. Thus we may think of language as an instrument that can be put to use. The grammar of the language characterizes the instrument, determining intrinsic physical and semantic properties of every sentence. The grammar thus expresses grammatical competence. A system of rules and principles consisting pragmatic competence determines how the tool can effectively be put to use (Chomsky, 1980, p. 224).

This point of Chomsky is later "shrewdly" (Hymes, 1989, p. 245) pointed out by Widdowson as "a kind of ability" (Widdowson, 1989, p. 130), which might be Chomsky's corrected answer to others' attacks. However, the study of form and meaning definitely cannot be constrained within the competence level.

It is now clearer to us what competence means to Hymes. In 1989 in his reaction to Taylor (1988)'s criticism of his introduction of the *ability for use* to Chomsky's definition of competence, Hymes said, "nothing depends on words. What is essential is to include more than knowledge, something that has to do with use" (Hymes, 1989, p. 247). Hymes admits that what he adds to the nature of competence *ability for use* is a state. From this, we can see that Hymes is not talking about performance. He is trying to extend and modify the nature of what he thought to be too much limited by Chomsky in his definition of competence. He associates that abstract notion of language with the society in which language exists. The introduction of the concept of *communicative competence* from a sociological perspective is very stimulating, which can be seen from the later modifications and proposals of competence frameworks in the applied linguistics field, although confusion accompanies the process of discussion in the employment of terms referring to the knowledge that underpins SLLners' behavior. It is obvious that Chomsky and Hymes in fact concern themselves with different things, as has been indicated in their works that the former is talking about the knowledge as a state while the latter is drawing in a dynamic component into the term "competence" and is interested in its relationship with the human society. Their discussion of the nature of the internalized language system turns out to prompt a lot of continuing interest in explaining the nature of a language bearer's internalized language system from different perspectives. It is like a stone thrown into the peaceful water, and bubbles and waves move since then. Among these continuing pursuits, the discussions around the components of communicative competence are the most influential in the applied linguistics field.

2.1.3 Components of the Communicative Competence

The above discussion of the nature of competence indicates how researchers disagree as to what competence is, which implies the disagreement on what should be learnt in second or foreign language learning. It also implies that the full understanding of the nature of the internalized language cannot be just seen from one perspective. Debates upon the above question extend to other fields such as applied linguistics whose main task is to solve language teaching problems, and the field of SLA whose task is to solve learning process problems.

As many articles have pointed out, during the past two decades or more, a good deal of thought and research has been concerned with the problem of discovering the linguistic and extra-linguistic abilities which make up communicative competence (see Bachman, 1990; Bachman and Palmer, 1996; Canale and Swain, 1980; Canale, 1983; Cziko, 1984; Celce-Murcia, 2008; Hymes, 1972; Li, 1987; Savignon, 1983; Widdowson, 1983;

Willis, 1990; etc.). Tracing the evolution of the CC theory during all these years from the sixties through the flourishing seventies to the eighties and nineties, two representative orientations relevant to the understanding of SL learning stand out, which make it necessary for us to give a brief introduction. One is the analytical orientation represented by the framework proposed by Canale and Swain (1980) and Canale (1983), and the other one is the use-based orientation represented by the model proposed by Li (1987) and L. F. Bachman (1990).

2.1.3.1 The introduction of the CC concept to the applied linguistics field

(1) Discussions with an analytical orientation

Canale and Swain (1980) and Canale (1983), in their attempt to measure their students' achievement in French, found that available grammar-based tests did not seem suitable for communicative immersion programs. They reviewed and elaborated Hymes' s theory of Communicative Competence and pointed out that Communicative Competence at least includes *grammatical competence* which covers lexis, morphology, sentence grammar, semantics, and phonology, *sociolinguistic competence* which "addresses the extent to which utterances are produced and understood appropriately in different sociolinguistic contexts depending on contextual factors such as status of participants, purposes of interaction, and norms or conventions of interaction" (Canale, 1983, p. 7), *discourse competence* which "concerns mastery of how to combine grammatical forms and meanings to achieve a unified spoken or written text in different genres" (Canale, 1983, p. 9), and *strategic competence* which has a compensatory function and an enhancement function. They argued that rules of grammar are meaningless (except presumably to the grammarian) without rules of use. Thus, Hymes' s idea of communicative competence develops from the components of linguistic and sociolinguistic competence to Canale and Swain (1980, p. 34) 's and Canale (1983, p. 5)'s four components, and in their view, communicative competence is clearly defined as including both *knowledge* and *skill* which obviously includes a dynamic element to the understanding of communicative competence.

Canale and Swain's work has been proved to be influential in the literature in this field although there are still arguments as to whether communicative competence consists of only one general factor or more. There are also some arguments around the explanation of CC in Canale and Swain's framework. One of the issues is concerned with the understanding of *the ability for use* in Hymes' s term. In Canale and Swain's model, this is excluded from their model as they stated:

> However, we hesitate to incorporate the notion of ability for use into our definition of communicative *competence* for two main reasons: (i) to our knowledge this notion has not been pursued rigorously in any research on communicative competence (or considered directly relevant in such research), and (ii) we doubt that there is any theory of human action that can adequately explicate "ability for use" and support principles of syllabus design intended to reflect this notion (Canale and Swain, 1980, p. 7).

However, Hornberger expresses a different opinion. He points out:

> Canale and Swain exclude Hymes' s ability for use from their framework for communicative competence on the grounds that it is not practical for application in syllabus design and that it suggests linguistic deficit (Canale and Swain, 1980: 7). However, these reasons seem unconvincing to me. First it is not clear that potential differences among speakers in ability for use gives any more rise to the notion of linguistic deficit than do potential differences in knowledge. Second, given that one of the factors of ability for use that Hymes names, motivation (1972: 283), is considered significant for language acquisition (cf. Gardner and Lambert's integrative/instrumental distinction (Lambert et al., 1968)), it seems counter-productive to exclude it from a model of communicative competence which aims to inform an understanding of second language acquisition (Hornberger, 1989, p. 226).

Hornberger goes on to give an example of his own case to show that motivation takes a role in communicative competence. Hymes admits that *ability for use* is a state when he comments on Hornberger's article (1989). This means that Hymes still admits the distinction between competence and performance. Later, another pair of terms also appears correspondingly, i.e. *communicative competence* and *communicative performance* (the coined term corresponding to the term " communicative competence "). *Communicative competence* refers to the internalized linguistic knowledge and rules of the use of that knowledge. It is different from the actual use. The success of one's actual performance depends on his internalized knowledge of grammar and use. So, the nature of communicative competence emphasizes the appropriateness in using language. But if one wants to use language appropriately, he has to possess the ability to use it appropriately — i.e. to have the internalized knowledge of how, when and where to use language. He should have the potential to realize that knowledge in communication, i. e. he should have the ability for use (Hornberger, 1989). Otherwise the case would be like what Widdowson (1989) said when talking about the problem of the Structuralist Approach, — "what was promoted was the ability to manifest language as usage rather than to realize it as use" (p. 131). From this point of view, it is without doubt that *ability for use* should not be excluded from communicative competence.

Although Canale & Swain (1980) and Canale (1983) expressed their hesitancy in including *the ability for use* into their framework, the identification of the strategic competence and the inclusion of the idea of skill in their explication indicate that researchers gradually pay attention to the process of learners' appropriate use of language in communication, although the nature of strategic competence is still not fully researched in this framework. In Canale (1983), strategic competence is defined as follows:

> Strategic competence: mastery of verbal and nonverbal strategies both (a) to compensate for breakdowns in communication due to

insufficient competence or to performance limitations and (b) to enhance the rhetorical effect of utterances (Canale, 1983, p. 339).

This definition indicates a perception of the dynamic nature of language use in communication, and strategic competence is mainly relavant to language use rather than language learning process in this line of thinking. The insight that the discussion around the CC concept has brought was soon re-contextualized for second/foreign language teaching and learning by means of a new applied language intervention approach — the Communicative Approach (CA), a reaction against the SA. The CA aims to enable learners to become communicatively competent. The communicative orientation of CA carries with itself a humanistic nature and bases its practice on the learner's needs, which provides very strong theoretical support for the language learning for specific purposes. As for English learning, it is usually called *English for Specific Purposes* (ESP). Widdowson devotes much of his attention to the study of this field. In developing his theory for ESP, Widdowson finds that both Chomsky's and Hymes' s definitions of language competence are analytic in nature. They both view language competence in an analyst's perspective rather than a user's (Widdowson, 1983, p. 23). What Hymes objects to Chomsky is only the inadequacy of Chomsky's interpretation of his term in not accounting for other aspects of language apart from the knowledge of sentence structure (Widdowson, 1983, p. 23). Widdowson then chooses to use another term "language capacity" which means the ability to exploit the resources for meaning in a language which have only partially been codified as competence. According to Widdowson (1983, p. 25), Hymes' s idea of capability is essentially ethnographic, which emphasizes analysis and assessment, while the term "capacity" he uses is ethnomethodological in his sense. Widdowson (1983) explained further that, "That is to say, it is the ability to use the knowledge of language as a resource for the creation of meaning, as is concerned not with assessment but interpretation." (p. 25). In Widdowson's sense, when we apply theory into practice, we cannot just analyze what is right or wrong, but what is intended to be expressed. According to Widdowson, for both Chomsky and Hymes, "what is referred to is a conformity to pre-existing rules of behavior as if instances of language use were only tokens of types of knowledge structure. What the concept of competence does not appear to account for is the ability to create meanings by exploiting the potential inherent in the language for continual modification in response to change" (Widdowson, 1983, pp. 7–8). Thus, Widdowson said that "it is the ability that I refer to in using the term 'capacity'" (ibid). Widdowson claims that the CC model "is not a model of member knowledge of language use, but one which provides the means for analyzing member behavior from outside" (Widdowson, 1983, p. 24). Widdowson's following statements give a very clear explanation of the difference between the term "capacity" he used and the term "competence" Chomsky and Hymes employed in their senses of language competence.

> Whereas 'competence' carries with it the implication that behavior is determined by rule almost as if humans simply responded to linguistic and sociolinguistic control, 'capacity' carries with it the assumption that human beings are in control of their own destiny and exploit the rules at their disposal for their own ends. One might claim that both competence and capacity allow for creativity. But the creativity referred to in discussions of linguistic competence refers to the generative mechanism of grammar which allows for the production and reception of sentences never previously attested. The creativity associated with capacity refers to the ability to produce and understand utterances by using the resources of the grammar in association with features of context to make meaning, which is a function of the relationship between the two. Such utterances will not always be in direct correspondence with sentences at all and in this respect will not be always sanctioned by the system (Widdowson, 1985, p. 8).

With respect to second or foreign language learning, Widdowson's idea, which emphasizes the creative use of the target language in context, is worthy of special attention. It carries with it a more cognitive-functional view of the relationship construction between language form and its function, and emphasizes the ability to make use of language resources to create meaning in language use on the basis of the interaction between language bearer's internal knowledge and the social variables, and hence lays a good foundation for a deeper understanding of the CA, although his view is still analytical by nature, as Taylor (1988, p. 165) points out. Till this stage, the understanding of the nature of communicative competence has moved from an analytic perspective to a more dynamic explanatory perspective. Hence, a learner possessing or lacking CC in second language development may manipulate communicative tasks in different ways and cause different effects to occur.

Along the line of discussing the nature of language competence, there are still many others who have contributed to the understanding and modification of the terms, such as Corder (1981), Stern (1983), Savignon (1983), Brumfit (1984), etc. By the end of the 1980s, Taylor (1988) made a very influential synthesis of the different employment of terms and understandings around *competence* and *communicative competence* and finally proposed to let the term *competence* keep its original meaning in Chomskyan sense, while using *proficiency* in the applied linguistics field to indicate its dynamic nature, although this suggestion did not seem to receive warm responses from the applied linguistics field.

(2) Discussions with a use-based orientation

Following the line of Canale and Swain (1980) and Canale (1983), when it comes to the 1990s, inspired and nourished by the achievements in functional linguistics, pragmatics, textual linguistics, cognitive psychology, second language acquisition, and corpus linguistics, an attempt to introduce and apply the concept of communicative competence into language teaching, language learning and language testing gradually makes the dynamic nature of the CC more explicit. Taking into consideration the Chinese teaching and learning situations, Li (1987, p. iv) puts forward her modification of communicative competence in teaching which consists of *linguistic competence*, *pragmatic competence* and *cognitive and affective capacity*, i. e. the form of the target language, the use of the form, and the content clothed in the form (Li, 1990a, p. 48). Apart from the ideas expressed by other researchers, this model particularly reflects a dynamic view of language. "Language is communication, and learning a language is learning to communicate" forms the basis of this framework. This understanding of language and language learning distinguishes itself from other models in that language is not considered to be a tool which suggests something ready-made, but something that every user has to create and construct for himself every time he uses it (ibid). Thus, language as communication is a process which is dynamic in nature, and the process "of acquiring a language and that of increasing and refining one's cognitive and affective capacity are intrinsically concurrent and contribute to each other's development" (ibid). Thus, another component is included into the concept of communicative competence, i. e. *cognitive and affective capacity*. Language form and its function are taken as a whole which works along with learner's cognitive development. Language is learnt in communication, and communication cannot take place without content. Learner's development of communicative competence helps him to develop his whole-person competence.

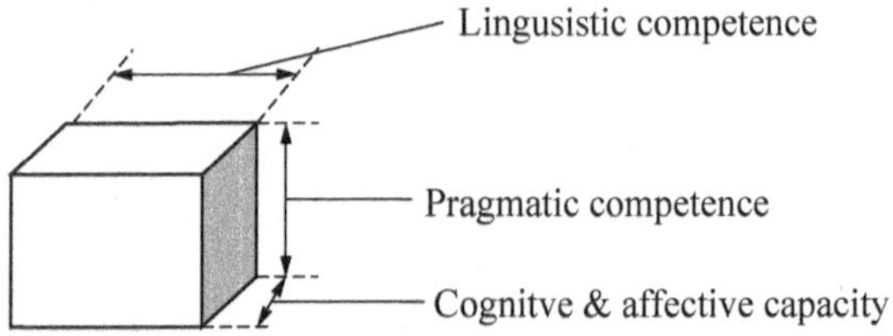

Figure 2 – 1 A three-dimensional model of communicative competence (Li, 1987, p. v)

Obviously, in this explanation, CC is elaborated from the perspective of language use and language education. The ability for use in included and the inclusion of cognitive and affective capacity into CC adds an explicit communicative, functional and humanistic color to the concept. CC in this understanding is considered as an entity which is integrative in nature. Unlike Canale & Swain (1980)'s framework which is still much constrained within language itself, this model targets CC as a higher goal of second language education. The fact that the discussion of the CC theory prevails for over 40 years in the applied linguistics field is partly because it is incorporated into second language acquisition research, and partly because it is introduced and adapted for language teaching and testing practices, which makes it easily accessible to practitioners. Among the many adapted models, the most influential one is the model expounded by L. F. Bachman (1990). According to Bachman (1990), *Communicative Language Ability*, as Bachman (1990) renamed, at least subsumes three components: *language*

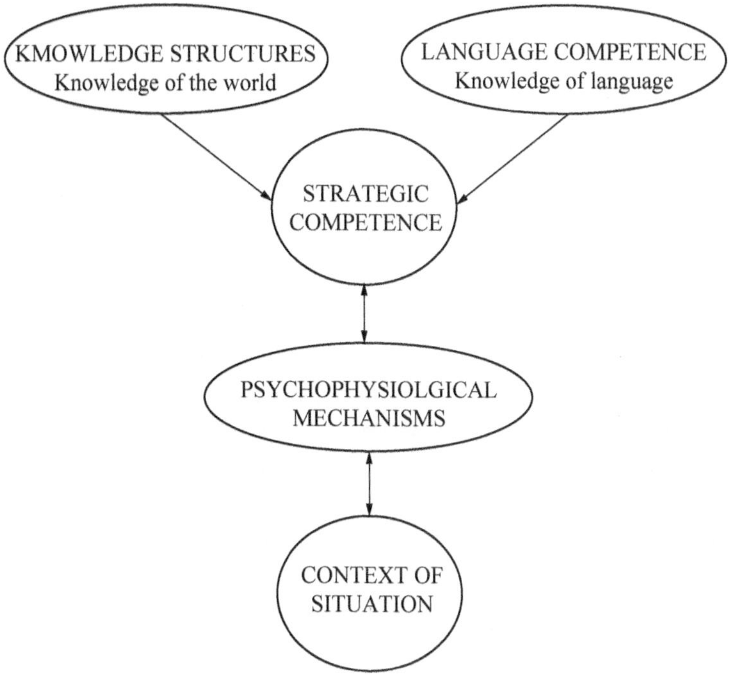

Figure 2-2 Components of CLA in communicative language use (Bachman, 1990, p. 85)

competence, *strategic competence*, and *psychophysiological mechanisms* (Bachman 1990, pp84-108). As illustrated in Figure 2-2, *strategic competence* here is given a different role which acts as the key link of the three components. It performs a macro function, which is the manipulating approach in language production and comprehension.
As Bachman (1990) defines,

> Strategic competence is the term I will use to characterize the mental capacity for implementing the components of language competence in contextualized communicative language use. Strategic competence thus provides the means for relating language competencies to features of the context of situation in which language use takes place and to the language user's knowledge structures (sociocultural knowledge, "real-world knowledge") (p. 84).

Strategic competence here is viewed as operating mechanisms in language use apart from its compensatory function and enhancement characteristic. It consists of three components: *assessment*, *planning*, and *execution*. This understanding of the role of *strategic competence* in communicative language ability enables the whole model a use-based operable guide which moves far away from the original perception of Hymes (1972) 's CC, but maybe closer to the direction that Hymes (1972) points to. From the perspective of use and language testing, Bachman therefore further expounds that the component *language competence* consists of *organizational competence* and *pragmatic competence*, while *grammatical competence* and *textual competence* are included into *organizational competence* and *illocutionary competence* and *sociolinguistic competence* are classified into *pragmatic competence* (See Figure 2-3).

In Bachman (1990), language competence is only one of the important components in the use process, and *grammatical competence* is taken as one means of organization. The model indicates two elements in *language competence*, i. e. form and meaning. Forms are mainly used for organizing whereas meaning

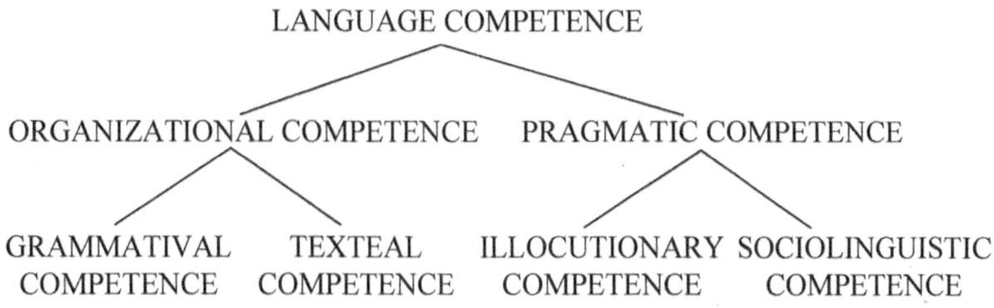

Figure 2-3 Components of language competence (Bachman, 1990, p. 87)

is realized in speech acts and appropriate choices of language forms in correspondence with social activities. Form and meaning are of equal significance. To put this understanding in line with second language development, a learner's second language development involves both the acquisition of organizational competence and that of pragmatic competence. One can easily sense the influence of meaning-oriented linguistics development since the 1960s.

There are also researchers who believe that there is only one factor in language competence, i. e. the UCH (Unitary Competence Hypothesis). Oller (1976) puts forward a theory of an "expectancy grammar" or grammar-based expectancies in testing, which means that communicative competence is only one holistic factor and cannot be separated. Thus in testing, only one factor can be tested. But this theory has met with problems. Cummins (1979, 1980) has pointed out that Oller's theory of a unitary proficiency concept is based on an interpretation of language test data. Language tests have a certain academic or cognitive character. What is tested is only "a cognitive/academic language proficiency" (CALP), which is why the tests highly correlate with each other, for they all have the same academic characteristic. Hence, Cummins points out that what these tests fail to capture is another quality of language use, i. e. "basic interpersonal and communicative skills" (BICS). Thus, Cummins believes that at least there exist two components in language competence: CALP and BICS. Oller's unitary competence theory has been proved to be without basis by statistical results. He admits that "The idea of an exhaustive global factor of language proficiency was wrong"

(Oller, 1983, p. 35). Another problem for the concept of Unitary Competence is pointed out by Vollmer (1983), i.e. the equivalence of "proficiency" to the concept of "competence". Vollmer pointed out that in the UCH "...the proficiency (measurement) and the ability (psychological construct) levels are tacitly mixed and defined by one another" (Vollmer, 1983). For all existing problems, however, the concept of CC was in fact widely researched, elaborated and applied in foreign language teaching and testing fields in the past more than 40 years, and has been set as the target of communicative language teaching.

To sum up, the introduction of communicative competence into the applied linguistics field has inspired a huge mass of studies which have shaped the thinking and professional practice of most researchers in the applied linguistics field since then. However, one needs to notice that it is not the term itself that matters, rather, the perception of the nature of the knowledge that works behind language users that has motivated researchers to crowd into this discussion. The conundrum of the nature of language user's knowledge system has also initiated another strand of exploration which focuses on the discussion of form and meaning from a process-oriented perspective in SLA.

2.2 Form, meaning or the mapping?

Another strand of research around the nature of the knowledge working behind learners' behavior is from the perspective of second language acquisition. In terms of what should be learnt and what kinds of knowledge are necessary for language comprehension and production in communication, in the field of second language learning, researchers have been debating around which should come first between form and meaning in the learning process or whether it is the mapping between form and meaning that should be attained for language use. The discussion of these problems has been around in one guise or another since 1960s among L1 and L2 research fields, as has been pointed out by VanPatten (2004). And this discussion finally led to a conference in 2002 where around 50 papers were presented. Along this line of enquiry, two approaches turn out to be worthy of notice: *rule-based approach* vs *usage-based approach*.

2.2.1 Rule-based approach

SLA researchers are more interested in the learning process, hence, the discussion moves to the study of how learners could finally gain the competence that could enable them to employ it and how learners employ the knowledge they have had in communication. Under such circumstances, competence is considered as either a system of form or a system of meaning or the interaction between the two. This idea has also been in accordance with the discussion of CC and language teaching and testing. The line of enquiry with a SLA orientation starts from the 1980s when researchers in SLA believed that there were two types of processes in second language development: *acquisition* and *learning* (Krashen, 1981, 1982), and when attention is called to be given to L2 instruction and input (Ellis, 1984; Felix, 1981; Krashen, 1981, 1982; Long, 1983; Saleemi, 1989; etc.). This line of inquiry continues throughout the 1990s (Myles, Mitchell & Hooper, 1999; Pica, 1991; Radford, 1997; VanPatten, 1990, 1994, 1996; White, 1998; etc.) till the 21st century (Bardovi-Harlig, 2000, 2010; S. Carroll, 2001; Hawkins, 2001; Marsden & Chen, 2011; Odlin, 2008; Sonbul & Schmitt, 2012; Toth, 2006; VanPatten, Williams, Rott & Overstreet, 2004; White, 2003; etc.) and still prevails at present.

In general, this line of inquiry follows a generative tradition (Pinker, 1994; Radford, 1997; VanPatten, 2004; etc.) which holds a contrastive view of competence and skill, and claims that they prefer the choice of such terms as *underlying competence*, *underlying mental representation*, *the developing system* or *interlanguage* to refer to SLLners' knowledge system, although these terms are also employed by researchers with a usage-based orientation with different meanings. Large amount of research in this line is around finding the universal rules in L1 and L2 acquisition, hence, the study of form is given special attention. Form is defined as "a surface feature of language or a surface manifestation of an underlying representation" (VanPatten,

Williams & Rott, 2004, p. 1), and meaning is taken as "concrete, displaced, or abstract referential value such as number, temporal reference, agency, aspect, and lexical reference" (VanPatten, Williams & Rott, 2004, p. 2), while the connection between form and meaning, which is the focus of attention in this strand of research in the 21st century, is defined as "a situation in which a form encodes some kind of referential meaning" (ibid).

However, it is still unclear as to how form corresponds to meaning in the acquisition process, because form may have one single meaning, may also have multiple meanings, and the same form can encode different meanings in different contexts. Besides, the same forms may share meanings. One more complicated phenomenon that has been identified by L2 researchers in SLA is that L2 forms can also be connected to meanings that are not L2-like (VanPatten, Williams & Rott, 2004, p. 4). With such complicated issues in front, researchers with this orientation start from the exploration of how learners process the different kinds of input given. In terms of the nature of the knowledge that supports learners' performance, this group initiates their work by first of all identifying the different types of form-meaning connections, and moves on to find out how these connections were established in the acquisition process. The study of form-meaning connections is considered as a fundamental aspect of both first and second language acquisition, according to VanPatten (2004), because "All but a few L2 learners pursue meaning first, in an effort to communicate and to understand the world around them" (ibid, p. 4). It is obvious that this view has moved away from the old dichotomous way of focusing on either form or meaning, rather the interactions of the two, hence the different understandings of the nature of the knowledge—how form-meaning connections are established in the acquisition process rather than a set of static rules. However, now that this group claims that they stick to the generative tradition and aims to find the universal rules governing the whole SLA process, we classify them as rule-based group.

2.2.2 Usage-based approach

Within the same strand of enquiry but with different assumptions about language learning is what they themselves claimed as the *usage-based perspective* (N. Ellis, 2004, p. 51). This line of research is a continuation of the cognitive tradition since the 1970s with its various tribes linked with constructivism (J. R. Anderson, 1983; N. Ellis, 2003;). In relation to the identification of two processes in SLA following the rule-based approach, this line of research also saw an identification of two terms describing the language acquisition process: *knowledge* and *control*, among which, *knowledge* is further compartmentalized into: *explicit knowledge* and *implicit knowledge* (Bialystok, 1978, 1979; Krashen, 1982; etc.), and *control* refers to the processing of the knowledge. Followed this identification was a number of publications and arguments about the nature of the two types of linguistic knowledge representation and whether there existed an interface or not between these two types of knowledge in language acquisition and use (N. Ellis, 1993; R. Ellis, 1984, 1994a; Hulstijn, 1984; McLaughlin, 1983; Odlin, 1986; Robinson, 1994; etc.). These issues continue to be the concern of the connectionists, the applied linguists, functional and cognitive linguists and emergentists at present, but with "a shift of emphasis from knowledge as static representation stored in particular locations to knowledge as processing involving the dynamic mutual influence of interrelated types of information as they activate and inhibit each other over time" (N. Ellis, 2003, p. 6).

Thus, the study of the nature of the two types of knowledge together with the ways of language knowledge processing in SLA turns out to be a meeting point for enquires with different starting points in this line. The dissociation nature of the two types of knowledge has been examined from a psychological perspective by Reber (1976, cited from N. Ellis, 2003) which concludes that "Implicit learning is acquisition of knowledge about the underlying structure of a complex stimulus environment by a process which takes place naturally, simply, and without conscious operations. Explicit learning is a more conscious operation where the individual attends to particular aspects of the stimulus array and volunteers and tests hypotheses in a search for structure." (N. Ellis, 2003, p. 3)

In terms of the interface or non-interface problem, Schmidt (1990) 's noticing hypothesis motivates subsequent continuing research efforts in the applied linguistics field on the role of consciousness in SLA. "The shortcomings in uptake and the consequently limited endstate of naturalistic learners, together with the demonstrable role of noticing in SLA, obliged in turn the rejection of the extreme 'no-interface' position" (N. Ellis, 2003, p. 5). The converging of different disciplines on the nature of the two types of knowledge has led to a better understanding of learners' language knowledge representations and the complexity nature of the knowledge. There are still such complicated issues around this area as how these types of knowledge are formed in the learning process, how they influence each other in the forming and accessing processes, and how they transfer to each other, and how they conspire to make learners able to accomplish communicative tasks or fail to do so, etc. However, a basic understanding has been formed, i.e. these two types of knowledge are different in nature, and they can come into mutual influence in processing. In fact, a recent publication by N. Ellis, O'Donnell & Römer (2013) has indicated that a learner's language knowledge representation involves not only linguistic form, but also the learner's cognition and language usage, while language usage is considered as a complex adaptive system. This view of a learner's language knowledge is obviously from a broad cognitive perspective, in which different ways of form-meaning mapping are the focus of attention.

2.3 A critique of the previous theories

The question we discussed in this chapter is one of the fundamental questions that have been puzzling researchers in the past 60 years or so, and is still a question confusing us. However, the review helps to make clear that the previous dichotomous way of understanding the nature of the underlying language system needs to be reassessed. Things are easy to be separated, but not easy to be put together again, especially when second language acquisition is concerned. The above discussion of the underlying language system from different perspectives exhibits the complex nature of language form and its functions. As J. R. Anderson (1985) once pointed out, one reason that this issue [the issue of language competence] is still unclear, is that linguists differ as to what should be covered under the topic of competence. Now that language has its multi-aspects and performs various functions, different angles in theorizing the issue of language competence emerge reasonably.

The competence-performance debate leads to the emergence of a complete new term *communicative competence* which moves far away from the original meaning of the distinction, but stimulates a vast ocean of new ideas around the nature of the language user's underlying system. The enlightening proposal of the different components in CC throughout the whole discussion has inspired both L1 and L2 language acquisition researchers, and has clarified such concepts as *competence*, *skill*, *proficiency*, *capacity* and *the ability for use*, although it is still not clear how those components interact with each other to make language users able to communicate. A basic agreement has been reached after the proposal by Canale & Swain (1980) and Canale (1983) that communicative competence is the underlying system which includes both *knowledge* and *skill*. In Canale (1983, p. 5), knowledge " refers here to what one knows (consciously or unconsciously) about the language and about other aspects of communicative language use; skill refers to how well one can perform this knowledge in actual communication." And communicative competence is different from actual communication. The inclusion of skill into the underlying system of knowledge gives the concept of CC a more dynamic nature, although Canale and Swain (1980) and Canale (1983) stress that the four components they propose only serve as an illustration of what CC includes. Four basic components have been identified in Canale and Swain (1980)'s and Canale (1983) 's framework for the application in language teaching and language testing:

grammatical competence, *sociolinguistic competence*, *discourse competence* and *strategic competence*. With the inclusion of skill into CC, the dichotomous distinction between competence and performance has been subtly integrated into a new way of viewing the language user's language system, and this view has been furthered later on into "multicompetence" (V. J. Cook, 1996) for second language acquisition.

Many other later frameworks are developed on the basis of this one. The nature of CC and skill has also been further expounded in different frameworks, such as in Li (1990a) 's framework, the commonly-mentioned four types of skills (listening, speaking, reading and writing) are further clarified as "only the surface manifestation of processes that take place beneath the surface" (Li, 1990a, p. 53), while CC in language learning suggests the comprehensive underlying knowledge and ability for use in communicative contexts. CC is holistic in nature, while skills can be separated. The mastery of some compartmentalized skills in language learning does not indicate the mastery of a language, for language should be learned as communicative competence, and communicative competence is "something that certainly goes deeper than the surface and cannot be compartmentalized" (Li, 1990a, p. 54). The components of CC are actually the different dimensions of it rather than unrelated separate entities. Thus, CC is integrated but not discrete in nature. The holistic integrative nature of CC has been given special attention with further discussions.

It is still not clear how these components interact with each other although there are attempts incorporating new components or reorganizing components and explaining the interaction of different components in different fields (Li, 1987; Bachman, 1990; Celce-Murcia, 2008), and these attempts manifest, from another angle, the confluence of recent developments of linguistics, applied linguistics, and cognitive psychology. It is here that second language acquisition studies fill in.

The different components coming from the debates around the nature of competence and performance which is analytical in nature are changed into the topic of the processing of different types of knowledge or different connections or mappings between form and meaning in second language acquisition field. Although with contrastive views as to how the underlying system comes between the rule-based approach and the usage-based approach, what they are all pursuing is the connections or mappings between language form and its meaning, and how those connections are established in the acquisition or learning process, which indicates a typical dynamic processing and systematic view. The nature of the knowledge a learner needs to acquire, in this line of inquiry, to its latest insight, is the relationship between form and meaning rather than either of them alone (N. Ellis, 2003, 2004; N. Ellis et al, 2013; VanPatten, 1996, 2004; etc.).

The two underlying components of CC — *knowledge* and *skill* in the applied linguistics have changed into *knowledge* and *control* in the cognitive-psycholinguistic tradition, while *knowledge* here refers to *information* or *mental representations* or such different types of knowledge as *explicit linguistic knowledge* (ELK) and *implicit linguistic knowledge* (ILK) (Bialystok, 1978), and *control* refers to the processing of the different types of knowledge. In line with this tradition are the well-known Information-processing Model, the Monitor Model and Bialystok's SLL model [①] which are later modified as the input processing theory (VanPatten, et. al., 2004) and other recent research based on the cognitive-functional perspective (N. Ellis, 2004; N. Ellis et al, 2013, etc.). The early discussion of *declarative knowledge* (which refers to the knowledge of the facts of language, e. g. grammatical rules, vocabulary, pronunciation, etc.) and *procedural knowledge* (which refers to rules of how to do things) (J. R. Anderson, 1980) and of *acquired knowledge* and *learnt knowledge* (Krashen, 1985) has been channeled to the discussion of implicit knowledge and explicit knowledge (Doughty, 2004; Doughty & Long, 2003; N Ellis, 2003, 2004; N. Ellis et al., 2013; Gass, 2004; Larsen-Freeman, 2004; VanPatten, 1996, 2004; Williams, 2004; etc.), although a non-interface view was held strongly by Krashen (1985). However, when looking back, wisdom

① Detailed description of these models can be seen in Ellis, 1985.

in earlier works is still shining. The possibility of the interface between explicit knowledge and implicit knowledge has already been pointed out since the 1980s.

Bialystok believes that in SLL learnt knowledge is not so unimportant as Krashen assumes, but might be converted into acquired knowledge through practice. In Bialystok's understanding, the nature of both ELK and ILK is as follows: (Bialystok chose the term "analyzed knowledge" and "unanalyzed knowledge" in her later works.)

> ...Explicit Linguistic Knowledge contains all the conscious facts the learner has about the language and the criterion for admission to this category is the ability to articulate those facts. These may include some grammar rules, some vocabulary items, pronunciation rules, and so on. Implicit Linguistic Knowledge is the intuitive information upon which the language learner operates in order to produce responses (comprehension or production) in the target language. Whatever information is automatic and is used spontaneously in language tasks is represented in Implicit Knowledge (1978, p. 72).

Thus, ILK is the proceduralized linguistic knowledge that can be employed directly in communication, while the ELK is the conscious knowledge of the rules of language when it has not been converted into the ILK. This does not mean that the ELK is not necessary or has no role in communication. It may function as a monitor and can be used as a source for the ILK learning under certain conditions. According to Bialystok, three functions are assigned to ELK, that is, ELK can perform as a buffer of new information about the language, can act as a store for explicit information that is always represented there, and as an "explicit articulary system" (Bialystok, 1978, pp. 72 – 73). In explaining the first function, Bialystok (1978, p. 72) hypothesizes that,

> For example, new words or vocabulary items which are presented in a classroom, or encountered in any other explicit situation, would at first be represented in Explicit Linguistic Knowledge.

> After continued use, the information may become automatic and transferred to Implicit Linguistic Knowledge, but the initial encounter, because of its explicitness, requires that it is represented in Explicit Knowledge (Bialystok, 1978, p. 72).

Obviously, an interface position is held here. And this position has been strengthened by the probabilistic cognitive-functional view in SLA which emphasizes the learning of constructions relating form and meaning (Cadierno, 2004; N. Ellis, 2004; Williams, 2004; etc.), and Schmdt (1990)'s noticing hypothesis which postulates that a conscious involvement is required for the conversion form input to intake.

The introduction of cognitive element into the discussion of the acquisition of different types of knowledge has also been reflected in the above-mentioned applied-linguistics-based framework of communicative competence, such as Li (1987) 's understanding of CC as consisting of *linguistic competence, pragmatic competence* and *cognitive and affective capacities,* which notices the role of learners' cognitive effort in second language learning and use. It is here that we find the intersection between applied linguistics and cognitive-functional view of SLA studies in explaining the knowledge conversion problem and the nature of the knowledge undergirding learners' behavior. The latest research on the form-meaning connections or mappings or the interfacing of explicit knowledge and implicit knowledge in SLA from different perspectives has finally been pointed to the understanding of a kind of language-based developing system in which different types of competencies conspire to make it accessible to the learner in his use, while in attaining or employing this system, learner's cognitive effort also plays an important role. The competencies that a learner needs for comprehension and production cannot only be constrained within the purely linguistic part, rather, such linguistic-related areas as socio-cultural conventions, formulaic language use, strategic planning and employment of different resources in language learning and use, and discourse competence which is actually a realization of all kinds of competencies in language use

(Celce-Murcia, 2008; Tarone, 2007; Swain & Deters, 2007). In actual language use, each component might play a different role, but it is the effective interaction of all those components that make it possible for successful language communication to occur, and in this interaction the role of the owner of the interacted system is active.

However, the review also reflects the limitations of the research on the underlying system. First, there are still disagreements on the role of grammatical competence and its relationship with other competencies in second/foreign language learning theories. It is in fact the problem of the relationship between language form and its meaning. Just as Spolsky pointed out, "Communicative competence theories have not yet clarified the relationship between function and structure, ..." (Spolsky, 1989, p. 144). Second, many CC theories have identified the different components of communicative competence, but have not described clearly how these components interact with each other, and how to delimit the boundaries of these components. This appears as a serious problem as researchers probe further. Third, all these theories are more theoretical than empirical. Few empirical studies have been conducted to see how different understandings of the internalized integrative system or different types of mental representations bring about different learning results in second/foreign language learning. Thus little evidence is found to verify these theories. Fourth, the employment of various terms in the explanation of the nature of the internalized system reveals the multi-aspects of the underlying system on the one hand, but causes confusion in understanding on the other hand.

2.4 The present study and the previous review

The present study aims to explore the nature of the Chinese secondary school EFL learners' final attainment after their six or more years' time and effort have been spent. The research is carried out by means of an experiment conducted within a conceptual framework. The foregoing review aims to provide a theoretical basis for the establishment of the working conceptual framework from the aspect of what should be learnt.

Although pointed out by Spolsky (1989) that the componential frameworks have oversimplified Hymes' original idea, these frameworks are theoretically and practically more acceptable than others where language teaching and learning are concerned. With an understanding of the different types of knowledge necessary for language comprehension and production and the consideration of the present research purpose, the author adopts the general terms for the components of communicative competence put forward by Canale and Swain (1980) and Canale (1983) as part of the theoretical basis for establishing the working conceptual framework for this study, but with some modifications of the framework, some addition of Li (1987) 's understanding of CC and an understanding of SLLners' second language system development from the perspective of SLA. This decision is based on the following thinking.

(1) Canale & Swain (1980)'s and Canale (1983)'s framework provides for us an explicit and detailed picture of what competencies are included in the learner's internalized knowledge system which are necessary for language learning and use. Communicative competence, according to this framework, consists of four components: *grammatical competence, sociolinguistic competence, discourse competence* and *strategic competence.* Grammatical competence is one of the necessary components of communicative competence, but not the whole. Although analytical in nature, this framework explicates clearly the difference in content between the CC-oriented SL learning and many other approaches.

(2) This framework orients itself at the discussion of the nature of the internalized language system by incorporating the developments both from the linguistic field and psycholinguistic and intercultural communication fields, whose purpose corresponds well with the purpose of this research although it still needs to be modified and adapted. It makes clear that both knowledge and skill are included in this framework which somewhat reveals the development and discussion in the cognitive-psycholinguistic tradition. This makes it appear more prospective and tolerant of

later modifications.

(3) It is also of instructive value in language teaching practice. With these componential competencies in mind, language teaching should not be directed to one kind of competence only, but all kinds of competence. The integration of these types of competence for the learner can only be achieved by responding to genuine communication needs and interests in realistic second language situation. Language learning should therefore be directed to the learning in a contextualised situation which involves meaningful and genuine communicative interaction rather than a decontextualised situation which involves mainly the learning of discrete linguistic forms.

However, as has been pointed out in the previous part of this chapter, there are still problems in this model. The exclusion from this model of the *ability for use* weakens its power in its explanation of language use, and restrains itself within its analytical nature. There is still some confusion in the framework about the interrelationships among the components and the understanding of strategic competence which limits its function within a compensating role. Besides, this framework does not explain how form and meaning relationship is established in learning and in use, and it is here that the cognitive-functional ideas of SLL (N. Ellis, 2004; Williams, 2004; etc.), Li (1987, p. iv)'s identification of "cognitive and affective capacity" (CAC) in SLL and the identification of the general planning role of strategic competence by Bachman (1990) are of great value, and will be incorporated into the framework for this research in explaining the relationship between learners' language learning process and their attainment.

To sum up, we then can draw a basic conclusion about the nature of the internalized language system that works behind our learners' performance. From the discussion above, it is clear that for either a successful first language user or a second language user, the system he/she employs should not be a static rule system or a store of discrete units or unrelated competencies, otherwise, it will be hard to explain the textuality, fluency, effectiveness and efficiency of his/her discourse in communication. Nor should his/

her system be non-developing or non-interfacing in the learning or acquisition process, otherwise it will be hard to explain his/her maturing process in his/her language comprehension and production during his language learning process. SLLners' interlanguage system is a special case in this development, in which some properties or types of knowledge of the system might have been integrated in different ways so that they are represented in different manners in learners' minds and hence cause difficulties in learners' language employment. Hence, we assume that if the stored system is systematic and the form-meaning relationship is well established, this system can be easily retrieved, and hence the textuality, fluency, effectiveness and efficiency can be guaranteed in the learner's employment of the system. On the contrary, if the stored knowledge is not interconnected and form-meaning mappings are not established, problems will occur in learners' language performance. Therefore, an internalized system which can guarantee successful communication should enable learners to employ freely and automatically not only the facts part, but also procedures which can guarantee not only the compensating function, but also the holistic planning function both in learning and use, and the sizing up of different contexts with its various senses: textual, topical, spatial, temporal, psychological, interpersonal, social, and intercultural (Li, 1987, p. v), and even an advanced stage of explicitly explicating his/her own language behavior. In terms of learning, in order to achieve this goal, various components should be included, including the content knowledge (e.g. world knowledge and cultural knowledge) which may facilitate the development of learners' cognitive and affective capacities which are essential in language learning and use to a certain extent. A learner's language system which lacks the nature of the above description may lead to his/her poor performance in communicative tasks.

2.5 Summary

This chapter has reviewed theories respecting the nature of the internalized language system from different perspectives. The review starts from the initial distinction between *competence* and *performance* made by Chomsky in terms of linguistics to Hymes' s re-explication and adaptation of competence from a sociological angle. The review goes on exploring the arguments around the different types of knowledge constructed by learners in different learning processes in relation to second language acquisition from linguistic, applied linguistic and cognitive-functional perspectives. At the final stage, a critique is provided about the different understandings. The relation between the review of previous theories around the nature of the internalized language system and the present study has been discussed.

When we come to this point, the following questions occur naturally: How can the different components of the internalized system interact with each other? How can we explain the different employment of the different types of knowledge in learners' language use? What are the possible factors that may affect the whole process of language learning and language using? These questions will lead us to our enquiry into second language learning processes which will be dealt with in the following chapter.

Chapter 3
Pursuing an Understanding of Second Language Learning Processes

Apart from the questions concerning what should be learnt, another set of questions is concerned with how learners can attain what they need for successful language communication. This chapter will present discussions respecting those identified factors and how their relationship and their interactive effect on learners' final attainment are understood by research from different perspectives.

3.1 Theories of naturalistic second language learning

3.1.1 The distinction between naturalistic learning and classroom learning

In the field of SLA, there usually appear pairs of terms in relation to different kinds of learning, such as *second and foreign language learning*, *formal and informal learning*, *formal training and apprenticeship*, *naturalistic and classroom language learning*, *naturalistic second language acquisition and instructed second language acquisition*, and so on. Each pair of terms reflects more or less a different perspective on language learning. Seeing language learning from an educational point of view, then terms of "formal training and apprenticeship" are employed, of which the former refers to "learning which has been induced or influenced by some form of deliberately planned social intervention" (Stern, 1983, p. 19), and the latter mainly refers to learning by doing things. A psychological view of language learning might result in "formal and informal language learning", of which "Formal learning involves some kind of studial activity on the part of the learner—for example, an attempt to learn *about* the language by obtaining information about explicit rules of grammar" (R. Ellis, 1990, p. 2), and "Informal learning takes place through observation and direct participation in communication— learning is a process of discovery which takes place spontaneously and automatically providing certain conditions have been met" (ibid). However, from a sociolinguistic perspective, researchers might use the terms "naturalistic" and "classroom" language learning (Fishman, 1964 cited from R. Ellis, 1990, p. 1).

R. Ellis (1990) provides a good review of the above-mentioned terms. As to the pair of terms of "classroom and naturalistic L2 learning", Ellis points out that they are explained in a view of domains, which means "constellations of factors that affect the way language is used" (p. 1). The domains of these two terms can be distinguished with reference to such factors as *location*, *participants*, *topics* and *purposes* (R. Ellis, 1990, p. 1). Ellis explains that "naturalistic L2 learning" is characterized by a greater range of settings, participants, topics and purposes although it is possible to envisage exceptional cases of each type of learning where the reverse applies—the classroom can provide the richer, more diverse learning experiences.

The review of theories in this chapter is based on a basic distinction among the following three terms: *naturalistic L2 learning*, *mixed classroom L2 learning* and *classroom L2 learning*. Naturalistic L2 acquisition and mixed classroom L2 learning, to the best of the author's knowledge, are mostly discussed in the field of SLA, while classroom L2 learning only attracts researchers' interest recently. Naturalistic second language acquisition refers to the learning of a target language by communicating orally with native speakers of the target language, i.e. learners have many opportunities to be exposed to the target language. Mixed classroom learning refers to the learning carried out "in the context in which a learner learns the target language through classroom instruction in the target language community and thus has many opportunities to use the target language by participating in natural communication situations" (Wu Xudong, 1994, p. 2). Classroom L2 learning, however, refers to the learning of the target language in classrooms by way of the teacher's help — instruction, and thus it is also called "instructed learning". Learners of this type receive input mainly from their teachers, and have few opportunities to use the target language in communicative situations, while in the first two learning situations, learners can receive input from other target language speakers or learning partners. Learners in the first two situations could learn a second language in a subconscious way — *implicit learning* as it is addressed in SLA field, while learners in the third situation are usually told what they are learning about the language — *explicit learning* in correspondence with implicit learning. We then have two lines of theories: theories on naturalistic second language acquisition and mixed classroom learning, and theories on classroom L2 learning.

3. 1. 2 Studies on the internal processing mechanism

A great number of studies about SL/FL learning come from the comparison between L1 and L2 acquisition processes at the beginning in SLA. Related to the question of what constitutes language competence is the question of how language is acquired and how knowledge of language is put to use. Questions like whether SLA is like first language acquisition in terms of language processing and storing, whether SLA is guided by fundamentally different mechanisms, and why SLLners vary so much in terms of outcome if there are processes and mechanisms common to L1 and L2 acquisition, etc. are frequently examined from different perspectives. In order to find out the key to second language acquisition process, researchers turn to ask how children acquire their first language at the beginning.

Most of the research on L1 acquisition is based on Chomsky's theory of Universal Grammar (UG). In terms of child L1 acquisition of knowledge of language, Chomsky argues that the acquisition of a grammar is only possible if it is guided by some kind of innate structure, specifically linguistic in nature, usually called Universal Grammar (UG). Therefore, not all knowledge of language has to be acquired, because some of it is already "built in". Linguists as Chomsky should aim at finding the principles and parameters that shape our linguistic knowledge (Chomsky, 1981).

> The theory underlying UG assumes that language consists of a set of abstract principles which characterize core grammars of all natural languages. If children have to learn a complex set of abstractions, there must be something other than the language input to which they are exposed in order for them to learn with relative ease and speed. UG is postulated as an innate language faculty that limits the extent to which language can vary. That is, it specifies the limits of a possible language. The theoretical need for an innate language faculty is based on a negative argument. The claim is that on the basis of language input alone, children cannot attain the complexities of adult grammars (i. e. the input underdetermines ultimate acquisition). Innate linguistic properties fill in where the input fails (Gass, 1993, p. 106).

According to the theory underlying UG, universal principles form part of the mental representation of language. It is properties of the human mind that make language universals the way they are. The universal principles are then the physical state and they root in the human mind. These principles and parameters not only specify a language which is different from other systems, but also guarantee the internalization of a specific language by exposure to the input. For child L1 acquisition, as Gass summarizes, these properties fill in when input fails. Thus the process of child L1 acquisition can be schematized as: **Input → UG → L1 grammar.**

It is apparent that any child L1 acquisition seems to grow with relative ease and speed, while adult L2 learning usually grows with low speed and much difficulty. Besides, children could internalize such a complex language system within two or three years. Researchers are interested in the great difference between child L1 acquisition and adult L2 learning. According to Goodluck (1991)'s summary, the following factors have been identified to be working in the L1 acquisition process:

(1) **The innate UG effect**: Evidence in current studies shows that the UG does contribute to child L1 acquisition. The innate or biologically equipped LAD is in an active state in child L1 acquisition①. Evidence of children's *orderly progression of stages* has been found②. This suggests that the child has priority in learning a first language. Once the principles and parameters project correctly in the child's first language, they will guarantee the easy learning of L1. This is one part an adult language learner cannot match. Researchers are then interested in whether LAD are still working in L2 learning.

(2) **The Age factor**: Theories and empirical studies of language acquisition show that human beings have a language learning critical period although there is still an argument as to what the critical age is (Krashen, 1985; White, 1989). The "critical age" hypothesis holds that once the child goes beyond this age, the ability of language learning will be impaired. It has been observed that from the teens onwards, most people exhibit a decreasing ability to learn a second language. That might be one of the reasons that it is relatively hard for an adult learner to learn a second language. This inspires researchers to explore whether it is the age that obstructs L2 learning.

(3) **The input difference**: The input children receive has been observed to be different from that of the adults' language when they communicate among themselves. There is a phenomenon of "care-taker" language or "motherese". The "care-taker" or "motherese" language has the characteristics of

---

① The problem of whether UG is dead in L2 learning is a hot topic among SLA researchers. There is no agreement up to now. For more reference, see L. White, 1989.

② It has been observed that in different areas of grammar, there is a distinct sequence in which children develop their linguistic abilities. See Goodluck, 1991, p. 144: "For example, babbling emerges before first words; a one-word stage generally precedes the emergence of multi-word utterances; and specific morphemes and rules emerge in appropriately the same order across different children learning the same language."

simple-structured (few embedded structures since the *Subjacency* principle in the UG does not allow children to learn complicated structures at an early time), soft-sounded, matching children's style, etc. Besides, mother's speech forms are characteristically fluent and intelligible, with fewer hesitancies or mumbled or muffled utterances than speech to adults, grammatical, with very few utterances that are not well formed by the rules of the adult grammar, and short (the average length of utterances of mothers to two-year-old children in Snow's original study was approximately 6. 5 words, compared to 9. 5 in the speech of adults to ten-year-olds) (Goodluck, 1991, p. 160). But it has also been observed that the input to children is always beyond their current ability. Sentences with embedded structures are often used by adults and heard by children although they could not use them at the beginning. Yet, they could still understand and carry out any instructions of their parents. This description of the features of the input received by children lays the foundation for Krashen's *Input Hypothesis* (1985).

There is another typical feature of the input to children which forms a strong argument for the position that the child is equipped with a highly structured grammar-forming mechanism. Input can be divided into *positive* evidence (i.e. evidence that a particular form exists in a language) and *negative* evidence (i.e. information about what is inappropriate in some way, possibly non-felicitous, ungrammatical, difficult to parse, etc.). Children are seldom exposed to the speech concerning the correct rules for the language to be used. Thus children are encouraged to form rules and hypotheses and try their hypotheses without being frequently corrected. What they often hear is mainly *positive* evidence. Children are never told that in the sentence "John told Bill to take good care of himself", the first two words must be analyzed as subject noun phrase and verb, and the reflexive pronoun "himself" must refer to "Bill". The input children receive lacks information about sentence structures and meanings, yet children are still able to learn the rules of their language. Meanwhile, children are also seldom exposed to speeches about what is ungrammatical (see Goodluck, 1991, p. 142). However, children can easily manage to avoid ungrammatical sentences or errors and learn the correct grammar of their language. This kind of input is invoked by Chomsky and others as a point in favor of a learning mechanism in which the child's innate knowledge of principles of grammar plays a major role in guiding development (Chomsky, 1965).

The input to children is rich in content and not limited to any one particular topic or particular setting. It involves every aspect of life which is necessary for children's living. Thus language to a child is a tool for living. In addition, in terms of the quantity of exposure, adults cannot match with children. Children are not pitied for the overload of language exposure.

(4) **Meaning-oriented learning**: Children's L1 learning is characterized by meaning-orientation. Children learn a language in an unconscious way and acquire language competence when they try to communicate with others. It is of living necessity for children to learn a language. Children do not attend much to how sentences should be formed and they have little chance to be told to do so. This gives us some inspirations about second language learning.

The above review and summary of the literature on children L1 acquisition could give many clues to second language learning researchers. The disparate achievements between L1 learners and second language learners cause researchers to ask how the first language learners acquire their mother tongue on the one hand and stimulate them to establish theories about SLA or SLL on the other hand. The next section will give a brief review of the relevant theories in the field of SLA which might help us to obtain a clear picture of FLL in China.

3.1.3 Research on L2 acquisition

A great deal of review work has been done on the existing SLA models (R. Ellis, 1985, 1994b; Larsen-Freeman and Long, 1991; VanPatten, 2010; etc.), this chapter does not attempt to repeat all those theories here, but only attempts to present the main theories briefly so as to establish the relationship between the theories in SLA and the present study. The study of second language learning process is characterized by attention to learners' individual factors, and learning process factors. Hence, theoretical models are mostly established from a learner's point of view. A brief review of some influential models and factors that have been studied can exhibit the characteristics of this kind of research.

(1) Cognitive-psychological theories

Cognitive-psychological theories in general learning aim to explain how humans create and use knowledge; hence, basically, it is not domain specific. Quite a number of cognitive-psychological researchers are interested in the individual differences such as learning styles, understanding, aptitude, motivation, and language restructuring process which leads to the study of information processing, and fluency development, etc. Within this framework, language learning utilizes the same mechanisms for learning other subjects. Applied to SLA, cognitive-psychological models are characterized by the distinction of two systems in knowledge representation and ways of acquiring or learning a language. Within these models, terms like *language acquisition* and *learning*, *conscious* and *subconscious learning*, *controlled* and *automatic processing*, *acquired knowledge* and *learnt knowledge*, *declarative knowledge* and *procedural knowledge*, and *implicit knowledge* and *explicit knowledge* are frequently cited and discussed. Different pairs of terms represent different explanations of the internal representations of the knowledge system and the internal processes. Works of such scholars as Peter Skehan, Jan Hulstijn, Rod Ellis, Nick Ellis, Richard Schmidt, Peter Robinson, Robert DeKeyser, Ellen Bialystok, Rossman Mclaughlin, Stephen Krashen, etc. have exerted heavy influence upon SLA research. The review below will only focus on three relevant models proposed by S. Krashen, E. Bialystok and R. Mclaughlin.

i) Krashen's Monitor Model

Five well-known constructs about second language acquisition have been posited in this model: (1) The Acquisition-Learning distinction, (2) The Natural Order Hypothesis, (3) The Monitor Hypothesis, (4) The Input Hypothesis, and (5) The

Affective Filter Hypothesis. One fundamental distinction made by Krashen which has caused a lasting stir in SLA field is the distinction between *acquisition* and *learning,* although the influence of this concept is weakening when it comes to the 21st century. Here *acquisition* is a subconscious process identical to the process children utilize in acquiring their first language whereas *learning* is a conscious process that results in "knowing about" language (Krashen, 1985). *Acquisition* occurs automatically when learners engage in natural communication where the focus is on meaning and where there is comprehensible input. *Learning* occurs as a result of formal study where learners focus on the formal properties of the target language. Krashen thus identifies two distinct types of linguistic knowledge operating in the learner's mind: *acquired knowledge* and *learnt knowledge. Acquired knowledge* is composed of rules of the target language which the learner can call upon automatically, but *learnt knowledge* is mainly metalinguistic knowledge which can only be used to monitor output generated by means of *acquired knowledge.*

Krashen emphasizes *acquisition* over *learning* in general except that when he refers to the advantage possessed by adult learners in learning in classrooms. According to Krashen (1985), the input, as one of the most important factors affecting L2 learners' learning, must be at a level that is comprehensible to them, i.e. at the *i +1* level, just beyond what the learner can fully understand; this input is comprehensible, but contains structures that are not yet fully understood, although this proposal has been criticized on the basis that there is no clear definition of *i +1*, and that factors such as interest or presentation can also affect whether input is actually turned into intake. The role of formal instruction is minimized and the knowledge received from it only has the role of a monitor which can only work when there is enough time to give enough attention to it. The learner improves or progresses along the "natural order". The Affective Filter hypothesis embodies Krashen's view of the facilitative, but non-causal role of such affective variables as motivation, self-confidence and anxiety in second language acquisition. According to Krashen, lack of motivation, low self-esteem, debilitating anxiety, and so on, can combine to raise the filter, to form a mental block, which prevents the comprehensible input from reaching the LAD (Krashen, 1982, p. 31). The main idea expressed in his theory can be explicitly summarized by Krashen's own statements as follows:

> People acquire second languages only if they obtain comprehensible input and if their affective filters are low enough to allow the input "in". When the filter is "down" and appropriate comprehensible input is presented (and comprehended), acquisition is inevitable. It is, in fact, unavoidable and cannot be prevented — the language "mental organ" will function just as automatically as any other organ (Krashen, 1985, p. 4).

The model presented by Krashen is in fact an attempted realization of the cognitive psychological theory of language learning and an application of the UG-based L1 acquisition hypothesis into SLA. The Monitor Model has motivated quite a number of empirical studies among which Seliger's (1979) findings are very thought-provoking. In Seliger's study, it has been found that there do exist two types of rules which result in different output. Learners can often articulate formal rules of grammar but cannot use them correctly in spontaneous communication or vice versa. However, Seliger also found that rules of grammar learnt under formal instruction do not only perform a role as a monitor. On this basis, Seliger holds a weak-interface position rather than a non-interface position between *acquisition* and *learning*.

However, the Monitor Model also manifests its weaknesses (Gregg, 1984; McLaughlin, 1987) in the following aspects: (1) it is hard to carry out any empirical studies to prove that there does exist a distinction between *acquisition* and *learning*; (2) the minor role given to formal instruction has been challenged when successful learning occurs in foreign language learning contexts; (3) the over-emphasized role given to comprehensible input is also challenged when research indicates the efficacy of output and interaction in language acquisition process (Lyster, 1994; Swain,

1993, 1995; etc.).

Nonetheless, the fundamental distinction between acquisition and learning exerts great influence on SLA research. The two hypothetical learning processes imply more than the theory itself really indicates. The theory has also made an attempt at giving a systematic and inspiring explanation of the interactive relationship among such identified factors that might affect the acquisition and learning processes, i.e. the nature of input, the affective filter, acquired knowledge, learnt knowledge, and output.

ii) Bialystok's SLL Model

Like Krashen, Bialystok (1978) defined two types of linguistic knowledge operationally: *Explicit Linguistic Knowledge* (ELK) and *Implicit Linguistic Knowledge* (ILK), which has been pointed out in Chapter 2.

Different from Krashen, who distinguishes two distinctive types of knowledge, Bialystok, however, further explains her uses of the terms as a continuum, which means that one kind of linguistic knowledge can be converted into another through continued use and practice. Thus, to Bialystok, these two kinds of linguistic knowledge stay at the two ends of the continuum, but not distinct from each other. With further studies, she later chooses to use another pair of terms: *analyzed* and *unanalyzed*, which shows more clearly the nature of a continuum. In Bialystok's model, there is another kind of knowledge which might influence SLL, i. e. *Other Knowledge*. This refers to knowledge of social culture, or knowledge of the world, or knowledge of the mother tongue, etc. The "Other Knowledge" can be incorporated into the ELK and the ILK, which indicates that the aim of SLL is communicative competence rather than mere linguistic knowledge. The relationship between these two kinds of knowledge and factors influencing the acquisition of these types of knowledge is represented in the following model (see Figure 3 - 1).

In this model, Bialystok identifies the strategies of *formal practicing*, *functional practicing*, and *inferencing*. She virtually identifies two kinds of learning approaches: form-based learning and function-based learning. Starting from *Language Exposure*, Bialystok attempts to explain the relationships among factors such

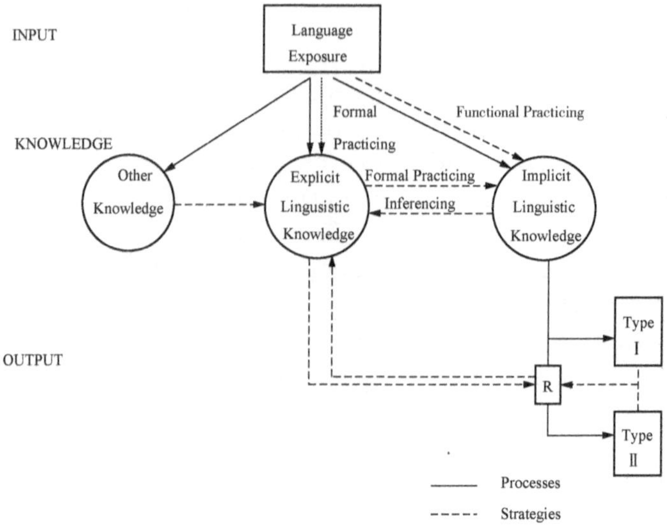

Figure 3 - 1　Bialystok's model of second language learning (Bialystok, 1978, p. 71)

as *language exposure*, *learning strategies*, and *language output*. According to Bialystok (1978), different types of linguistic knowledge are brought about by different learning strategies, and different tasks involve the employment of different types of knowledge. Thus, the target language must be experienced or encountered, the information gained may be represented in three ways, and two types of language responses may be subsequently formed—Type I and Type II, which are subsumed in the general response cell "R". Bialystok points out that Type I responses are spontaneous and immediate, whereas Type II responses are deliberate and occur after a delay. Different types of language behaviour and different degrees of proficiency may be associated with each type of response. In her later works, she develops another model to explain the relationship between knowledge and the control of knowledge, which is in fact an elaborated model for the explanation of how learners process the knowledge represented in their minds. In developing this model, Bialystok (1988, p. 37) explained second language learners' process of knowledge from two dimensions: *knowledge* and *control*, i.e. the automatic processing of the non-analyzed and analyzed knowledge and the non-automatic processing of these kinds of knowledge. By doing this, she attempted to explain learners' differences in language proficiency. In other words, Bialystok describes language proficiency with reference to an analyzed factor and an automatic factor. The analyzed factor concerns the extent to which the language learner is aware of the structure of her linguistic knowledge. Analyzed knowledge can be operated on by the learner and so is available for language uses of the kind required in formal education. The automatic factor concerns the learner's relative access to knowledge. It is reflected in easier access and more fluent performance. Automaticity is achieved through practice, therefore, in this model, practice takes a particular role in facilitating the transfer of ELK to ILK. Bialystok states that the learning context will also influence the kind of acquisition that takes place. Informal L2 learners are more likely to emphasize automaticity, and formal learners will stress analyticity. As has been mentioned in Chapter 2, there exist two kinds of knowledge in the learner's mind according to cognitive theories: declarative knowledge and procedural knowledge. Cognitive theorists believe that their task is to provide answers for procedural knowledge, i.e. the control procedures and their application, or in Bialystok's term — the automatic factor.

Bialystok's theory is one of the most relevant theories to classroom L2 learning in cognitive models. In her theory, factors under consideration are mainly practice, classroom interaction and formal instruction in learning and the role of different types of knowledge in output. As she points out in her 1988 article, practice is one of the key strategies to the development of automaticity. According to Bialystok, practice can help to activate mental nodes, strengthen connections, increase speed of access and thereby reduce errors. Cognitive learning theory emphasizes the need for practice in real operating conditions. Only in this way will the learner succeed in achieving automatic control of her knowledge for use in authentic communication.

Bialystok's model also emphasizes the provision of adequate opportunities in the classroom for the proceduralization of knowledge. Her model explains that most classroom learners fail to achieve automaticity because classrooms do not really prepare students for participation in ordinary face-to-face interaction, and most classrooms do not provide conditions needed to ensure that full automatization of L2 knowledge takes place.

As for formal instruction, Bialystok's model emphasizes that formal instruction can help to increase the learner's analyzed knowledge. The focus on specific linguistic structures facilitates learners' restructuring of language system and the building of propositional representations of L2 knowledge. Learners are then able to participate in decontextualised language use which needs analyzed knowledge.

Thus in Bialystok's theory, four kinds of learning strategies have been identified in her model (1981b): *formal and functional practicing, monitoring and inferencing.* Three main factors are identified in her 1988 paper with respect to second language learning: *practice, classroom interaction* and *formal instruction.* However, although this model has identified the efficacy of ELK, it neither explains clearly how formal instruction works to facilitate the transfer, nor pinpoints the role of affective factors which are mentioned in Krashen's model.

The basis of Bialystok's theory is not very different from that of Krashen's, as has been acknowledged. However, her theory makes different contributions to the SLL research. One difference lies in that the two types of knowledge are at the different ends of a continuum in her model. From the model in 1978, it can be seen that the ELK can be converted into the ILK after continued use and practice, which indicates an identification of the role of frequency, practice and formal instruction in classroom learning. The knowledge obtained from formal instruction does not merely function as a monitor, but can perform as a source of Implicit Linguistic Knowledge. This could provide some explanations for second language learning that takes place in classrooms. This understanding has been furthered by later studies which can be seen from Norris & Ortega (2000) 's meta-analysis of 49 empirically rigorous studies which in sum demonstrated that focused L2 instruction resulted in substantial target-oriented gains and that explicit types of instruction were more effective than implicit types, and that the effectiveness of L2 instruction was durable. Another difference lies in that her model makes an attempt to provide explanations of the relationship between knowledge and use. It attempts to explain not only how knowledge is represented, but also how knowledge is retrieved and produced, as is manifested in the two types of responses.

However, there are still many problems existing in her model. One of the problems is about the nature of the two kinds of knowledge as is pointed out by Odlin (1986). Odlin points out that Bialystok's position on the nature of the ELK is not as clear as Krashen's. But this point is clarified by Bialystok herself later on. Another point pointed out by Odlin is that Bialystok, like Krashen, assigns an unimportant role to Explicit Linguistic Knowledge in communicative competence. Odlin points out that metalinguistic knowledge often has communicative functions. He uses evidence of children in communication to illustrate his point. He finds that children have metalinguistic awareness in communication. Therefore, metalinguistic knowledge also plays a role in communication.

Both Krashen and Bialystok's theories attempt to cover all factors that might be involved in SLA/SLL from a cognitive perspective. However, the following theory is a bit different, which attempts to explain SLA from one single perspective.

iii) Mclaughlin et al's Information Processing Model

A different model from the above-mentioned two is the information-processing model from the perspective of cognitive psychology. This theory considers language learning process as a process of information. The pair of terms frequently used by researchers like Mclaughlin, Stevick, Rossman, etc. are *controlled process* and *automatic process*, which are explained by Anderson (1985) as follows:

> Automatic processes complete themselves without conscious control by the subject. ...Many aspects of driving a car and comprehending language appear to be automatic. Controlled processing seems to require conscious control (Anderson, 1985, p. 45).

These two terms are related to several assumptions about human mind and language learning. The two assumptions about the workload requirements in second language learning are: (1) human minds are limited-capacity information processors, which restrict what can be attended to at a given point in time, and how information is processed in terms of an individual's knowledge and expectations; (2) human minds develop ways of organizing information, which help them assign more attention to some tasks and less attention to others which have been well-practised (Mclaughlin, Rossman and Mcleod, 1983, pp. 143 – 144).

Another assumption is about the human memory, i. e. humans have a short-term memory and a long-term memory. The short-term memory is a working memory which is used to handle input and output in a short time. Miller (1956) argues that human short-term memory is rather limited in capacity which can only store seven plus or minus two items for a short period. He goes on to point out that items in short-term memory are equivalent to "bits" of information in information theory, which means that items in memory can store more than minimal amount of information depending on the individual's learning history and on characteristics of the input. It is pointed out that in fact humans have the ability to chunk information so as to solve the problem of the limited capacity of short-term memory. The organization of long-term memory is still under argument. Cognitive psychologists do not agree as to whether the system is organized in terms of associative networks or hierarchical structures.

According to the above assumptions, information processing by human minds is restricted by time and attention. Thus there exist two kinds of processing: *controlled processing*, which refers to a temporary activation of nodes[①] in a sequence. *Controlled processing* is thus tightly capacity-limited, and requires more time for the activation of nodes, and *automatic processing* is the

① Here nodes come from what Schneider (1977) conceived of memory as a large collection of nodes that become "complexly interassociated" through learning. Each node is a grouping or set of informational elements. Most of the nodes are inactive and passive and, when in this state, the interconnected system of nodes is called long-term store (LTS).

activation of certain nodes in memory every time the appropriate input is present (Mclaughlin et al., 1983). Controlled processing needs time and attention. However, once controlled processing becomes automatic processing, the learner has moved out of difficult levels.

When this theory is applied to second language learning, it holds that learning at the initial stages involves the controlled processes with focal attention to task demands, e. g. the slow development of skills at the beginning when the learner tries to automatize the various components of performance. When the learner becomes more familiar with the situation, the attention will be eased and the processing will need little time. Besides, in the initial learning, learners often focus attention on formal properties of language. With the improving of their performance skills, their learning will gradually become routinized, and then information processing will become automatic (Mclaughlin et al., 1983, p. 142). Empirical studies (for details, see Mclaughlin, 1983) on automaticity in lexical retrieval and in syntactic processing indicate that more proficient learners use different techniques to decode lexical items in memory (Mclaughlin et al., 1983, p. 148).

The information-processing model, like other cognitive models, considers language learning as the processing of information which follows the flow of "input — internal — processing — output" targeting at automaticity. Levels not at or approximate to the target levels are at the stage of controlled processing. The difference between this model and others is the method this model uses: this model is based on empirical studies. Besides, this model emphasizes internal processing and outside training. Thus practice is given a particular role in this model. The claim of aiming at automaticity is in fact based on the distinction between declarative knowledge and procedural knowledge[①] made by Anderson (1985), i.e. aiming at the

① According to Anderson (1985), declarative knowledge refers to knowledge about facts and things, while procedural knowledge refers to knowledge about how to perform various cognitive activities. Procedural knowledge fundamentally has a problem-solving organization.

attainment of procedural knowledge which guarantees automaticity. The discussion and research on memory, attention and learning strategies in this model have exerted great influence on SLA theory development. Along this line together with the development of cognitive linguistics is the new developing ideas of constructivism, connectionism and emergentism in language acquisition studies which emphasizes the role of practice, frequency effect and construct formation and the form-meaning mappings (Christiansen and Chater, 2001; Lakoff, 1987; Langacker, 1987, 1991; Larsen-Freeman, 1997; Nick Ellis, 2002; Leech, 2011; McClelland, Rumelhart, and the PDP Research Group, 1986; MacWhinney, 1999; etc.). This line of discussion has the tendency of moving from the focus of the inside to the interplay of the internal mechanism with the sicial environment.

iv) Summary of the cognitive models

Cognitive SLA models in the ealier period were heavily influenced by the UG theory, L1 acquisition theory and cognitive psycholinguistics, but influence from the studies with a functional orientation can be seen in recent years. Some of the achievements by these models are summarized below.

1) The identification of two kinds of learning processes, viz. subconscious acquisition and conscious learning, form-based learning and function-based learning, controlled processing and automatic processing, etc. Although researchers still disagree as to the nature of learning processes, the identification of two types of learning processes contributes a great deal to research on SLL/FLL.

2) The role of formal instruction is elaborated to some extent through researchers' arguments around the interface or non-interface position of the two types of knowledge corresponding to the different ways of learning. Research in the past 30 years have found enlightening results that formal instruction does play a role in facilitating second language acquisition (Norris & Ortega, 2000).

3) Factors such as language exposure, learning strategies, practice, frequency and affective filter have been noticed to influence SLL process.

Different from the focused attention on the interactional effect on second language development among the learner's internal factors, the following perspective of SLA studies is interested in the interactional effect among social-cultural factors and the learner's internal processing factors.

(2) Sociocultural perspective of SLA

Theories with this perspective can find their sources from both the cognitive-psychological studies, such as the Russian cultural-historical psychologist Lev Vygotsky's and his followers' works and the works of the functional schools with different orientations, such as J. R. Firth's and systemic functional linguist M. A. K. Halliday's and his followers', which hold the conviction that language, as a social and cultural phenomenon, is acquired and learnt through social interaction. For classroom learning, this perspective views *classroom* learning as "a developmental process mediated by semiotic resources appropriated from the classroom ..." (Donato, 2000). This perspective can also find traces from the studies in the pragmatics discipline, such as the works of John Austin's and John Searle's Speech Act theory and Sperber & Wilson's relevance theory. The above-mentioned figures did not write extensively about second language acquisition per se, but their analyses of the interrelationship between thinking processes and language processes, between linguistic systems and social contexts, etc. have provided a foundation for understanding the interrelationship between thinking and language processes involved in communicating meaning in a second language.

The pervasive influence of this perspective can be detected from the different proposals about communicative competence in the applied linguistics field, and the Socio-cultural Theory school in second language development represented by the following figures as James Lantolf, Steven Thorne, Amy Ohta, and Richard Donato, and the SLA models like *the Acculturation Model, the Accommodation Model,* and others. The socio-cultural tradition of approaching SLA has not been neglected (as is evidenced from works like van Lier, 1996; Lantolf, 1993, 1996; Newman & Holzman, 1993; etc.) as complained by Firth & Wagner (1997), but is given more attention after Firth & Wagner (1997). The central construct in this line of inquiry is the term *mediation*, which "refers to the idea that humans possess certain cultural tools, such as language, literacy, numeracy, and others, that they purposefully use to control and interact with their environment" (VanPatten, 2010, p. 152). Another important construct for this line of inquiry is the Zone of Proximal Development (ZPD) proposed by Vygotsky (1978) which refers to "the distance between the actual developmental level as determined by independent problem solving and the level of potential development as determined through problem solving under adult guidance or in collaboration with more capable peers" (1978, p. 86). Researchers in this line of inquiry like Aljaafreh and Lantolf (1994) give high acclamation to the construct of ZPD, and describe it as "the framework, par excellence, which brings all of the pieces of the learning setting together — the teacher, the learner, their social and cultural history, their goals and motives, as well as the resources available to them, including those that are dialogically constructed together" (p. 468).

SLA research with socio-cultural orientation is instantiated in different models because of their various foci of interest. Apart from the enthusiastic attempt of applying Vygotskyan theory into SLA research in recent years (Lantolf, 1995, 2006; Lantolf and Thorne, 2006; etc.), in the early Acculturation Model, for instance, according to Schumann (1978, p. 34), "second language acquisition is just one aspect of acculturation and the degree to which a learner acculturates to the target language group will control the degree to which he acquires the second language." Thus, acculturation is in fact a process of becoming adapted to a new culture. Social and psychological distances are believed to determine the learning of a second language. Social distance is the result of various factors which affect the learner as a member of a social group in contact with the target language group, whereas psychological distance is the result of various affective factors which concern the learner as an individual. Social factors are primary, while psychological factors only come into play in cases where social distance is indeterminate.

Another SLA model with the socio-cultural orientation is the Accommodation Model which shares some assumptions with the Acculturation Model, but with a number of differences. It derives from the research of Giles and his associates (see Ellis, 1985 for ref.) into the intergroup uses of language in multilingual communities. Giles holds that motivation is the primary determinant of L2 proficiency. He considers the level of motivation to be a reflex of how individual learners define themselves in ethnic terms. Thus such key variables are found to govern the level of motivation: identification with intergroup, inter-ethnic comparison, perception of ethno-linguistic vitality, perception of ingroup boundaries, and identification with other social categories.

In sum, this group of theories is characterized by the attention to the interplay of the social and psychological factors in second language learning, which can be considered as a complement to the innate theories in explaining SLA processes, although this on-going line of research is still limited in its influence. Language here is not considered as input, rather a resource for participation in the kinds of activities which our everyday life comprises. And "participation in the activities is both the product and the process of learning" (Zuengler & Miller, 2006, p. 38). The particular interest of this line of inquiry in the function and use of language, the social-cultural influence on language learning and the learner factor from a humanistic point of view helps to reveal a different picture of second language learning processes.

3.1.4 Factors involved in SLL process and relationships among them

The examination of naturalistic SLA research reveals that the following factors are of essential concern in SLA, such as learners' factors as learners' *attitude*, *motivation*, *anxiety*, *self-confidence*, *cognitive style*, etc., conditional factors such as *exposure to the target language*, *the nature of input*, and *instruction methods*, and processing factors in learning processes, such as *learning strategies*. These factors are interwoven with each other to influence SLA process. Although definite answers are still far from us as to how these factors influence the process of SLA, the above-mentioned studies are inspiring attempts in this area. Do these factors also work in classroom SLL/FLL? The following review of classroom or instructed SLL/FLL research may assist us in understanding research in this area.

3.2 Theories of classroom second language learning

3.2.1 Theories about classroom learning

Studies on formal classroom second language learning are not new, but a case of intensive interest in recent years, when research findings indicate that explicit learning also plays a role in second language acquisition. Classroom SLL research is concerned with whether formal classroom instruction intervention works to facilitate second language acquisition. Long (1983) provides a comprehensive review of 12 studies in instructed second language learning and concludes that "the effect for instruction holds 1) for children as well as for adults, 2) for intermediate and advanced students, not just beginners, 3) on integrative as well as discrete-point tests, and (4) in acquisition-rich as well as acquisition-poor environments" (p. 374). Ellis (1990) developed a model of instructed L2 learning, and Stern (1983) gives an outline of a learning model which is mainly about classroom learning. The following discussion will take Ellis' model as an example.

Rod Ellis (1985, 1990) posited nine hypotheses about such factors as *instructional input*, *learning style*, *L2 knowledge* and *control*, and the relationships between these factors in classroom L2 learning on the basis of a review of research and discussions about the role of formal instruction in classroom second language learning. Two initial premises lay the foundation for Ellis' later discussions, i. e. (1) L2 knowledge is differentiated, and (2) different kinds of instruction typically result in different kinds of L2 knowledge. This theory allocates a significant role to explicit knowledge while maintaining a weak interface position between explicit knowledge and implicit knowledge for providing a basis for consciousness-raising tasks (Ellis, 1991) that require learners to derive their own explicit grammar rules from the data they are provided with. According to this model, explicit knowledge functions as an acquisition facilitator which serves to sensitize the learner to the existence of non-standard forms in her/his target language and thus facilitates the acquisition of the target language system. The significant role of explicit knowledge in learning determines the significant role of instructional input. This model claims that both meaning-focused and form-focused instruction can facilitate learning, but explicit knowledge is derived largely from form-focused instruction and implicit knowledge is derived largely from meaning-focused instruction. Learners develop their control over their L2 knowledge by practising in "real operating conditions" (Ellis, 1990, p. 192). Besides, according to Ellis (1990), output also serves as a kind of input to the language-processing mechanisms. Ellis' model allows deviant output and states that this kind of output can also facilitate the acquisition of correct forms given corrective feedback. This model explains that there are two ways for the acquisition of implicit knowledge: (1) by meaning-focused instruction, and (2) by being taught directly provided that one of the following conditions is met, i. e. (a) the learner is developmentally "ready", or (b) the target forms are not subject to developmental constraints.

After a comprehensive survey of research on instructed learning, Ellis (2006) generalizes ten principles for successful instructional practice in terms of the following aspects as *input sufficiency*, *learners' meaning orientation*, *learners' necessary attention to form*, *balancing implicit knowledge and explicit knowledge relationship*, *attention to learners' "built-in" syllabus*, *input variety*, *opportunity for output*, *opportunity for interaction*, *attention to individual differences*, and *means of proficiency assessment*. These aspects actually cover most of the factors involved in classroom L2 instruction.

3.2.2 Factors involved in classroom L2 learning

In sum, holistically, two types of instruction have been identified from the review above, i.e. *form-focused instruction* and *meaning-focused instruction.* Different types of instruction may result in different types of knowledge representation, hence different types of final attainments. Another identified factor of wide interest is the strategy of *practice.* This is a strategy often advocated in the Audiolingual Methodology. However, practice in cognitive classroom L2 learning theories obtains a different sense. Practice in the Audiolingual Methodology emphasizes the controlled practice of specific forms in specially contrived exercises, while practice in cognitive SLL theories emphasizes real and high frequent communicative use of language. Among the different ways of practicing, *task-based classroom interaction* is given priority. It is believed that learners' procedural knowledge can only be attained by providing them with adequate opportunities to interact with each other as in natural discourse. *Languaging,* as Swain and Deters (2007) discuss verbalisation or output in another way, can also be considered as a type of language production practice and also plays an important role in facilitating L2 acquisition. In terms of learners' individual differences, *learning style* has also been identified as an important factor in manipulating learning process. Learning style, according to Ellis (1990), refers to the learner's affective and cognitive orientation to learning. "Only learners with a positive affective orientation to learning the L2 are likely to benefit from the instruction" (Ellis, 1990, p. 188). Therefore, if a learner is not cognitively suited to the type of instructional input provided, even if he/she is receptive to the input, learning may still not happen. A predominently form-based input may hold back the learner from focusing on communication. Ellis then concludes that "learners who find that their learning style is incompatible with the instructional style may develop anxiety and so lose confidence and motivation, perhaps even to the point of abandoning instruction" (ibid). Thus, in classroom L2 instruction, *types of practice, nature of input, learners' individual differences including their cognitive style*, *learning strategies*, *focus of attention*, *ultimate learning orientation*, and *the means of assessment* all play a role in affecting learners' second language development.

3.3 Factors influencing SL/ FL learning processes

3.3.1 Summary of factors from the review

The above review of naturalistic and classroom L2 learning theories helps us elicit the following factors that are mostly considered among these theories, which can be seen in Table 3-1.

Table 3-1 Factors mostly considered in the field of SLA

Learner factors	UG, L1, age, aptitude, intelligence, motivation, attitude, anxiety, cognitive style, learning style, personality characteristics, focus of attention, knowledge orientation, etc.
Processing factors	strategies in learning and production
Conditional factors	input type, practice type, assessment type, etc.

Note: For details, see review by Ellis (1985, 1990), Larsen-Freeman and Long (1991) and Wu (1994)

3.3.2 Factors singled out for the present study

Taking into consideration the scope and feasibility of the study, five of the factors are finally selected for this study, i.e. *motivation, attitude, learning strategy, outside class language exposure,* and *classroom instruction method.* This research will be limited to the study of the relationship of these factors with the chosen subjects' final attainments, whereas such factors as intelligence, aptitude, cognitive style, and personality will not be covered for reasons stated above. The age factor is not considered, either, for the subjects under study are known to be adolescents or young adults. They generally went to school at the same lawful age and began to learn a foreign language at about the same time. Age differences in secondary schools are not as significant as that of adult EFL learners in night schools or other open schools. Most of the subjects under study here were born in Guangzhou and speak Cantonese and the common speech of the Chinese language

(Putonghua).

Since this research concerns an EFL learning situation, the factor of *classroom instruction* is of particular importance. This has been widely acknowledged by many researchers (Celce-Marcia, 2008; Pienemann 1989, etc.) in this field. *Learning strategy* is to be considered for the reason that few studies can be found about classroom secondary school EFL learners. The *affective factor* is mostly discussed in the field of SLA, but research results seem to be rather contradictory. *Outside class language exposure* is supposed to occur seldom in Chinese EFL learning situations, but it is not known whether it is true at present after the implementation of the open-policy in China.

3.3.3 A brief review of the factors for this study

(1) Motivations and attitudes

In the field of SLA, motivations and attitudes have been widely studied under different learning situations to account for learner's variation in his/her attainment in second/foreign language learning. In Krashen (1985)'s Monitor Theory, motivations and attitudes are included in "the Affective Filter", while in Ellis (1990)'s instructed SLA model, they are under the heading of "learning style". The study of motivations and attitudes centres on whether there exists a strong relationship between these variables and learners' final attainments, and if there is, how these variables affect learners' final attainment. In addition, attitudes and motivations are regarded as being related to each other for it accords with the common sense that a positive attitude towards second/foreign language learning will motivate the learner to extend the effort required to learn a second/foreign language.

One of the frequently-quoted studies of motivations is the one conducted by Gardner and Lambert (1972). Having drawn support from the concept of identification① during their study,

① In L1 study, Mowrer (1950) attributes a child's success in acquiring an L1 to the child's quest for identity, initially with members of the child's immediate family and then later with members of the larger speech community (cited from Larsen-Freeman and Long, 1991, p. 173).

Gardner and Lambert proposed a construct of " integrative motivation " and introduced another concept " instrumental motivation ". According to them, learners can be both instrumentally motivated and integratively motivated. They further hypothesized that motivations of an integrative orientation, in particular, make for more successful learning than motivations of an instrumental orientation. Their Montreal and Maine studies support some of their hypotheses (Gardner and Lambert, 1972). However, this latter statement is challenged by their studies in other language learning contexts. Students learning English as a foreign language in their Philippine study are found to be highly successful despite their having instrumental rather than integrative motivation.

In their early studies, motivations and attitudes are not separated by Gardner and Lambert. Correlations are found between learners' motivation-attitudinal variables and their achievements. Other studies have reached similar conclusions at this point. However, there is also evidence contrary to these findings, such as Carroll's (1962, 1966) and Savignon's (1972) studies. Carroll studied groups of students in an intensive language course — the " Five University Summer Programme in Middle Eastern Languages " — in 1958 and 1959. The method Carroll used was to correlate students' scores with their responses to a questionnaire on their liking for foreign languages. Carroll found that the correlation was not significant. Thus he concluded that whether or not a person liked the foreign language he studied was not related significantly to his achievement (Carroll, 1962).

Studies in Malaysia by Antonia Chandrasegaran (1981), however, gave different results. In her two groups of students, attitude turned out to be the least useful of the attitudinal-motivational variables as a predictor of competence in Group A (the national schools). But for Group B (the national-type schools), significant correlations were found between attitudes and competence. Another result is that motivational intensity was found to be the best predictor of competence in Group A (those students from the national schools where Bahasa Malysia is the language of instruction, and English a compulsory subject.), while for Group B (those students from the national-type schools where English as a medium of instruction is being replaced by Bahasa Malaysia.), intensity of motivation had no bearing on competence.

All those investigations reviewed above indicate that different learning situations might bring out different kinds of results as far as the effect of these variables is concerned. This study is about an EFL learning situation, hence, the research results obtained from this study will provide further evidence.

(2) Learning strategies

Research on learning strategies came from an interest in learners' errors at the outset. It is believed that a learner's systematic errors provide evidence of how language is learnt and what strategies or procedures the learner is employing in his discovery of language (Corder, 1967, p. 25). However, the use of error analysis is largely speculative, and cannot provide a full understanding of language learning process. Later researchers (e.g. Schumann, 1976), therefore, advocate direct investigations into learners' cognitive processes. This line of research has once been focused on successful second language learners' learning strategies (Stern, 1975, 1983; Rubin, 1975). Stern's study (1975) finally concludes that the good language learner "constantly searches for meaning by whatever method available" (p. 314), while the poor learner "does not treat his failure to understand as a challenge". The methods used by Stern and many other researchers are mainly classroom observation and interview of learners. However, it has been found that "strict observation in language learning classrooms does not reveal language learning strategies or specific techniques" (Naiman, Frohlich, Stern and Todesco, 1978), whereas the interview method and questionnaires are found to be more effective and widely adopted later (Oxford, 1990).

Learning strategies are also considered to be responsible for different types of knowledge representation. Bialystok (1979), for instance, believes that different kinds of knowledge are obtained by different learning strategies. Explicit Linguistic Knowledge is obtained by form-based practice, while Implicit Linguistic

Knowledge is obtained by function-based practice. Bialystok's follow-up experiments (1979, 1983) make her conclude that "the learner's intuition (his implicit knowledge store) must be developed and encouraged, and efficient strategies for consulting explicit knowledge must be trained. ...Concentration on only the formal aspect of language and rule formation not only precludes important aspects of the language but ignores as well the learner's great intuitive source" (Bialystok, 1979, p. 101). Learning strategies under this study are based on Oxford (1990)[①] 's inventory which divides learning strategies into two large groups: *direct strategies* and *indirect strategies.* The former refers to strategies "that directly involve the target language" (p. 37). "All direct strategies require mental processing of the language" (ibid). The latter refers to those strategies "that underpin the business of language learning". Grouped under *direct strategies* are *memory*, *cognitive*, and *compensation strategies,* while under *indirect strategies* are *metacognitive*, *affective*, and *social strategies.* Each type of strategies is further divided into some sub-strategies.

---

① For details, see Oxford (1990) on pp37 – 149. Definitions for the six types of strategies are provided here.

(1) Memory strategies: refer to strategies that help students store and retrieve new information. Four types of sub-strategies are included here: creating mental linkages; applying images and sounds; reviewing well; and employing action.

(2) Cognitive strategies: are used to enable learners to understand and produce new language by many different means. They consist of four sub-strategies: practising; receiving and sending messages; analyzing and reasoning; and creating structure for input and output.

(3) Compensation strategies: allow learners to use the language despite their often large gaps in language. Two types are included here: guessing intelligently and overcoming limitations in speaking and writing.

(4) Metacognitive strategies: provide a way for learners to coordinate their own learning processes. Three sub sets of strategies are included here: centering your learning; arranging and planning your learning; and evaluating your learning.

(5) Affective strategies: refer to emotions, attitudes, motivations, and values. Three sub types of strategies are included here: lowering your anxiety; encouraging yourself; and taking your emotional temperature.

(6) Social strategies: strategies involved in the learning of the target language in communication. Three sets of sub strategies are included here: asking questions; cooperating with others; and emphasizing with others.

Memory strategies, in this study, are mainly related to vocabulary learning. Two sub-strategies are included here: *memorizing word by associating sound and spelling*, and *memorizing words by associating the old with the new*. The selection of these two strategies is based on the idea that vocabulary learning is always considered as one of the most important and most difficult aspects in EFL learning in secondary schools in China. With respect to *cognitive strategies*, two sub-strategies are covered in this study: *the employment of translating and summarizing in learning*. It is assumed that frequent uses of these strategies are helpful for the training of learners' EFL writing. Two *compensation strategies* are chosen here to be studied: *overcoming the limitation by applying gestures in communication* and *guessing intelligently when failing to understand*. Two *metacognitive strategies* are included here: *making plans in EFL learning* and *self-evaluation*. Two *affective strategies* are listed here: *discussing feelings with others* and *self-encouragement*. Two *social strategies* are investigated here: *asking questions* and *cooperating with others*. Thus totally there are twelve strategies to be investigated in this research. These strategies are believed to be mainly employed by second language learners in other learning contexts. They are selected in this study to see whether these strategies are also available among Chinese secondary school EFL learners and whether they have any effect on these learners' final attainment. The findings will be used to help us analyse whether the chosen subjects show a difference in their learning approaches from those students in naturalistic setting.

(3) Outside class language exposure

Both theories and common sense make us believe that large amount of exposure contributes to the success of language learning. Krashen's Monitor Theory and Bialystok's SLL model reflect the opinion of this kind. There are two reasons for selecting outside class language exposure as a factor under this study. First, it is aimed to check whether there really exists high exposure among Chinese secondary school EFL learners.

Secondly, it is aimed to find out whether the amount of exposure correlates with these learners' final attainment. Literature review shows that there is evidence to support the view that more listening, reading, or other ways of target language contact is related to learners' achievements. Chandrasegaran (1981) made an investigation about Malaysian second language learners and found out that "There is a definite link between degree of exposure to English and competence in the language" (p. 59).

(4) **Classroom instruction (the instructional focus)**

There has been a lot of research before the 1970s about language instruction methods. Since the 1970s, the shift of focus from research on classroom instruction to learners, however, has led researchers too far away from the attention to the effect of classroom instruction. The research on learners and learning process does achieve a lot in helping researchers understand the nature of second language learning. But to see more clearly the nature of learners' achievements, the understanding of the nature of the input that learners have obtained in classroom situations is also important. However, how instruction affects second/foreign language learning is also a large topic which cannot be dealt with in such a study. This research, therefore, only selects some important parameters to help us to infer the instruction approach employed among the selected schools. The parameters chosen are: (1) learners' choice of methods after class to consolidate their learning in class, (2) learners' evaluation of their strengths and weaknesses in their language competence, (3) learners' preferred activities in class, (4) teachers' employment of activities in class, (5) homework types assigned by teachers, (6) teachers' focus in teaching in class, (7) teachers' ways in handling the errors students make in class and in homework, (8) native language use in class by teachers and learners, (9) teachers' allotment of time in class, and (10) opportunities for interaction in class between teachers and students and among students themselves.

It is assumed in this study that instruction is the most important means of knowledge input in Chinese secondary school EFL learning. Hence, any study concerning EFL learning in

China need take this factor into consideration. Research on classroom instruction in the past usually employed the method of large-scale comparisons between teaching approaches, but in the field of SLA, instruction is usually investigated by direct observation, controlled longitudinal studies, interviews, questionnaires, etc. The first three methods are impossible here in this study due to limited time and personnel. But questionnaire is feasible. With the exploration into the nature of the learners' underlying knowledge as the main aim, the investigation part will be regarded as supporting data.

In terms of whether instruction helps and how it works in aiding learners to attain what they need for communication, Ellis (1985), Long (1983), Chaudron (1990), Larsen-Freeman and Long (1991) and Norris & Ortega (2000) have provided comprehensive reviews of theories and research on this topic. Findings tend to indicate that classroom instruction does play a role. Nonetheless, researchers still disagree as to how different types of instruction influence the nature of learners' final attainment, and how the interplay of instruction, learners' affective factors and learning strategies work together to influence the learning process.

3.4 SLA theories and the present study

The review of learning process theories in this chapter helps us single out such factors as *motivation*, *attitude*, *learning strategy*, *outside class language exposure* and *instruction method* as the focus of attention for the present study. It also helps us establish the following ideas about foreign language learning process, which will lay the foundation for our conceptual framework in this study.

(1) The aim of EFL is to internalize the target language system within a meaningful communication-oriented context.

(2) Second language acquisition basically follows two distinct processes: implicit learning and explicit learning, with the former indicating the subconscious meaning-oriented learning and the latter referring to the conscious form-oriented learning. Both processes are believed to contribute to the internalization of the target language system when they are meaning-oriented.

(3) Different types of instruction influence learners' selection of different learning approaches, and hence different kinds of attainments. Meaning-based instruction might channel learners' selection to meaning-based learning approach, while form-based instruction might induce learners' selection of form-based learning approach.

(4) Social and psychological factors like cultural difference, educational policies, learners' motivations, attitudes, etc. are found to play a role in second language acqusition.

(5) Individual factors like age, intelligence, aptitude, cognitive style, personality might have much influence on the rate or success of a foreign language learner in learning the target language.

(6) The final success of FLL is the result of the interaction of the above mentioned possible factors.

3.5 Summary

This Chapter gives a review of some representative theories on second/foreign language learning processes around two lines of inquiry: naturalistic second language acquisition and classroom second language learning. SLA theories in early times are mainly concerned with the former situation, while classroom second language learning arouses interest when research findings indicate the existence of two types of learning processes: implicit learning and explicit learning. Both influential theories from the cognitive-psychological perspective and the socio-cultural perspective are reviewed in this chapter. Factors which are mostly concerned in this field are drawn on the basis of the review and relevant factors for this research such as *motivation*, *attitude*, *learning strategy*, *classroom instruction* and *outside class target language exposure* are singled out and discussed. With the preceding chapter and this chapter as theoretical bases, Chapter 4 will provide the working conceptual framework for the following experiment and investigation.

Chapter4
A Working Conceptual Framework for the Research

4.1 Introduction

Discussions in Chapters 2 and 3 have revealed that different understandings of the nature of the competence that is necessary for SLLners' communication and the nature of learning processes may be channeled to different theoretical assumptions about second language development. Based on the review and discussions in the foregoing chapters, in terms of the nature of the targeted competence for SLLners, this study adopts the componential view of communicative competence as its basis, among which five major components are included: *grammatical competence (GC) sociolinguistic competence (SLC), discourse competence (DC)* and *strategic competence (SC)*) and *cognitive and affective capacity (CAC)*. In terms of learning processes, two types of learning, i. e. *form-based learning* and *meaning-based learning* are identified, and five major factors, i. e. *motivation, attitude, learning strategy, classroom instruction* and *outside class target language exposure* are singled out for this study. This chapter aims to make an attempt to establish the realationshiop among all the above-mentioned factors and processes so as to provide a guiding framework for the subsequent investigation.

4.1.1 The necessity to establish a working conceptual framework

It is the following considerations that have made the author believe it necessary to establish a working conceptual framework.

First, overview of related literature indicates that few systematic studies have been conducted concerning the problems raised in this study in the FLL context. Thus substantial and explanatory FLL models are rarely found. This causes inconveniences to this type of studies. Secondly, this study has touched upon an area that covers a variety of topics; hence, it is practically necessary to delimit the focus of attention for the present study. An establishment of a framework can function as a guide to the study. Thirdly, there is a need to specify the relationships among the factors under study and the different results brought out by the various kinds of interplay of these factors. The establishment of a working framework could provide a systematic guideline for the present and even future research. The framework aims to explain why the learners under this study perform as they did, and what might be the sources of the underlying competence and what might be the factors that bring about the different types of knowledge. Thus, the framework will reflect the process of the learning and the competence resulted from it.

4.1.2 Characteristics of Chinese secondary school EFL learning

As has been pointed out by Brumfit (1981), English is rarely taught in secondary schools in the most efficient way possible, and most of the reasons for this are historical and administrative. Chinese secondary schools demonstrate a similar picture. To illustrate this point, a brief account of the known facts about situations in Chinese secondary schools is given below.

(1) Affected by the NEE, EFL learners in secondary schools devote most of their school time to the preparation for the NEE. Under this practical pressure, Chinese EFL learners' motivation, attitude, learning strategies and the teachers' instruction methods manifest a different picture from those in other situations. The influence of socio-cultural and psychological factors here might play a particular role in these learners' second language development.

(2) As has been pointed out in Chapter I, the lack of theories and research in language teaching and learning have resulted in a

lot of problems in practice. The author's observation and personal language learning experience indicate that in most Chinese secondary schools, EFL teaching is still intuition-based. Little consideration is given to the balancing of factors among instruction and practice, form and meaning, teachers and learners, mother tongue use and the target language use, listening and speaking, reading and writing, etc. It is the usual case that in secondary school English classes teachers explain rules and texts all the time with learners sitting there listening or reading after teachers or doing exercises rigidly according to teachers' instruction. Learners are not given sufficient opportunities to exploit their potential for learning in class. EFL classes in Chinese secondary schools are mostly teacher-centered. Form-oriented teaching and learning predominate in most classes.

(3) Most English teachers in secondary schools have few opportunities to be well-trained in EFL teaching. Wu's (1994) investigation of EFL learning and teaching in a university in Fujian has indicated this phenomenon. Based on these characteristics and the discussions in the previous chapters, we propose the guiding framework for this research in the next section with the purpose of clarifying the goal of FLL and establishing the interrelationship of factors working in the learning process.

4.2 The working conceptual framework

The figure below is a visual metaphor of the conceptual framework, rather than a theoretical model, because it occurs that it may demonstrate some relationships at the expense of others. The framework here follows the general cognitive process of "input — internal constructing — output" with the functional modifications of other factors in the process. The factors to be represented in the framework in this study are: *Input*, *Affective Filter* (including attitudes and motivations), *Internal Constructing* of different types of knowledge and the interaction among factors including *Learning Strategies* (shortened as LS), *Affective Filter* (affective factors), types of knowledge construction and knowledge sources such as *GC* (grammatical competence), *SLC* (sociolinguistic competence), *DC* (discourse competence), *SC* (strategic competence) and *WK* (other general world knowledge) and *CAC* (cognitive and affective capacity), and the *Output* which is composed of *GCP* (GC-based performance) and *CCP* (CC-based performance). Their relationship is manifested in Figure 4. 1.

The framework is both descriptive and explanatory in nature. By descriptive, we mean that it incorporates some key factors suggested by the literature to have relevance for second/foreign language learning. By explanatory, we mean that it postulates the processes describing the nature of the effect of these factors and the interactions among them. The framework demonstrates three levels of the learning process: *Input*, *Internal Constructing*, and *Output*. In the framework, the solid lines represent the obligatory processes, while the thick dotted lines represent the optional processes and the thin dotted lines are for outlining the three levels.

The *Input* refers to the data or language resources a learner receives and from which he/she can learn. It is assumed here that there are three kinds of input: *form-based input*, *meaning-based input* and *input of world knowledge*. The input of world knowledge is inevitable in any kinds of learning and it is clothed in the form of the language. *Form-based input* focuses its attention essentially on linguistic forms which include English morphological, lexical, syntactical and phonological knowledge. Learners usually receive this kind of input in decontextualised situations rather than in communication-oriented contexts. The input of world knowledge here may occur, but is limited in its depth and breadth. Thus, if sufficient meaningful practice is not guaranteed in communicative situations, learners who only receive this type of input are not expected to be able to communicate effectively because it is possible that they might have only attained the grammatical competence. Form-based input is usually found in traditional EFL classes where learners' attention is mainly directed to the learning of discrete linguistic forms.

Meaning-based input focuses its attention on the learning of a language in meaningful contexts. " Learning through communication" is its main principle. Learners who receive this kind of input are usually provided with a lot of opportunities to practise using the target language they are learning. Learners learn the target language by doing things in multi-modal situations, i.e. by performing communication-oriented tasks either in productive mode or in receptive mode or in mixed modes, with appropriate meaning realization as their final goal. This kind of input is assumed to be close to the nature of actual communication through language, and hence to be able to activate acquisition-related factors to co-work to facilitate learners' final internalization of the target language, i.e. the attainment of communicative competence. The input of world knowledge here is indispensible and may occur at any time when learners are involved in learning either consciously or subconsciously. It is a kind of knowledge which is closely related to learners' self development under different kinds of input. This kind of knowledge enjoys particular attention in meaning-based input, because meaning-based input focuses its attention on real communication, and communication cannot take place without content. Language forms are embodied in content basically. Even the forms that learners encounter in form-based input cannot be devoid of content unless instructors purposely strip them down to discrete rules, which is not an uncommon phenomenon in classroom instructions.

Outside class language exposure is also included here as a kind of input. The exposure can be meaning-based or form-based. However, in this research, the meaning of exposure is restricted to the learner's communication-oriented target language contact after class. Thus it is assumed that a large amount of exposure is helpful for the internalization of CC. However, in China, it is postulated that EFL learners enjoy few opportunities to be exposed to the target language after class. This will be examined in the investigation. EFL learning in China mainly takes place in classrooms which is the main means to receive input under teachers' instruction. In cities or some more developed areas, students may have opportunities to receive input from the outside, such as by means of interacting with native English speakers, listening to radios, watching TVs or by means of computers. However, EFL learners in secondary schools in China are fully occupied by preparing for the NEE. Therefore, even though they had the opportunities, they might not be able to make good use of them. Therefore, this study assumes that the nature of the input is a factor of significance for the final internalization of the target language system in the Chinese EFL context.

The **Internal Constructing** level subsumes the *Affective Filter*, the choice of *learning strategies* and the actual *learning processes* which involves the interaction among different types of knowledge. The Affective Filter is a term adopted from Krashen (1985) which refers to learners' anxiety in learning, learners' attitudes and motivations towards the target language and the learning of the target language, learners' anxiety in learning, etc. It may function as a hindrance or facilitator for the internalization of the target language system. As Krashen points out,

> When it [the filter] is "up", the acquirer may understand what he hears or reads, but the input will not reach the LAD. This occurs when the acquirer is unmotivated, lacking in self-confidence, or anxious, when he is "on the defensive" (Stevick 1976), when he considers the language class to be a place where his weaknesses will be revealed. The filter is down when the acquirer is not concerned with the possibility of failure in language acquisition and when he considers himself to be a potential member of the group speaking the target language (Smith 1982a, 1983) (Krashen 1985, pp. 3-4).

The study of the Affective Filter in this study is only regarded as a kind of supporting data. Two of the factors in the Affective Filter were investigated: attitudes and motivations. It is assumed that the Affective Filter might influence the learner's choice of different learning strategies. The Affective Filter is considered to be significant in the explanation of the success or failure of the Chinese EFL learners because of the special effect of the NEE as has been discussed above.

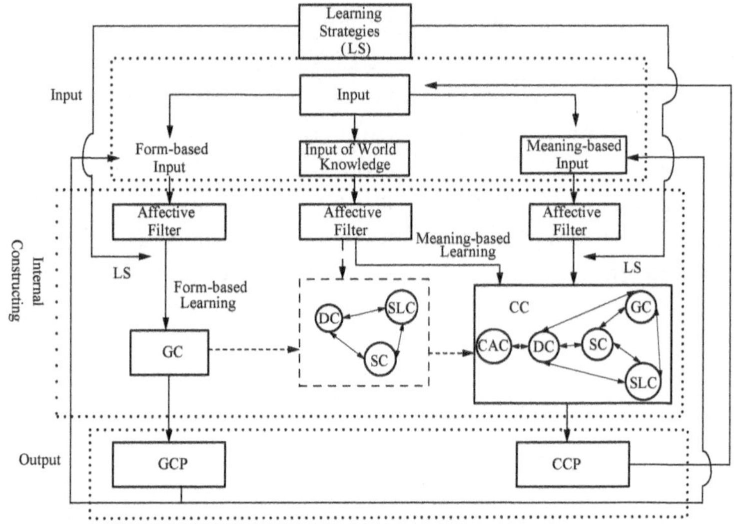

Figure 4 - 1　A Working Conceptual Framework for EFL Learning

Learners' choice of different learning strategies have been understood as correlating with their learning processes, and hence affecting the nature of their final attainment. Also, learners' choice itself may be influenced by the instruction processes they experience and their affective factors, which will in turn influence his/her learning approach. Different learning approaches may then result in different types of attainments. This research attempts to touch upon some of the learning strategies from a very general point of view, i.e. to inquire into whether learners' affective variables play a role in channeling them to their choice of different strategies and whether their frequency of choices is related to their final attainments. For the present study, a working definition has been given in Chapter 1. One point that merits attention is that researchers have found differences between learning strategies and communication strategies. But it is still hard to distinguish them absolutely. This study does not make an attempt at this point.

Two kinds of learning processes are represented in this

framework: *Form-based Learning* and *Meaning-based Learning*. By *Form-based Learning*, we mean the type of learning whose attention is directed at the learning of language forms mainly during the whole process, and whose main language learning activities are around the understanding and memorizing the facts or rules about language rather than around how to use the target language in communicative contexts. The underlying beliefs of this approach is that language can be finally acquired by means of large amount of practice around the memorizing and understanding of the rules and words of discrete units without necessarily putting language in situated contexts. It is assumed that knowledge of explicit nature (GC here) is mainly induced under this learning approach. By *Meaning-based Learning*, we mean the type of learning whose attention is targeted at the learning of language implicitly by providing learners with meaning-rich communicative contexts where learners learn the target language by using the language to accomplish communication-oriented tasks. Learning is posited to take place in the process of learners' engagement in communicative tasks, and language form is supposed to be acquired implicitly by learners when their consciousness can be raised in communication-oriented tasks. It is postulated that knowledge of implicit nature can be induced under this learning approach mainly.

Form-based Learning is compatible with *Form-based Input*, and *Meaning-based Learning* is in accordance with *Meaning-based Input*. Learners, influenced by the instruction processes and their choices of different learning strategies, may develop different learning processes. Form-based learning focuses its attention on discrete language forms. It emphasizes the learning about language. Instruction in this process basically follows the Traditional Grammar-Translation Methodology which regards language learning as a subject learning, or by the Structuralist Approach which emphasizes the practice of discrete linguistic rules. The result of this kind of learning will be mostly the attainment of grammatical competence mainly, which is mainly explicit. It is assumed here that most of the knowledge attained in this kind of learning process will be explicit knowledge that can be easily accessed by decontextualized linguistic tasks. It might also be employed for communicative tasks, but in a rather limited sense. Formed-based learning might also result in some implicit knowledge after time and effort have been spent, but also in a very restricted sense. Thus, learners with this kind of knowledge can perform discrete-point grammatical tasks well, but will find it hard to accomplish communicative tasks. Meaning-based learning occurs when the learner's attention is on the use of the target language. The meaningful context is characterized by the learning of rules of "use" as well as rules of "usage" which can guarantee the appropriate choice of language in real communication. The context for this kind of learning is mainly at the discourse level. Learning in this approach provides learners with the ability to organize their language in a cohesive and coherent way, i.e. to make their conversations or compositions consistent in meaning and structure, because learners in this learning process the target language form in a content-rich meaningful contexts, which can help learners associate language form with its meaning, hence assist them in their construction of their conceptual systems. Since "learning through communication" is emphasized, learners can also develop their strategic competence which might assist their learning and facilitate their communication. The strategic competence is in fact the knowledge to help learners to process different kinds of information in learning and in communication. Thus, this kind of knowledge can also be learnt and developed. Once learners acquire this kind of competence, they can employ it to facilitate their learning process. The strategic competence includes both learning strategies and communication strategies. The development of strategic competence can thereby help their learning of new language phenomena. Meaning-oriented interaction in class between teachers and learners and among learners themselves is advocated in this kind of learning process. Since production is considered as a way of learning in this approach, learners committing errors is taken as one of the indispensible elements of the learning process. Here, production does not mean oral production only, but also production in written mode. Learners' production of the target language is also a kind of input to themselves. Hence, the lines from both GCP and CCP are also connected to *Form-based Input* or *Meaning-based Input* or to the Input box for further choice. GCP is assumed to contain mainly the explicit knowledge about language, hence, learners' production here will be mainly as a type of grammatical knowledge input to either Form-based Input or Meaning-based Input, while CCP may contain content knowledge apart from linguistic knowledge, hence, it can go back to the Input box for learners' choice. In brief, Meaning-based Learning emphasizes the learning of the target language grammatical system in discourse or in meaningful contexts. Language instruction functions as a facilitator to help learners process input and provide learners with necessary opportunities for using the knowledge they encounter in meaningful contexts. Thus the integrated process of all kinds of knowledge is like the upward spiral movement and directs to the end of the final internalization of the target language system. This level is also called by some researchers as learning strategies (Bialystok, 1978). But, this research still considers it as the learning processes since it involves many other factors.

Different types of knowledge or competencies, i.e. GC, SLC, DC, SC and CAC, are also represented in the framework in the knowledge constructing process. In Form-based Learning, GC is the focus of attention and the target, while in Meaning-based Learning, the interaction among GC, SLC, DC, SC, and CAC is the target with the goal of achieving a type of integrated knowledge of implicit nature which can be called CC. In the interaction among different types of knowledge, SC plays the planning and processing role to retrieve the necessary types of knowledge to process, and it involves the whole process of knowledge construction and production, while DC is the knowledge which can help learners to process language at discourse level. DC here is the key element among the components, because all other competencies are supposed to work together finally toward the establishment of DC, without which learners will feel particularly difficult to construct large units of language, and hence difficult to produce large cohesive and coherent discourses. CAC is added to CC in particular in this framework in addition to the four components proposed by Canale and Swain (1980) with the basic conviction that learners' cognitive and affective capacity is an indispensible element in EFL learning, as has been pointed out by Arnold (1999), Li (1987), Goleman (1995), Feuerstein, Falik, Rand & Feuerstein (2006), etc. Without the development of CAC, meaningful communication cannot be guaranteed, if we aim language learning at successful communication. Hence, the induced knowledge system under Meaning-based Learning approach is the result of a chemical integrating process, which involves the transformation of the learner's conceptual systems and the developing of his/her whole personality. If learners are fully engaged in this process, their language learning process is actually a whole experience of a new culture. Thus, if GC is the dominant attainment by the learner, he is supposed to be only able to accomplish grammatical tasks well, while communicative tasks will be very difficult for him. SLA research results demonstrate that the nature of learners' internal knowledge system is divided into two types: Explicit Linguistic Knowledge (ELK) and Implicit Linguistic Knowledge (ILK). ELK, in this case, corresponds to GC while ILK corresponds to CC. As far as the nature of the underlying knowledge is concerned, it is assumed that the knowledge that underpins automatic language processing is implicit, and the knowledge which can be consciously employed and analyzed is explicit. Bialystok (1978) proposes three functions of the ELK, viz. (1) as a buffer for storing new information for later practicing and transferring to implicit knowledge; (2) as the store for information which is always represented explicitly; (3) as an "explicit articulatory system", which is in fact represented as implicit knowledge, but can be made conscious or explicit for specific use. These three functions of the ELK provided by Bialystok shows that knowledge learnt in classrooms can be converted into the ILK after continued use or practice. From this point of view, if given certain conditions, the knowledge learnt in the form-based learning process in classrooms can be converted into implicit knowledge. In the framework, the condition for the possible transfer from GC to CC is represented by the box in the middle with dotted line which contains the interaction among DC, SLC and SC. That is, provided that GC is integrated into the interaction of DC, SLC and SC, GC can be converted into CC after time and effort when sufficient conditions are met.

Different learning processes result in different types of knowledge which in turn underpin learners' different types of **Output** — the third level in the framework. In this framework, two types of output have been identified: GCP and CCP. It is assumed that GCP is the type of performance that is undergirded by GC, while CCP is undergirded by CC. Learners who engage themselves in form-based learning will mainly attain GC, for they learn the target language mainly by means of memorizing rules and lexis and practising mechanically the sentence structures without much attention to the use of the knowledge in meaningful contexts. Those who engage themselves in meaning-based learning will attain CC which is the integration of GC, SLC, DC, SC and CAC, hence, the accomplishment of communicative tasks is guaranteed. Constrained by their limited capacities, learners who only attain GC will find it easier to accomplish grammatical tasks than communicative tasks, for communicative tasks involve the employment of more competencies within limited time.

4.3 Questions and hypotheses in the experiment

Based on this framework and the research purposes stated in Chapter 1, two kinds of tasks were therefore devised, i.e. the Knowledge Task (KT) which is decontextualised in nature, and the Writing Task (WT) which is contextualised in essence. Learners' performance on the KT was regarded as a sort of GC-based performance, while their performance on the WT was considered as a kind of CC-based performance. Learners' performance on the same linguistic forms in both tasks was to be compared so as to find out what they have attained. We assume that differential focus of attention in language learning results in a continuum, although our operationalization of the tasks with different focus is by necessity dichotomous and cannot capture clearly the underlying connections between the two types of language tasks which is inherent in viewing them as a graded phenomenon in terms of this group of learners' final attainment. Details of the design of the experiment will be presented in Chapter 5. To specify our purpose, the sub-questions and the hypothesis for the experiment are presented below.

4.3.1 Research questions in relation to the experiment

(1) How well do the learners perform in the decontextualised task as a whole?

(2) How well do the learners perform in the contextualised task as a whole?

(3) In the two kinds of performance results as a whole, is there a significant difference demonstrable by statistics?

(4) In the results of the learners' performance on the components in the KT and those in the WTK (the basic grammatical forms and lexical items generated by the learners for their accomplishment of the WT), is there a significant difference demonstrable by statistics?

(5) Which of the components in the KT and in the WTK are relatively more difficult for the learners in both types of performance?

(6) Is there any correlation between the decontextualised task performance result and the contextualised task performance result for the chosen subjects?

(7) How much can the contextualised performance result be accounted for by the decontextualised performance result?

(8) Are there any differences in the two types of performance results among the top one quarter, the average two quarters and the bottom one quarter learners?

(9) What types of knowledge have the learners attained?

(10) Does the lack of CC result from the lack of GC only?

(11) What stage are the learners at as far as their CC is concerned?

4.3.2 Hypotheses in the experiment

The first group of hypotheses is concerned with the difference between the learners' performance on the same linguistic features in the two kinds of tasks. The second group of hypotheses is concerned with the nature of the relationship between the two kinds of performance. And the third group of hypotheses is about the nature of the relationship between GC and CC. The answers to the third group of hypotheses are based on the answers to the second group of hypotheses.

Null Hypothesis One:

There is no significant difference between the learners' performance in decontextualised situations and performance in contextualised situations on the same linguistic forms.

The Alternative Hypotheses to Null Hypothesis One:

(i) The learners' performance in decontextualised situations is better than their performance on the same linguistic forms in contextualised situations.

(ii) The learners' performance in decontextualised situations is poorer than their performance on the same linguistic forms in contextualised situations.

Null Hypothesis Two:

There is no relationship between the students' performance in decontextualised situations and performance on the same linguistic forms in contextualised situations.

The Alternative Hypotheses to Null Hypothesis Two:

(i) There exists a positive relationship between the students' performance in decontextualised situations and performance on the same linguistic forms in contextualised situations.

(ii) There exists a negative relationship between the students' performance in decontextualised situations and performance on the same linguistic forms in contextualised situations.

Null Hypothesis Three:

The students' successful performance in decontextualised situations entails successful performance on the same linguistic forms in contextualised situations.

The Alternatives Hypothesis to Null Hypothesis Three:

The students' successful performance in decontextualised situations does not entail successful performance on the same linguistic forms in contextualised situations.

It is assumed that the acceptance or rejection of the above hypotheses would help us answer the above questions. The answers to the first eight questions listed above and question (11) depend on statistical analyses. The answers to questions (9) and (10) depend on the answers to the hypotheses, which were to be postulated from the experimental results.

4.4 Questions and hypotheses in the investigation

The investigation was to provide background information for the questions under investigation. There were five factors to be investigated: (1) classroom instruction (or the nature of classroom input), (2) outside class language exposure, (3) attitudes, (4) motivations, and (5) learning strategies. The results in this part were to be considered as the supporting data for the experiment.

4.4.1 Research questions in relation to the investigation

(1) To what extent are the selected students motivated and of favorable attitudes towards English learning in general?

(2) To what extent do the selected students experience exposure to English after class?

(3) What kinds of SLL strategies are more frequently employed among the subjects?

(4) What kinds of methods do the learners usually choose after class to strengthen their learning in class?

(5) What do the learners think they are strong at in English learning?

(6) Which of the classroom activities do the students prefer?

(7) What kinds of activities do the teachers usually employ in class?

(8) What sorts of homework do the teachers usually assign to their students?

(9) What are the foci of teaching in class by the teachers in these selected schools?

(10) How do the teachers in these schools handle the errors their students made in class and in homework?

(11) What language do the teachers and the students usually use in class?

(12) How do the teachers allot their time in class in these schools?

(13) How often do the students interact with each other and with their teachers in class in English?

(14) What is the nature of the input given to the students under study?

(15) What are the factors that contribute to successful EFL learning in the Chinese context?

(16) What are the factors that hinder effective EFL learning in the Chinese context?

The answer to (14) depends on the answers to questions (4) to (13), while the answers to questions (15) and (16) are to be inferred from all answers to the questions before them and the hypotheses below.

4.4.2 Hypotheses about the relationships between the experimental results and the factors under investigation

(1) The students' attainments correlate with their strong motivations in learning.

(2) The students' attainments correlate with their favorable attitudes towards the learning of the target language.

(3) The students' attainments correlate with the intensity of their outside class language exposure.

(4) The students' motivations correlate with their choices of learning strategies.

(5) The students' attainments correlate with their following

strategies: (a) memory strategies, (b) cognitive strategies, (c) compensation strategies, (d) metacognitive strategies, (e) affective strategies, and (f) social strategies.

(6) The form-based input in class is less effective than the meaning-based input in facilitating the internalization of the target language system.

The answers to the first five hypotheses will help to reveal the nature of the relationship between the investigated factors and the students' two types of performance in the experiment and how some of the factors are related to one another and influence the students' choice of learning approaches, and hence influence their final attainments. The answer to statement (6) will then be based on inferences from the answers to the first five hypotheses, the answers to the questions raised in 4. 4. 1. and the results from the experiment, and it will be discussed in Chapter 7.

4. 5 Summary

This chapter has made an attempt to establish a working conceptual framework for the following experiment and investigation, which also functions as the theoretical basis for the whole research. In the framework, the relationships among the factors to be studied and the learners' final attainments have been demonstrated. A brief discussion has been given to each level in the framework. Based on the framework and the research purpose, sub-questions and hypotheses for the following experiment and investigation have been presented. This leads to the next chapter — the design of the experiment and the investigation.

Chapter 5
Design of the Research

5.1 Initial thinking

5.1.1 Research methods

The call for going into classrooms to collect real data has resulted in many research results around instructed SLA in recent years. Both qualitative and quantitative approaches have been employed for this kind of research, which accords with Punch (1998, p. 150) in pointing out that within any given piece of research a combination of elements from different designs can overlap. Qualitative approach cherishes researchers' values and the negotiating process in approaching truth, and advocates holistic interpretation on the basis of observation and description of facts, while quantitative paradigm values empirical verification and strict methodological protocols, and advocates the use of controlled experiments to collect data for objective analysis. Among them, cross-sectional studies help us observe things on the horizontal level, while longitudinal studies help us see the development (see Gui, 1993).

However, every method has its merits and demerits. Qualitative methods appear to be subjective because of its limited samples and subjective analysis, but it may help to approach the object from a more holistic perspective. Quantitative methods, on the other hand, appear to be objective and robust, but most experimental studies in social sciences cannot be justified in accordance with real scientific experimental criteria. We embrace a more lenient model of research methodology in accordance with the post-modernist understanding of scientific research which, on the one hand, respects the means of collecting data by employing the experimental or quasi-experimental methods, while at the same time does not reject qualitative reasoning, which respects individual's understanding. Studies which are too much dependent on the data obtained from experiments may risk the danger of being unable to control extraneous variables, and result in biased conclusions because of the complexity of the objective world itself, while research which is only based on subjective reasoning risks the danger of biased epistemology. The choice of a research approach and methods is based on the nature of the research questions, the goal and the feasibility of research. This study aims to explore the nature of the knowledge attained by the Chinese middle school EFL learners and the possible operating factors and principles underlying the learning process. Due to the limitation in time, space, funds, and personnel, a quasi-experimental design and a follow-up investigation are employed, which encompasses both quantitative and qualitative reasonings. The experiment is quasi-experimental and quanlitative in nature, because the study was carried out in natural classrooms, hence the factors under study are not rigidly controlled as they might occur in labs; however, it is still a data-driven procedure and follows relatively rigorous procedures of experimental studies. The follow-up investigation was supplementary to the explanation of the experiment and qualitative in nature, because it is based on the students' self-reports and narrative accounts. On a whole, the research is cross-sectional, which studies only one level of the middle school EFL learners and bases its conclusions on the learners' one-stage performance. What intrigues the researcher is not the performance itself, but the underlying knowledge and factors operating the performance, which helps to reveal the learning process.

5. 1. 2 Background knowledge of the participants under study

By middle schools here, we refer to those high schools or middle schools, i.e. the schools whose students are normally at their 16 to 18 years of age. The circumstances of middle schools in China generally can in fact function in itself as a very important variable in the study of EFL in China. But it is not the goal of this research. Taking into consideration the effect of this variable on EFL learning and its relevance to this study, some of the features need to be summarized here with regard to the design for the experiment and the investigation.

(1) Little research has been conducted on middle school EFL learners in China, which means little literature or research results to turn to, necessary preliminary data for understanding the general situations of middle school EFL learners were necessary. This required a number of questions in the investigation part.

(2) In most Chinese middle schools, learners are put into either science classes or arts classes. However, since this research focused its attention on group performance, this difference was not to be considered when designing the experiment and the investigation.

(3) Whether in cities or the countryside in China, middle schools are graded in levels. Generally, there are two levels: *key schools* and *ordinary schools*. Students in *key schools* are mainly those who have passed a certain cut-off score in general examinations covering all subjects learnt in their junior secondary schools, and who have applied to study in key high schools, while students in *ordinary schools* are mainly those excluded from key schools. For those who have obtained rather low scores in the junior secondary school graduation examinations, they will have no chance to go to middle schools. In some places, there are three graded levels, such as in Guangzhou: *key schools*, *ordinary schools* of which there are *second-class schools* and *third-class schools*. Different levels of the schools have different social status and are treated differently by the local government. This is an important condition which results in different learning outcomes. The research took this factor into consideration.

(4) Chinese senior secondary school EFL learners are preoccupied with preparing for the National Entrance Examinations to colleges or universities which are crucial for their future. Any time spent other than for this "central target" is regarded as a "waste" of time. Teaching and learning in middle schools are seriously affected by the preparation for the NEE. The

design also took this point into consideration.

The research was to be carried out in Guangzhou, where the author could obtain help from the City Education Bureau. Apart from this, the reform of the NMET (the English test in NEE, named as National Metriculation English Test; henceforth NMET) was first carried out in Guangzhou. It has been pointed out that the good washback effect could be easily seen in middle schools in Guangzhou (Li, 1990b). The findings of the experiment and the investigation could offer evidence for the examination of the washback effect the NMET has on middle school EFL teaching and learning.

The design of the research was to take the aforementioned points into account. The design followed two steps: the design for the experiment and the design for the investigation. The design for the experiment is to be discussed first.

5.2 Design of the experiment

The aim of the experiment was to probe into the nature of the knowledge attained by the Chinese middle school EFL learners, or specifically speaking, to find out whether there was any difference between the subjects' performance on the same linguistic forms in decontextualised situations and contextualised situations. Taking into account the aim of this research, the research methods and other aforementioned points, the following aspects were considered to be important for the design. Firstly, it was important to find a good method for measurement. Second, the knowledge to be measured should be within what the learners had been taught. Third, the forms to be used for measurement should not be too unfamiliar to these learners. Fourth, since little is known about what is going on in Chinese middle schools, universities, and colleges, it is not wise to choose too broad an area and too large a population. Hence, the following choices of subjects, instruments, forms and materials were made.

5.2.1 The sample for the experiment

Three factors were involved in deciding the number of the

sample: (1) the form of the experiment, (2) the reliability of the follow-up study — the investigation, and (3) the practical difficulties. Now that writing task was employed for observation, the sample should be constrained within a manageable level. However, the reliability of the investigation required a large number of subjects. Finally, a compromise was made and three middle schools which stand for three levels in Guangzhou were randomly selected by the City Education Bureau. Two classes out of each school — about 300 learners were to be chosen. Although the number of students from each school turned out not to be exactly the same, it was believed that this would not affect much the general tendency of variation among the whole subjects, for all these subjects would be put together as a whole and they would be ranked according to their performance in the experiment.

It was decided that school-leaving middle school students were selected for the study for the reason that they were believed to have already learnt all that was required in the syllabus in six years. Accordingly, they were believed to be able to cope with general communicative tasks, for they would soon take part in the decisive NEE in July. Thus they would have strong interest in doing any kinds of exercises which might be helpful in their preparation for the examinations.

The experiment was expected to be conducted in a sample of about 300 senior school-leaving students from three schools in Guangzhou. Both male and female learners were included, and the schools were all government-supported. As has been indicated above, in Guangzhou, middle schools are divided into three levels: *key secondary schools*, *ordinary secondary schools* which include second-class secondary schools and third-class secondary schools. The *key schools* are usually regarded as the top level schools, the second-class schools are of average level schools, and the third-class schools are regarded as the low-level schools. The standard for this classification usually depends on such factors as equipment, teachers' quality, the number of students entering colleges and universities each year, the number of junior secondary school students passing large-scale general examinations and being recruited to top-level high schools, etc.

The sample of these middle schools was randomly selected by the City Education Bureau. They are Guangzhou School No. 2 (the top level), Guangzhou School No. 28 (the average level) and Guangzhou School No. 11 (the bottom level)①. As predicted, the number of students in the three schools is not equal, i.e. there are more students in one class in School No. 28 and School No. 11, and fewer students in one class in School No. 2. Among the three schools, 80 of the students were selected from School No. 2, 100 of the students were selected from School No. 28, and 106 of the students were selected from School No. 11. The total number of the school-leaving students in the three schools is 630. The sample makes up 43.49% of the total.

However, when the experimental papers and the investigation papers were collected, it was found that some of the students did one but not the other, thus they had to be sifted out. This will be dealt with later in the next chapter.

5.2.2 Instruments for the experiment

5.2.2.1 Decision on instruments

To take the time of the seniors in the third year for the experiment was not an easy task. In order to gurantee the reliability of the investigation, the tasks were designed in particular to match well with the NEE format so as to be carried out as a kind of formal test practice for the preparation of the NEE. However, this experiment was not to assess the total achievement of the middle school English learners, rather, it only aimed to make comparisons between two kinds of results through two types of tasks. Therefore, it was not necessary to devise it according to a standard measurement test, but a test for determing mastery for research purpose.

---

① Although this investigation was conducted in 1995 which only represents the basic classification of school levels at that time, interestingly, however, the basic ranking among these schools does not change much after over ten years except the names. No. 28 Middle School now restores its original name, i.e. Zhiyong Middle School, while No. 11 Middle School gains a new name, i.e. Nanhai Middle school, and No. 2 Middle School still keeps its old name and remains within the first six key schools in the city.

5. 2. 2. 2 Decision on the choice of skill for observation

Owing to the nature of this research, the choice of a skill in production mode would help us see clearly the nature of the knowledge undergirding the performance. As a form of production, it is relatively easier in writing tasks to control the implementation procedure and the linguistic features for observation than in speaking tasks although it is also time-consuming. As a skill which is holistic in nature, writing involves the employment of the different components of communicative competence — the integration of GC, SLC, DC, SC and CAC, hence it is considered here as an appropriate indicator of this group of learners' language productive ability and attributes which are related to their language learning process.

5. 2. 2. 3 Brief review of studies on writing

Writing, in essence, is a process of the integration of different kinds of competencies. As an integretive productive skill, writing involves the employment of the kinds of competence which are structural, rhetorical and instrumental (Allen, 1980, cited from Bialystok, 1981b). Different ways of developing this skill will lead to different kinds of language production. Therefore, by examining learners' language production in written mode can assist us in understanding learners' learning experience. Kroll (1993) provides a full survey of studies concerning the writing process in the early 1990s and finds that most of the research is mainly concerned with advanced learners or case studies about university students. Research findings show that L2 writers have a similar composing process with the L1 writers in some studies, while in other studies different results are obtained. The use of L1 when writing in L2 is "often an intentional (e.g., Johnson, 1985), sometimes an organizational (e. g., Lay, 1982), and occasionally a stylistic strategy (e.g., Cumming, 1987)" (cited from Kroll, 1993, p. 49). Besides, " A lack of competence in writing in English results more from the lack of composing competence than from the lack of linguistic competence" (cited from Kroll, 1993, p. 48). In the United States, since 1945 — the beginning of the modern era of second language learning, there is a succession of approaches or orientations to L2 writing. Chronologically, four main approaches can be listed: *the controlled composition approach, the current-traditional rhetoric approach, the process approach* and *the English for academic purposes approach.* According to Silva (1993b), the controlled composition approach accompanies the oral approach which focuses on listening, speaking, and reading, while writing functions only as "the handmaid of the other skills", "which must not take precedence as a major skill to be developed" (Rivers, 1968, p. 241 cited from Silva, 1993b, p. 13). Learning to write in a second language is seen as an exercise in habit formation. There is no concern for the purpose or the audience in writing. The current-traditional rhetoric approach was introduced when the controlled composition approach could not meet the increasing need of producing extended written discourse. It is found that there is more to writing than just building grammatical sentences and what is needed is a bridge between controlled and free writing. This approach is a combination of the basic principles of the current-traditional paradigm from native speaker composition instruction with Kaplan's theory of contrastive rhetoric in which Kaplan defines rhetoric as "the method of organizing syntactic units into larger patterns" (Kaplan, 1967, p. 15 cited from Silva, 1993b, p. 14). The major concern of this approach is the logical construction and arrangement of discourse forms. Classroom instruction focuses students' attention on language form. For instance, students in this approach are asked to choose alternative sentences within the context of a given paragraph or longer discourse. Thus according to this view, writing is basically a matter of arrangement, of fitting sentences and paragraphs into prescribed patterns. Learning to write involves becoming skilled in identifying, internalizing, and executing these patterns. The writer fills in a preexisting form with provided or self-generated content (Silva, 1993b, pp. 13 – 14).

The introduction of the process approach is motivated mainly by the dissatisfaction with the controlled composition approach and the current-traditional approach. According to this approach, "composing means expressing ideas, and conveying meaning. Composing means thinking" (Raimes, 1983, p. 261). Thus controlled composition approach seems largely irrelevant to this goal, while the prescriptivism and linearity of the current-traditional rhetoric approach discourages creative thinking and writing. The process approach sees writing as a "non-linear, exploratory, and generative process whereby writers discover and reformulate their ideas as they attempt to approximate meaning" (Zamel, 1983, p. 165 cited from Silva 1993b, p. 15). When being applied to the classroom, learners are encouraged to work through their composing processes with minimal interference, ample time and the teacher's help in developing their viable strategies for getting started. Learners are encouraged to draft and revise their work repeatedly. Writing here is a creative and recursive process somewhat similar to that by first language writers.

The introduction of the English for Academic Purposes Approach comes from the criticism of the process approach which is attacked for its overemphasis on the psychological functioning and its negligence of the sociocultural context. The process approach emphasizes meaning and claims that form depends on meaning. The text produced by the process approach is a product of secondary, derivative concern, whose form is a function of its content and purpose. Another point for the process approach which is attacked is that it does not adequately address some central issues in ESL writing. Reid (1984a; 1984b cited from Silva 1993b, p. 16) has suggested that the process approach "neglects to seriously consider variations in writing processes due to differences in individuals, writing tasks, and situations; the development of schemata for academic discourse; language proficiency; level of cognitive development; and insights from the study of contrastive rhetoric" (Silva 1993b, pp. 16 – 17). Thus from the orientation of the English for Academic Purposes, writing is the production of prose that can be acceptable at an American academic institution, and learning to write is a part of becoming socialized to the academic community — finding out what is expected and trying to approximate it. The writer has a purpose whenever he writes, while the reader is a seasoned member of the hosting academic community who has well-developed schemata for academic discourse and clear and stable views of what is appropriate. The produced text is then a conventional response to a particular task type or falls into a recognizable genre. The context is the academic community and the typical tasks associated with it.

In brief, different products reflect different approaches and different understandings of second language learning. Several points may be elicited from the simple review of the writing approaches for the use of this study. First, writing is a complex process which involves many characteristics, such as the writer himself, the task, the context, and the audience. Thus, the study of writing should take all these factors into consideration. Second, the upward spiral development from the focus on linguistic forms themselves to the gradual recognition of the effect of language production context and the importance of audience reflects the multiplex nature of writing. Then, writing with a communicative purpose not only involves the use of linguistic forms, but also the employment of knowledge of the target culture, knowledge of discourse and knowledge of how to cope with one's own deficiencies. Third, a writing task type is a mirror of the underlying principles one advocates. Any choice or design of writing tasks should first be based on a clear idea of the purpose of writing.

5.2.2.4 Tasks in the experiment

Based on the previous understandings of the writing skill and the research purpose, two types of tasks were decided and designed for the experiment, i.e., the knowledge task (i.e. the test of learners' knowledge of the controlled linguistic forms) (KT) and the writing task (i.e. the two communication-oriented writing tasks) (WT). The grammatical forms and lexical items needed to encode the essential ideas contained in the WT (hereafter GL) are the controlled linguistic forms in the experiment. For convenience, the design started first from the WT.

Taking into consideration the factors like the sampled learners' English proficiency and their particular attention to the NMET, controlled writing or guided writing task was employed as one of the tasks in the experiment (WT). By *guided writing task* here, it refers to the type of writing task which is designed for students to accomplish within fixed time period, but the task is usually designed with provided simulated authentic context for communication, guided information and requirements on the minimum employment of necessary linguistic features. In order to control the linguistic forms so as to make comparisons with the grammatical task in the experiment, the main content of the writing tasks was supplied in Chinese, but was presented in a rather discrete form to avoid possible translations. Requirements for the tasks were written in Chinese so that the subjects could understand the tasks easily. Two writing tasks were devised. One was in the form of a letter. The other was in the form of a brief report — a simple article written for publication in the Secondary School EFL Learners' Newspaper in Shanghai. Both tasks were made as authentic as possible. For details, see Appendix 1.

The KT was designed on the basis of the analysis of the minimally passable model versions of the WT. Two minimally passable versions of the two writing tasks were produced first by the researcher. Based on these two versions, the basic linguistic forms (i. e. GL) were elicited and they were used as the main content of the KT in the experiment. Two parts, i.e. vocabulary and grammar, are included which contain 23 items. The item types include: *spelling checking*, *identification of meaning*, *identification of parts of speech*, *giving grammatical forms*, *judgement of grammatical forms*, and *metalanguage test at both word level and sentence level.* The designing of the KT task followed the basic understanding of explicit knowledge which is defined as the declarative knowledge about language which is consciously held and accessed in controlled processing. The general level of the KT was fixed at the simplest cognitive level of recognition, simple recall and judgement with the purpose to examine the learners' explicit knowledge about the forms. The items were arranged from simple to complex or from complex to simple, i.e. from recognition of general concepts of language like *parts of speech* to recognition and recall of rules like *the rules of articles and verb conjugation.* The linguistic features in the KT were embodied in discrete forms with little language or sociocultural context provided. It is hence called a decontextualised task in this study. The detailed description of each item is presented in the Appendix. A simple description of the designing procedure is given below.

(1) Examining the secondary school EFL teaching syllabus—to make sure what grammatical forms and lexical items could be coped with by the students.

(2) Choosing topics — that might be interesting and rich in content and could be managed by adolescents.

(3) Devising writing tasks — selecting appropriate forms.

(4) Writing the minimally passable versions.

(5) Analyzing the versions: listing possible structures and vocabulary.

(6) Matching these structures and vocabulary with the secondary school EFL teaching syllabus.

(7) Devising the KT according to the listed possible structures and vocabulary.

(8) Revising all the items.

A pilot test was conducted to examine the feasibility of time setting and the face validity of the "test" among ten middle school graduates of the previous year. The result indicates that the assignment of time to each part and the difficulty of the tasks were within the students' language ability. The experiment was designed for at most 2 hours of which one hour was for the writing task and the rest was for the knowledge task. Time here is important because it is hard for the schools to arrange time and it is generally believed that if a test takes more than two hours, the students will usually feel bored.

Since the linguistic forms all came from the writing tasks, the KT should not be distributed before the WT. The KT was designed according to the order of grammatical difficulty and cognitive difficulty for the purpose of finding out at what grammatical level the learners were if they could not accomplish the WT. Thus, the sub-tests in the KT were arranged in order and printed on different pieces of paper so as to be distributed one by one in case one sub-test might influence the answer of the next one.

What needs to be discussed here is the reliability and validity of this "test". Since it is not a real test that aims at measuring learners' holistic knowledge of the target language, it is believed by the researcher that the "test" should not be evaluated by the traditional requirements in testing for reliability and validity. However, it does not mean that consideration of reliability and validity is unnecessary. This problem will be discussed from another perspective. In this experiment, to guarantee reliability, a relatively large sample was drawn, which has been discussed above. For the WT, two tasks were devised. Thus, with around 300 students, there were in fact about 600 scripts to be collected, which are actually a large sample for writing tasks. According to the factors that might influence the reliability of a test (Gui, 1987), the WT can be considered as reliable. In the KT, since the attention was on the knowledge about English, the learners were to be asked to recognize and recall the grammatical rules and the vocabulary required by the WT, and all items were in objective forms, which guarantee the scoring reliability. To guarantee the validity of the writing tasks, the tasks were devised with reference to the NMET formats. The contents were strictly restricted within the middle school EFL teaching syllabus, and the tasks have been analyzed and compared with the writing tasks in the NMET in the past. It was found that they were not very different in difficulty with respect to language and organization. The scoring for writing will be discussed below in another section in detail.

5.3 Design of the investigation

The investigation aimed to find out whether there was any relationship between the students' performance in the experiment and their ways of learning or to provide background information for the experimental results. The investigation employed the form of a survey, which makes possible the collection of data from a sizable sample of the population within a short period of three weeks.

5.3.1 The sample for the investigation

The students for the survey were the same group of participants selected for the experiment with the purpose of finding out their learning patterns and providing background information. It was expected that all the students who participated in the experiment would take part in the survey. Thus the expected number of students was the same as the number in the experiment. The teachers in the three secondary schools were to be requested to fill in a separate questionnaire for them.

5.3.2 The instrument for the investigation

The survey took the form of a questionnaire with multiple-choice questions mostly. The number of choices ranges from 3 to 23. Two questionnaires were designed: the one for the students (QL) was of primary concern, and the other for the English teachers in the three middle schools (QT) was just used as a supplement. The two questionnaires are presented in Appendix II together with a description of the component items.

5.3.3 The content of the questionnaires

Two points were to be first considered in the design of the questionnaires. First, research in the field of SLA has found that there are many factors affecting second language acquisition. In his framework for investigating SLA, Ellis (1985) points out that there are five major interrelated factors to be considered in the study of second language acquisition: (1) situational factors, (2) input, (3) learner differences, (4) learner processes, and (5) linguistic output, and each major factor consists of various sub-factors. Although there are differences between second language acquisition and foreign language learning, they share most of the features (Larsen-Freeman and Long, 1991). In this study, some of the factors that have been found to be important for SLA were adopted to see whether these factors also influence FLL. Second, FLL has its specific characteristics, especially in the context of China — a monolingual country. Middle school English learners are a special group of learners. Some of the factors which have been discussed a lot in SLA might not operate in the same way in the Chinese context. This opinion is also expressed by Young (1987) as stated below:

> Ways of teaching and ways of learning differ from one community to another. Yet most discussions of methods of teaching English to speakers of other languages (TESOL) and research into second language acquisition do not take these differences seriously. ... The conclusion which is drawn from this evidence [his work] is that many classroom techniques which work successfully in a Western cultural context will not work when applied to TESOL in a Chinese context (Young, 1987, p. 15).

Considering the feasibility and practicality of this study, factors like age, intelligence, aptitude, education policies, teachers' quality were not to be considered for the reasons that have been discussed under 3. 3 in Chapter 3. Thus, factors chosen for this study were: *Classroom instruction*, *learning strategies*, *attitudes, motivations*, and *outside class language exposure* (5 factors).

Although the questionnaire for teachers is not an important part in this research, however, teachers in Chinese middle schools play a special role in EFL learning. In Chinese middle school culture, teachers are like parents, taking care of everything of the students. Learners have great respect for and are obedient to them. Thus, teachers' personalities, their beliefs of EFL learning, their teaching methods and their assessment methods are closely related to learners' EFL development and eventually influence learners' choice of learning strategies. Taking all the above factors into consideration, the questionnaires were designed from three main aspects: teacher, learner, and environment.

In the questionnaire for learners, eight aspects were covered. They were (1) learners' background, (2) learners' learning experiences, (3) learners' attitudes and motivations, (4) learners' outside class language exposure, (5) learners' learning strategies, (6) learners' focus of attention in EFL learning, (7) learners' reports on their teachers' classroom instruction methods, and (8) learners' reports on their learning conditions. The items for (3) were based on Chandrasegaran's questionnaire (1981) but with some modifications. The items for the other aspects were written according to the researcher's experiences and interviews with some graduated students. Among the eight aspects, (1), (2) and (8) are only considered as a kind of background information, but not as variables under study. For details, see Appendix 2 for the description of items.

In the questionnaire for teachers, six aspects were included, i.e., (1) teachers' background, (2) teachers' knowledge of prevailing teaching approaches, (3) teachers' views of language competence, (4) teaching processes, (5) teachers' self evaluation, and (6) teachers' reports on teaching conditions. A description of each item is presented in the Appendix.

All items in the questionnaires were written in Chinese so as to avoid possible misunderstandings. Two instruction letters were produced and added to the front of the questionnaires so that teachers and students would understand what they were asked to do.

5.4 Data Collecting Procedure

5.4.1 The implementation of the experiment and the investigation

The experiment and the investigation were implemented during May and June in 1994 in Guangzhou in the above-mentioned three schools. In execution, there were two teachers in each class as invigilators. Each invigilator was given an instruction sheet and requested to write down any unexpected happenings and to observe the learners' writing processes. The experiment for the three schools was conducted at different time periods according to their own timetable, i. e. in the time they could arrange the "test".

The questionnaires were distributed to the students and the teachers in these schools after the experiment in each school and were collected within a week.

The teachers and students were interested in the results.

Therefore, after the execution of the experiments, immediate scoring of both tasks —the KT and the WT was carried out. To guarantee the validity of the scoring, two raters were requested to mark the writing papers. All the schools received the performance results in two weeks owing to the hard work of the researcher and the generous help of two other raters. The successful execution of the experiment and the survey guarantees the reliability and the validity of the experiment and the investigation.

5.4.2 The rating of the tasks

The scoring of the KT employed an objective scoring method, but the scoring of writing is always a "headache". Writing task is in nature a subjective test type. As Kroll (1993) points out that there are three processes involved in all tests of writing, and each has its nature of subjectivity:

> Of the three processes common to all tests of writing, (1) *the construction of questions* is clearly subjective, and carried out by humans; (2) *answering questions* is also clearly subjective and carried out by humans, even when human responses are limited by "objective" items; and only (3) *scoring* has both subjective and objective possibilities. Even then, "objective" scoring can be carried out only when humans have decided what the correct answers are (Kroll, 1993, p. 78).

The scoring, to some extent, depends on the form of the writing tasks. It can be objective if the task is not so free from control. However, there always exists a contradiction between task type and validity of scoring. If the task is directed to communication, the task should not be too much controlled since communicative tasks emphasize creativity in meaning transfer. Thus the construction of this kind of tasks will be mostly subjective and the answer will also be subjective. With regard to reliability, in the field of testing, objective scoring is preferred, of course. However, objective scoring cannot guarantee the solution of the problem of subjectivity. Sometimes, tasks of a subjective nature may best be scored by a subjective scoring procedure. To approach these problems, analytical rating method has been produced, which is now popularly used.

To employ the analytical method in this research, it is of first importance to decide on the factors needed to be considered in the scoring of the WT. The decision on the essential aspects in scoring writing tasks is based on the principles underlying language learning, teaching, and assessment. The aspects considered in the scoring of the WT in this research follow those in the communicative language testing, i.e. language proficiency is undergirded by componential communicative language competence. As has been mentioned, communicative language competence is composed of at least four components which are proposed in Canale and Swain (1980) and Canale (1983)'s framework, and summarised in three main factors in Li (1987)'s model. We, thus, decided on five aspects to be considered for the rating of the writing task, i.e. *message, organization, accuracy, appropriacy,* and *mechanics.* In addition to the analytical scoring, the impression method was also employed to check whether sufficient consideration for the holistic performance of the subject was given in rating. The above two methods guided the scoring of the two writing tasks. Detailed description of the scoring procedure for the WT papers will be given in the next chapter which is mainly concerned with the data in a statistical sense.

5.4.3 Data Coding

For the purpose of comparison, the linguistic forms produced by the participants in the WT need to be analyzed and classified so that they could be compared with the performance in the KT. Therefore, after the holistic scoring, a table for each student was drawn with the listed possible vocabulary and structures that have been used for the design of the KT. Based on this table, the learners' language responses in the WT were analyzed, categorized and marked. The criterion for judging a point to be correct or wrong depends on whether the student conveys the appropriate meaning to meet the task requirements. Thus, the final scores for each student's language responses in the WT were obtained. The procedure for the obtaining of this group of data will be provided in the next chapter.

The data for the investigation were also sorted and keyboarded in the form that was easily analyzed by the software SPSS and Microsoft Excel .

5.5 Summary

This chapter provides a detailed report on the design, the execution and the data collecting procedure of the experiment and the investigation for this research. It includes the sampling procedure, the decision on the instruments, the content of the tasks and the questionnaires, and the data collecting procedure for the experiment and the investigation. Therefore, the experiment was conducted in the form of task performance under testing situation among the sampled school-leaving students in three Chinese middle schools in Guangzhou. Two tasks in the experiment were devised: the KT and the WT. The investigation was carried out after the experiment among the same subjects by employing the questionnaire form. An additional survey of the teachers in these schools was also carried out. Finally, this chapter gives a brief account of how the data were collected and sorted. The results of the experiment and the investigation will be presented in the next chapter together with the answers to some of the questions put forward in Chapter IV.

Chapter 6
Presentation of Results

6.1 Data sorting

There are two sources for the data: one is the experiment, and the other is the investigation. All the data have been collected under conditions controlled by the design. A brief specification of the sorting of the data both from the experiment and the questionnaires is as follows.

6.1.1 Collating data from the experiment

As has been described in Chapter 5, the expected number of the students was around 300 and the sampling procedure was carried out by randomly selecting any two classes in each school. However, the number of the students in each class varies in each school. In No. 2 Middle School, there were about 40 students in each class, while in the other two schools, there were about 50 students or more in each class. For one reason or another, in each school, there were some students who were not available for the experiment and the investigation. Thus, altogether 274 test papers and questionnaires were distributed and the same number of papers was collected. After careful examination, incompletely filled questionnaires were rejected and partially finished test papers were given up, leaving 231 students for analysis. The distribution of students by schools is displayed below in Table 6-1 and Table 6 – 2.

Table 6 – 1 Distribution of the students by schools after leaving out those whose tasks were partially finished

School No.	No. 2		No. 11		No. 28		Total	
Category	Num	%	Num	%	Num	%	Num	%
Male	15	26.3	48	53.3	41	48.8	100	43.3
Female	42	73.7	42	46.7	43	51.2	131	56.7
Total	57	100.0	90	100.0	84	100.0	231	100.0

Table 6 – 2 Distribution of the students in each school before some of them were left out

School No.	No. 2		No. 11		No. 28		Total	
Category	Num	%	Num	%	Num	%	Num	%
Total	75	32.5	104	44.4	95	41.1	274	100

Of these 231 students, 57 of the students are from No. 2 Middle School which is considered by the City Education Bureau as one of the highest level secondary schools in the city; 90 of them are from No. 11 Middle School which is considered as one of the lowest level middle schools in the city, and 84 of the students are from No. 28 Middle School which is considered one of the average level schools in the city①.

(1) The scoring of the tasks in the experiment

A. Allocation of scores in the knowledge task (KT)

In both the KT and the WT, the total score is 100. In the knowledge task (KT), the 100 score is divided into six component scores for six subvariables, and the scores for each variable can be seen from the following table:

① The level assumed by the City Education Bureau is not definitely what it is in fact. There are many criteria. Thus, it might not be right to say that the English level in one school is definitely higher than another one. In fact, several students in School No. 11 and School No. 28 fall into the higher level group after the scores were sorted.

Table 6 - 3 Distribution of the scores for the six subvariables in the KT

Var. Name	Voc	Mph	Fct	Pron	Cont	Vfs	Total
Score	14%	27.5%	12%	5.5%	30.5%	10.5%	100%

Notes: Voc = vocabulary in the KT; Pron = pronouns in the KT;
Mph = morphological forms in the KT; Cont = basic grammatical concepts in the KT;
Fct = function words in the KT; Vfs = verb forms in sentence in the KT;

As has been discussed in Chapter 5, the purpose of the experiment was to find out whether there was any difference between the learners' two types of performance on the same linguistic knowledge in the contextualized and decontextualized situations. For comparison, the same scores for the subvariables in the KT were also allocated to each subvariable in the writing task as far as the same linguistic knowledge is concerned. Thus, we have two kinds of scores for the same lexis and grammatical features from the two kinds of tasks: linguistic knowledge score in decontextualized situation (variable names initialized with KT) and linguistic knowledge score in contextualized situation (variable names initialized with WTK). The scoring of the papers for the KT follows an objective process, but the obtaining of the scores for the WTK (the basic grammatical forms and lexical items generated by the learners for their accomplishment of the WT) corresponding to those for the KT involved both an objective process and a subjective one. The linguistic forms encoding the essential ideas of the two writing tasks (GL) were listed, categorized and printed on the table drawn for each subject at the outset. Then, the linguistic forms generated by the subjects for the accomplishment of the WT were then categorized and marked (The learners' expressions other than the listed ones on the table were also recorded on condition that those expressions convey the essential ideas accurately and appropriately.) according to the forms listed on the table. Then, for convenience, the lexical items or grammatical forms that were wrongly or inappropriately used by each student in expressing the essential ideas for the tasks were counted out first. The specifications for the counting of errors for each task are displayed in Appendix III. Then, the number of errors was subtracted from the number of the listed GL and the number of the linguistic forms correctly generated by the learners was obtained. The following table gives the idea of how the number of the linguistic forms correctly generated by the learners was transformed into scores matching those scores for each subvariable in the KT. For the GL appearing in both types of tasks and specifications of the data processing procedure, see the Appendix.

Table 6-4 Transforming the number of the linguistic forms correctly generated by the students into scores matching those for the subvariables in the KT

Number of the GL in the WT after being categorized:					
WTKVoc	WTKMph	WTKFct	WTKPron	WTKCont	WTKVfs
41	17	13	11	23	9
Transforming the learners' correct production of the GL into scores:					
WTKvoc = cr * 14/41;	WTKmph = cr * 27.5/17;	WTKfct = cr * 12/13;			
WTKpron = cr * 5.5/11;	WTKcont = cr * 30.5/23;				
WTKvfs = cr * 10.5/9;	WTKtotl = voc + mph + fct + pron + cont + vfs				

Notes: cr = the number of the GL correctly produced by the subjects;

B. The rating of the writing tasks from a holistic view

The analysis of the learners' linguistic expressions in their performance of the WT was mainly for comparison. In order to obtain a holistic view of the subjects' communicative competence from the writing skill, a more comprehensive scoring method was needed. Chapter 5 has provided a brief discussion of the scoring problem for the writing tasks. The process of writing is in fact a process of restructuring or organization of the knowledge of the grammatical system and knowledge of language related fields in written mode. Thus, the accomplishment of a writing task not only requires the accurate expression of the required ideas, but also requires the appropriate conveying of the ideas. The general requirements for punctuation and spelling may reflect one aspect of the writer's educational level. However, what is most important of all, of course, is the conveying of meaning for communication. Taking all these into consideration, as has been pointed out in Chapter 5, we have decided on five aspects to be considered for the marking of the writing tasks: *message*, *organization*, *accuracy*, *appropriacy*, and *mechanics*. The allocation of scores to each aspect was decided by the relative importance of each aspect. The most important principle was that the tasks were accomplished for communication. Thus, message transfer was the most important of the five aspects and should be allotted more scores. In this experiment, it has been held that meaning transfer is above all other factors. The principle behind this opinion is that the mastery of grammatical rules and vocabulary in language learning is not enough for communication without considering the use of these rules and words. However, since the learners under this condition are middle school learners, a basic knowledge of the English language system is also important. Thus, accuracy has its particular role in expressing ideas contained in the two writing tasks. Besides, the learners had been spending a lot of time learning grammar. The score assignment, therefore, should reflect the particular role of accuracy in writing for this group of subjects. Another important aspect in writing is the appropriacy in writing. Given the underlying principle stated above, appropriacy should also take on an important role in writing. Relatively speaking, *punctuation and spelling* were less important and therefore were allocated less scores. The two writing tasks in this experiment were scored together. Each task took 50 per cent of the 100 percent. The distribution of scores in rating the writing papers can be seen from Table 6 - 5.

Table 6 - 5 Distribution of the scores under each aspect for the rating of the writing papers

Aspects	Message	Organization	Accuracy	Appropriacy	Mechanics	Total
Scores	20%	12%	36%	20%	12%	100%

The scoring procedure could not avoid subjectiveness. It could never be as objective as the scoring of multiple choice items. To guarantee the validity and reliability of the scoring procedure, a combined scoring method was used. First, two raters were requested to score the papers and the final score for each subject was the average of the two raters' scoring results. Second, the analytical method was used together with the impression method. The raters were asked to follow three steps: i. e. (1) scoring holistically when first reading through the papers, (2) scoring analytically by reading it again, and (3) applying the impression method again to adjust the scores obtained by the analytical method. Thus, a score of a learner's performance in the WT could not be obtained unless the three steps had been followed. The analytical rating method was the one on which all scores are mainly based. The impression method was for the adjustment of scores. The two writing tasks were rated by two raters using a 100-point holistic plus analytic grading system. Specifications on the scoring procedure for the writing tasks are presented in Appendix 3.

(2) The treatment of the scores in the statistical analyses

Three sets of scores were obtained finally, i.e. the scores for the KT, the scores for the learners' generation of the required grammatical forms and lexical items in the WT, and the scores for the learners' holistic performance of the WT (WTTOTL). The scores for the KT and the WTK were used for comparison and other analyses, while WTTOTL was mainly used for grouping subjects into three groups: the top level group, the average level group, and the low level group. The use of WTTOTL in this way is based on that writing is a relatively comprehensive task as has been stated above. Although there is little research on the relationship between writing and other skills, some studies have shown that writing correlates highly with other skills, such as reading (Kroll, 1993).

6. 1. 2 Collating data from the investigation

The same subjects and the teachers in the three schools were requested to fill in the questionnaires. These data were analyzed after the experiment for the purpose of finding out the possible relationship between the factors under investigation and the students' scores in the experiment and the relationships among the factors themselves.

6.1.3 Analyses of the data from the experiment and the investigation

The sorting and the analyses of the data were performed by the Statistical Package for the Social Sciences (SPSS) with Microsoft Office as an aid in data transformation and graphics making.

In the experiment, descriptive statistics was applied first to give a general idea of the distribution of the scores. Paired samples t-test was used to compare the mean differences between the scores in both types of performance. Pearson Bivariate Correlation method was employed to compute the correlation of the scores obtained from the WT with the scores obtained from the KT. The Enter Multiple Regression method was used to determine how much the scores in the KT could account for the scores in the WT. With WTTOTL (the holistic score) as reference, three groups of students were obtained, i.e. the top one quarter, the middle two quarters and the bottom one quarter. One-way ANOVA was applied to examine whether there were differences among the three groups divided by WTTOTL and the three groups divided by schools in the two kinds of performance.

The statistical analyses of the data from the investigation were also carried out by employing some of the above-mentioned methods with the addition of the frequency distribution and the Chi square test. Pearson Bivariate Correlation method was applied again to compute the correlation of scores obtained in the KT and the WT with each of the independent variables in the investigation, i.e. the factors under study. The Enter Multiple Regression method was employed again to determine whether the amount of variance in the scores obtained from the two types of performance was due to each of the independent variables. Finally, the three groups divided by WTTOTL and the three groups divided by schools were treated separately to see if there existed any differences.

6.2 Presentation of the results from the experiment

In this section, the results of the statistical analyses of the data from the experiment will be presented in the order of the questions and hypotheses relating to the objectives of the experiment.

Question 1. How well do the students perform in the decontextualized task (here KT) as a whole?

Table 6 - 6 Distribution of the mean scores for all students (231) in the KT
(Means for all cases of all variables in original scores)

Variables	Means	SDs	Mini.	Maxi.	ValidN	Label
KTVOC	13.01	.83	9.5	14.0	231	KT vocabulary
KTMPH	24.47	2.23	12.5	27.5	231	KT mopholog. forms
KTFCT	8.50	1.51	3.8	11.8	231	KT function words
KTPRON	3.31	.98	.5	5.5	231	KT pronouns
KTCONT	26.32	2.46	16.0	30.5	231	KT basic gram. concpts
KTVFS	7.76	1.38	1.0	10.0	231	KT v. forms in sent.
KTTOTL	83.36	6.42	49.75	95.75	231	KT total score (100)

Number of valid observations (listwise) = 231.00

Table 6 - 7 Distribution of the mean scores for all students (231) in the KT in percentage form (i. e. each variable now taking 100 as the total score — transformed from Table 6)

Variables	Means	SDs	Mini.	Maxi.	ValidN	Label
KTVOCP	92.93	5.92	67.86	100.00	231	KT voc 100
KTMPHP	88.97	8.10	45.45	100.00	231	KT mph 100
KTFCTP	70.82	12.58	31.25	97.92	231	KT fct 100
KTPRONP	60.15	17.73	9.09	100.00	231	KT pron 100
KTCONTP	86.30	8.07	52.46	100.00	231	KTcont 100
KTVFSP	73.87	13.16	9.52	95.24	231	KT vfs 100
KTTOTLP	473.04	44.23	277.49	561.44	231	KT total 600

Number of valid observations (listwise) = 231.00

The students appeared to be very successful in the performance of the KT. Tables 6-6 and 6-7 show that the mean scores for all the subvariables in the KT except for KTPRON are over 70 percent. The poor performance in KTPRON is unexpected, but is not difficult to understand after further analysis. This will be discussed later in the next chapter. The total KT mean score amounts to about 83 percent. Obviously the students found it very easy to recognize and recall the tested grammatical forms and lexical items. The results in the percentage table (Table 6 – 7) may help us see how the students performed on the sub-tests of the KT. If we draw a cut-off line at the point of 60, which means that those who gained 60 or over 60 were regarded as having passed the "test", we find that 230 students out of 231 have passed the KT as a whole (for KTTOTL). That means about 99. 57 per cent have passed. As for the sub-tests, all of the students have passed KTVOC (100%), 229 out of 231 students have passed KTMPH (99. 13%), 193 out of 231 students have passed KTFCT (83. 55%), 112 out of the total have passed KTPRON (48. 49%), 229 out of 231 students have passed KTCONT (99. 13%), and 200 out of the total have passed KTVFS (86. 58%).

Question 2. How well do the students perform in the contextualized task (WT) as a whole?

The scores for the WTK have gone through a process of transformation as has been described above, i. e. to count the errors first and the errors were then subtracted from the number of the required GL and the number of the linguistic forms correctly produced by the learners was obtained then (Table 6 – 8). The raw scores matching the KT (Table 6 – 9) were transformed from Table 6 – 8. As Table 6 – 9 shows, compared with the mean scores in the KT, the mean scores in the WTK (i.e. the use of linguistic knowledge in context) are drastically lower. Most of the mean scores for the subvariables are lower than those in the KT as in Table 6 – 6, except for WTKPRON, which is unexpectedly higher than that in the KT. Further analysis will be given to this component to check the possible reasons underlying it. The same was done as that in Table 6 – 7 in order to help us see more clearly the subjects' performance in each component, and the percentages of the scores were again obtained, which gives each component equal weight for the purpose of direct comparison. Thus, it can be observed that only WTKPRONP is over 70%, while all the other components are around 60% or as low as 33%. Thus, if we also make 60 as the cut-off point like that in the KT, we find that for 231 students, only 62 have passed the "test" (26. 84%). For the components, 135 out of 231 subjects have passed WTKVOC (58. 44%), 18 out of 231 students have passed WTKMPH (7. 79%), 121 out of 231 students have passed WTKFCT (52. 38%), 212 out of 231 subjects have passed WTKPRON (91. 77%), 181 out of 231 students have passed WTKCONT (78. 35%), and 34 out of 231 students have passed WTKVFS (14. 72%). The subjects seemed to have much difficulty in producing the same linguistic forms in the WT which they could well recognize and recall in the KT. The total mean score does not amount to 60%.

Table 6 – 8 Distribution of the mean scores (the number of the GL correctly produced by the learners in the WT) for all students (231) in the WTK

Variables	Means	SDs	Mini.	Maxi.	Valid N
WTKVOC	25. 11	4. 93	13. 0	37. 0	231
WTKMPH	5. 74	3. 02	.5	14. 0	231
WTKFCT	7. 64	1. 65	3. 0	12. 0	231
WTKPRON	8. 42	1. 31	2. 0	11. 0	231
WTKCONT	15. 44	2. 71	7. 0	21. 0	231
WTKVFS	3. 76	1. 51	1. 0	8. 0	231
WTKTOTL	66. 12	11. 92	32. 50	98. 00	231

Number of valid observations (listwise) = 231. 00

With the five aspects in the analytic scoring as a guide and the impression method as an aid, the total scores (or holistic scores) of each student for the two writing tasks were also obtained which can be seen from Table 6 – 11. The results of the two raters' (WTTLCXP and WTTLYN) rating are also presented as reference. It can be seen from the means that the results of the two raters are not very different. The t-test for the means between the two raters' rating results indicates that the difference between them is not significant ($t = -1.31$, $p < .192$) when the criterion is set at $p <= 0.05$. The correlation between the two raters' results is marked ($r = .822$, $p < .0000$). The average of the two scores is the final score (WTTOTL) for statistical analysis. This indicates that the scoring procedure is reliable and valid.

Table 6 - 9 Distribution of the mean scores for all variables in the WTK for all students (231) (Mean scores transformed from Table 6 - 8 matching scores in the original form in the KT in 100)

Variables	Means	SDs	Mini.	Maxi.	ValidN	Label
WTKVOC	8.58	1.68	4.44	12.63	231	match-14
WTKMPH	9.29	4.89	.81	22.65	231	match-27.5
WTKFCT	7.05	1.52	2.77	11.08	231	match-12
WTKPRON	4.21	.66	1.00	5.50	231	match-5.5
WTKCONT	20.48	3.59	9.28	27.85	231	match-30.5
WTKVFS	4.39	1.76	1.17	9.33	231	match-10.5
WTKTOTL	53.99	11.21	23.31	85.27	231	matchKTtotal—100

Number of valid observations (listwise) =231.00

Table 6 - 10 Distribution of the mean scores for all students (231) in the WTK in percentage form (i.e. each variable in the WTK taking 100 as the total score — transformed from Table 6 - 8)

Variables	Means	SDs	Mini.	Maxi.	ValidN
WTKVOCP	61.25	12.02	31.71	90.24	231
WTKMPHP	33.77	17.79	2.94	82.35	231
WTKFCTP	58.79	12.67	23.08	92.31	231
WTKPRONP	76.54	11.92	18.18	100.00	231
WTKCONTP	67.14	11.77	30.43	91.30	231
WTKVFSP	41.77	16.79	11.11	88.89	231
WTKTOTLP	339.26	61.63	155.10	503.84	231

Number of valid observations (listwise) =231.00

From Table 6 - 11 and Table 6 - 6, it can be seen that the mean for the two writing tasks is also comparatively lower than the mean for the KT (i.e. WTTOTL 59.63 vs KTTOTL 83.36). Most of the students found it difficult to accomplish the two writing tasks although the grammar and lexis required by the WT is the same as that in the KT.

Table 6 - 11 Distribution of the holistic mean scores for the WT for all students (231)

Variables	Means	SDs	Mini.	Maxi.	ValidN	Label
WTTLCXP	59. 23	12. 53	26. 00	85. 00	231	Rater1 in 100
WTTLYN	60. 04	13. 38	22. 0	83. 50	231	Rater2 in 100
WTTOTL	59. 63	12. 36	25. 75	83. 25	231	Mean for 2 raters in 100
WTTOTLP	357. 79	74. 17	154. 50	499. 50	231	WTTOTL changed to 600

Note: Number of valid observations (listwise) = 231. 00

The mean difference between KTTOTL and WTKTOTL is 29. 37, and the difference between KTTOTL and WTTOTL is 23. 73. The mean difference between KTTOTL and WTKTOTL is greater than that between KTTOTL and WTTOTL. The SDs (standard deviation) in WTKTOTL and WTTOTL are greater than that in KTTOTL, which indicates a greater difference among the students' performance in the WT and a smaller difference in the KT.

Question 3. In terms of the two kinds of performance results as a whole, is there a significant difference demonstrable by statistics? (i. e. Is the mean for KTTOTL in the KT significantly different from the means for WTKTOTL and WTTOTL in the WT?)

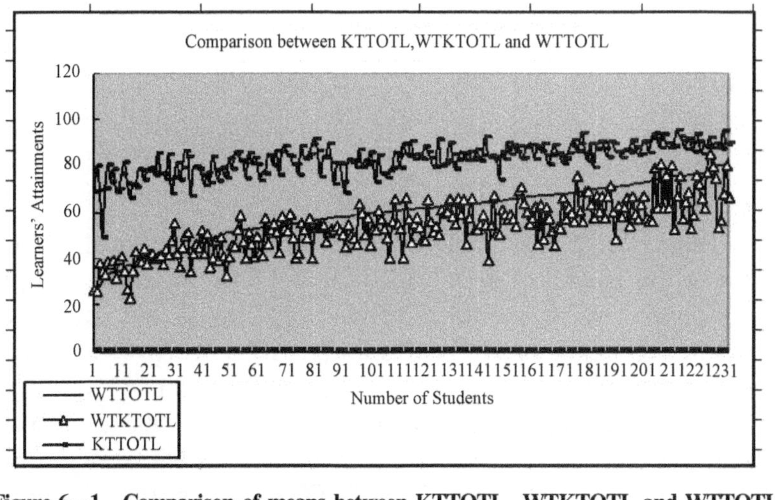

Figure 6 - 1 Comparison of means between KTTOTL, WTKTOTL and WTTOTL

The answer to this question and the following questions are in fact the answer to the null hypothesis stated in Chapter IV, i.e. there is no significant difference between students' performance on the same linguistic knowledge in the KT and the WT.

The mean tables and the above figure show that the means of KTTOTL, WTKTOTL and WTTOTL are different. In order to examine whether the differences are statistically significant, a two-tailed paired samples t-test was employed, hence the following results:

Table 6 - 12 Two paired samples t-test for KTTOTL and WTKTOTL

				Paired Differences					
Variables	Means	SDs	SEof Mean	Mean Difference	SD	SEof Mean	t-value	df	2-tail* sig.
KTTOTL	83. 3615	6. 421	.422	29. 3726	8. 635	. 568	51. 70	230	. 000
WTKTOTL	53. 9888	11. 205	. 737						

Note: The confidence interval at 95% is between 28. 253 and 30. 492. * $p < = 0.05$

Table 6 - 13 Paired samples t-test for KTTOTL and WTTOTL

				Paired Differences					
Variables	Means	SDs	SEof Mean	Mean Difference	SD	SEof Mean	t-value	df	2-tail* sig.
KTTOTL	83. 3615	6. 421	. 422	23. 7305	8. 877	. 584	40. 63	230	. 000
WTTOTL	59. 6310	12. 361	. 813						

Note: The confidence interval at 95% is between 22. 580 and 24. 882. * $p < = 0.05$

Table 6 - 12 and Table 6 - 13 manifest that the difference between the means of KTTOTL and WTKTOTL is statistically significant even at the level of $p < .000$. So is the difference between the means of KTTOTL and WTTOTL ($p < .000$). The difference between the means of WTKTOTL and WTTOTL is also statistically significant at the level of $p < .000$ (To spare space, the table form for this test is omitted.). Figure 6 - 1 also shows that when the learners' WTTOTL is low, the difference between the learners' KTTOTL and WTKTOTL is greater than that when the learners' WTTOTL is high. Combined with the results demonstrated in the mean tables above, it can be seen that the mean for KTTOTL is greater than the means for WTKTOTL and WTTOTL. The standard deviations for both WTKTOTL and WTTOTL are greater than that for KTTOTL, which indicates that the difference among the subjects in the WT is greater than that of the KT.

Question 4. Are the means of the components in the KT and those in the WTK significantly different in statistics?

Table 6 - 14 Paired samples t-tests between KTVOC and WTKVOC, KTMPH and WTKMPH, KTFCT and WTKFCT, KTPRON and WTKPRON, KTCONT and WTKCONT, and KTVFS and WTKVFS

				Paired Differences					
Variables	Means	SDs	SEof Mean	Mean Difference	SD	SEof Mean	t-values	df	2-tail * sig.
KTVOC	13. 0097	. 828	. 054	4. 4347	1. 447	. 095	46. 58	230	. 000
WTKVOC	8. 57501	. 683	. 111	95% CI (4. 247, 4. 622)					
KTMPH	24. 4675	2. 227	. 147	15. 1818	4. 348	. 286	53. 07	230	. 000
WTKMPH	9. 2857	4. 891	. 322	95% CI (14. 618, 15. 746)					
KTFCT	8. 4989	1. 510	. 099	1. 4440	1. 903	. 125	11. 53	230	. 000
WTKFCT	7. 0549	1. 520	. 100	95% CI (1. 197, 1. 691)					
KTPRON	3. 3084	. 975	. 064	-. 9015	1. 147	. 075	-11. 94	230	. 000
WTKPRON	4. 2100	. 655	. 043	95% CI (-1. 050, -. 753)					
KTCONT	26. 3203	2. 460	. 162	5. 8435	3. 621	. 238	24. 53	230	. 000
WTKCONT	20. 4768	3. 591	. 236	95% CI (5. 374, 6. 313)					
KTVFS	7. 7565	1. 381	. 091	3. 3701	1. 828	. 120	28. 01	230	. 000
WTKVFS	4. 3864	1. 762	. 116	95% CI (3. 133, 3. 607)					

Notes: KT subvariables = KTVOC, KTMPH, KTFCT, KTPRON, KTCONT, and KTVFS;
WTK subvariables = WTKVOC, WTKMPH, WTKFCT, WTKPRON, WTKCONT, and WTKVFS. $* p <= 0.05$

To spare space, the t-values for the components are summarized in one table (Table 6-14). Table 6-14 demonstrates that the differences between all the means for the components of the KT and those for the components of the WTK are statistically significant at the level of p <. 000. It also shows that all means of the subvariables in the KT are relatively higher than those in the WTK except for the component of pronouns. The standard deviations for all the means in the KT are relatively smaller than those in the WTK, which indicates that the difference among the students' performance in the WTK is greater.

Question 5. Which of the components in the KT and the WTK are relatively more difficult for the students in the two kinds of performance?

This question can be answered from the percentage mean tables, i.e. Table 6 – 7 and Table 6 – 10. From Table 6 – 7, it seems that KTFCTP, KTVFSP and KTPRONP are relatively more difficult, for the percentages of these three means are around 60% to 75% while the others are all above 80%. Table 6 – 10 shows a different picture. WTKMPHP, WTKFCTP and WTKVFSP appear to be relatively more difficult to the students with the mean percentages below 60% while the mean percentages for the other subvariables in the WTK are over 60% although they are still rather low compared with the percentages in the KT. In the WTK (Table 6 – 10), it seems that WTKMPHP is particularly difficult to the students, whose mean percentage is only 33.77%. It seems that the students found it very hard to use the morphological forms correctly when expressing ideas contained in the two writing tasks, although it was very easy for them to recognize and recall the rules of verb conjugation, noun plurals and the comparative and superlative degrees of adjectives and adverbs in the KT.

In both the KT and the WTK, function words (FCT) and verb forms in sentences including negative and inverted sentences (VFS) seemed to be more difficult than the other components for these students.

In the KT (Table 6 – 7), the percentage of KTPRONP is the

lowest in comparison with the other components, while in the WTK (Table 6-10), the percentage of WTKPRONP is the highest. It is still hard to determine without examining the papers themselves whether it is a more difficult component. It can be inferred here that it is relatively more difficult than other components in the KT.

Question 6. Is there any correlation between the students' decontextualized task (KT) performance and their contextualized task (WT) performance?

In order to find out whether the scores in the KT correlate with the scores in the WT, the Pearson Bivariate Correlation method was employed and the following results were obtained.

Table 6 – 15 Correlation coefficients of the KT variables with the WT variables (231 cases)

Variables	WT-TOTL	WTK-TOTL	WTK-VOC	WTK-MPH	WTK-FCT	WTK-PRON	WTK-CONT	WTK-VFS
KTTOTL	.7260**	.6408**						
KTVOC			.5111**					
KTMPH				.4581**				
KTFCT					.2108**			
KTPRON						.0504		
KTCONT							.3306**	
KTVFS								.3432**

** $p < 0.01$ (2-tailed)

Table 6 – 15 demonstrates that most of the KT variables correlate with the WT variables to a certain extent at the level of $p < 0.01$ except for the subvariables KTPRON and WTKPRON. For the total scores in the KT and the WT, KTTOTL correlates moderately with WTKTOTL. KTTOTL is also of marked relationship with the holistic score WTTOTL. This shows that the subjects who did well in the KT had a tendency to perform well in the WT.

As for the subvariables in the KT and the WTK, KTVOC

and KTMPH in the KT correlate moderately with WTKVOC and WTKMPH in the WTK, and KTFCT, KTCONT and KTVFS in the KT correlate weakly with WTKFCT, WTKCONT and WTKVFS in the WTK. There is one exception, i.e. the KTPRON in the KT is not found to correlate with the WTKPRON in the WTK. The low correlation coefficients show that for these subvariables, high scores in the KT cannot guarantee the subjects' good performance in the WTK. As for the variables KTPRON and WTKPRON, the case is rather different. The subjects' high scores in the KT do not tell anything about their performance in the WTK. For details, see the correlation matrix in Appendix 4.

In brief, the relationships between the KT variables and the WT variables are not very strong, although for some variables the correlation coefficients reach the moderate level.

Question 7. How much can the students' contextualized performance be accounted for by their decontextualized performance?

To gain a clear picture of the relationship between the subjects' performance in the KT and that in the WT, the Enter Multiple Regression analysis was employed to see how much the scores in the WTK and WTTOTL could be explained by the KT, which can help us see whether the subjects' success in the performance of the KT entails their success in the performance of the WT. The regression analysis was applied twice, i.e. one for the total variables and the other for the subvariables.

For both analyses, the KT variables were the independent variables and the WT variables were the dependent variables. For the total variables, regression analysis was carried out with KTTOTL as an independent variable and WTKTOTL and WTTOTL as dependent variables. The equation obtained for KTTOTL predicting WTKTOTL is: YWTKTL = B * KTTOTL + A. Here, A (the constant or the intercept) = −39.239614; and B (the slope) = 1.118364. The Enter Multiple Regression results are shown in Table 6 − 16.

Table 6 – 16 Multiple regression analysis for KTTOTL on WTKTOTL in the WT

Model	Variable Entered	Multiple R	R Square	Adjusted R Square	ANOVA F	Sig.* F.
1	KTTOTL	.64085[a]	.41069	.40811	159.58683	.0000

------------------------------------- Variables in the Equation[b] -------------------------------------

Variable	B	SE B	Beta	t	Sig t*	95% Confdnce Intrvl B	
KTTOTL	1.118364	.088529	.640847	12.633	.0000	.943929	1.292799
(Constant)	-39.239614	7.401656		-5.301	.0000	-53.823670	-24.655558

Note: a. predictors: (constant), KTTOTL; b. dependent variable: WTKTOTL; * p <=0.05

Table 6 – 16 indicates that there exists a significant linear relationship between KTTOTL and WTKTOTL (F <. 0000). The R Square tells us that KTTOTL can account for 41. 1% of the variance of WTKTOTL in the WT. Thus, for the same linguistic knowledge, the students' performance in decontextualized situations can only determine 41. 1% of their performance in contextualized situations. Their knowledge of the grammar and lexis does not correspond to their ability to use that knowledge. The equation obtained from KTTOTL predicting WTTOTL is: YWTTOTL = B * KTTOTL + A. Here, A (the constant or the intercept) = – 57. 472050; and B (the slope) =1. 404190. (see Table 6 – 17)

Table 6 – 17 Multiple regression analysis for KTTOTL on WTTOTL in the WT

Model	Variable Entered	Multiple R	R Square	Adjusted R Square	ANOVA F	Sig.* F
1	KTTOTL	.72595[a]	.52701	.52494	254.316	.0000

------------------------------------- Variables in the Equation[b] -------------------------------------

Variable	B	SE B	Beta	t	Sig. t*	95% Confdnce Intrvl B	
KTTOTL	1.404190	.087496	.725951	15.947	.0000	1.225205	1.570001
(Constant)	-57.472050	7.315274		-7.807	.0000	-71.289037	-42.461336

Note: a. predictors: (constant), KTTOTL; b. dependent variable: WTTOTL; * p<=0.05

Table 6 – 17 demonstrates that there also exists a significant linear relationship between KTTOTL and WTTOTL (F <. 0000). The R Square shows that KTTOTL could explain 52. 619% of the variance of WTTOTL in the WT. This indicates that the students' knowledge of the required grammar and lexis does play a part in their composition, but this part cannot determine their total performance, for this knowledge is only part of their whole communicative competence. Table 6 - 16 and Table 6 - 17 show that KTTOTL could explain the variance of the WT to some extent but the determination indices are not very high. Both R Squares are not over . 6000.

For the subvariables, the independent variables are KTVOC, KTMPH, KTFCT, KTPRON, KTCONT and KTVFS, while the dependent variables are WTKVOC, WTKMPH, WTKFCT, WTKPRON, WTKCONT and WTKVFS. To spare space, only the important figures are provided here and all the figures are summarized below in Table 6 - 18 and Table 6 - 19.

Table 6 - 18 Enter multiple regression analysis of the KT subvariables on the WTK subvariables

Dep. Var.	Step No.	Var. Entrd	Mult. R	R Square	Adjust. R	ANOVA F	Sig. * F
WTKVOC	1	KTVOC	. 51115	. 26127	. 25805	80. 99273	. 0000
WTKMPH	1	KTMPH	. 45807	. 20983	. 20638	60. 80943	. 0000
WTKFCT	1	KTFCT	. 21077	. 04442	. 04025	10. 64574	. 0013
WTKPRON	1	KTPRON	. 05044	. 00254	. 00181	. 58416	. 4455
WTKCONT	1	KTCONT	. 33059	. 10929	. 10540	28. 09735	. 0000
WTKVFS	1	KTVFS	. 34322	. 11780	. 11395	30. 57895	. 0000

$* p <= 0.05$

Table 6 - 19 The equation values for each pair of variables (KT subvariables on WTK subvariables)

Variables in the Equation

Variable	B	SE B	Beta	t	Sig t*
KTVOC	1. 038727	. 115419	. 511149	9. 000	. 0000
(Constant)	-4. 938549	1. 504602		-3. 282	. 0012
KTMPH	1. 005958	. 129001	. 458067	7. 798	. 0000
(Constant)	-15. 327596	3. 169340		-4. 836	. 0000
KTFCT	. 212209	. 065039	. 210767	3. 263	. 0013
(Constant)	5. 251399	. 561381		9. 354	. 0000
KTPRON	. 033906	. 044362	. 050442	. 764	. 4455

Continued

Variable	B	SE B	Beta	t	Sig t*
(Constant)	4.097781	.152985		26.786	.0000
KTCONT	.482616	.091048	.330586	5.301	.0000
(Constant)	7.774238	2.406805		3.230	.0014
KTVFS	.437928	.079194	.343223	5.530	.0000
(Constant)	.989580	.623890		1.586	.1141

* p< =0.05

Although Tables 6-16 and 6-17 show that KTTOTL could account for 41.1% of WTKTOTL and 52.7% of WTTOTL in the WT, Table 6-18 provides another picture for the accountability of the KT subvariables for the WTK subvariables. The R square coefficients show that all that the KT subvariables could account for the WTK subvariables is below 30% although most Sig. F values are at the level of .0000. The subvariable KTPRON in the KT is found to have no linear relationship with WTKPRON in the WTK.

Question 8. Are there any differences in the two types of performance among the top one quarter, the average two quarters and the bottom one quarter subjects?

To answer this question, all the analyses carried out for all students (231) were employed for the three groups. The results are shown in tables in a simplified form.

The three groups were obtained by sorting the WTTOTL scores first, and on the basis of the sorted scores, the first and the last one quarter of the subjects were obtained. This decision was based on the analysis of the frequency distribution of the students' total production score (WPTOTL) which indicates a rough normal curve with little skewness (-0.566) and kurtosis (-0.217). Thus, the average group is the largest one, while the top and the bottom level groups are smaller than the average one. The number of students in each group divided by this method is more or less equivalent to the supposed criterion demarcating scores for the good, average and poor levels (the good =over 70, the average

= around 52 to 70, the poor = below 52). The number of the subjects in the three groups is given in Table 6 – 20. The result of one-way ANOVA shows that these three groups are significantly different in statistics (F <. 0000).

Table 6 – 20 Distribution of the subjects in the three groups
(Sorted by WTTOTL)

Grp No.	Group A (Low)	Group B (Average)	Group C (High)
Studts. No.	1 – 58 (58)	59 – 173 (115)	174 – 231 (58)

The following tables present the statistical results for the three groups. Table 6 – 21 displays the means of the total variables for all the three groups. The means and percentages for the subvariables are presented in Appendix 4.

Table 6 – 21 Descriptive statistics for Groups A, B and C for KTTOTL, WTKTOTL and WTTOTL

Group	CaseN	Mean	SD	MINI.	MAXI.
KTTOTL:					
Grp A	58	77. 03	6. 33	49. 75	87. 00
Grp B	115	83. 66	4. 55	68. 75	93. 00
Grp C	58	89. 11	3. 20	79. 75	95. 75
Total	231	83. 36	6. 42	49. 75	95. 75
WTKTOTL:					
Grp A	58	41. 59	7. 24	23. 31	58. 99
Grp B	115	54. 59	6. 92	39. 52	71. 03
Grp C	58	65. 21	8. 56	48. 85	85. 27
Total	231	53. 99	11. 21	23. 31	85. 27
WTTOTL:					
Grp A	58	42. 41	7. 19	25. 75	52. 50
Grp B	115	61. 11	4. 33	53. 00	68. 25
Grp C	58	73. 92	3. 66	68. 25	83. 25
Total	231	59. 63	12. 36	25. 75	83. 25

From Table 6 – 21, we can see that the students in Group A, Group B and Group C generally performed better in the KT than they did in the WT. From the differences between the three variables (KTTOTL and WTKTOTL, KTTOTL and WTTOTL) in each group, we can see that these means show less difference in the higher level groups (Group B and Group C) and greater difference in the lower level group (Group A). Detailed data about their performance in the subvariables in the KT and the WT in the Appendix indicate a similar tendency except for the subvariables KTPRON and WTKPRON, which are compatible with the results for all cases.

As for the relatively more difficult components in the KT and the WTK, in Group A (the low level group) in the KT, KTPRON, KTFCT and KTVFS seem to be more difficult for this group of students than the other components. In the WTK, WTKMPH, WTKVFS seem to be very difficult for this group of students. They could only accomplish 18. 2% of WTKMPH and 26. 4% of WTKVFS in the WTK. For the other components in the WTK, the students did not perform well, either, except for WTKPRON with 70. 7% .

In Group B (the average level group) in the KT, the percentages of KTFCT and KTPRON are all below 60% , while in the WTK, the percentages of WTKMPH and WTKVFS are even below 45% . This indicates that these components are relatively more difficult than the others in the two kinds of performance.

In Group C (the top level group) in the KT, KTPRON seems to be comparatively more difficult than the other components for this group with the percentage of 71. 6%, while WTKMPH, WTKVFS and WTKFCT in the WTK are relatively more difficult than the other components for this group of students with percentages of 49. 2% , 57. 1% and 66. 3% respectively.

In summary, it can be seen that the pronouns in the KT seem to be difficult for all groups, while in the WTK, the use of morphological forms and verb forms in sentences is difficult for all groups.

After the first test of the differences among the three groups in the performance of each variable in the KT and the WT, the next step is to test whether the results of the KT variables and the WTK variables and WTTOTL are significantly different in each group in statistics. Two samples paired t-test was again applied here to test the differences of the subjects' performance in the KT and the WT by each group. The t-test results for the total mean score variables for each group are displayed here while the results for the subvariables in the KT and the WTK are omitted. Table 23 shows that for all three groups, the differences between KTTOTL and WTKTOTL and WTTOTL are significant at the level of p <. 000.

The t-test values for the differences of all groups in the subvariables have also been obtained. The t-values between the variables in Group A are: t1 (KTVOC and WTKVOC) =32. 31, t2 (KTMPH and WTKMPH) =36. 05, t3 (KTFCT and WTKFCT) =5. 98, t4 (KTPRON and WTKPRON) =− 6. 46, t5 (KTCONT and WTKCONT) =14. 61, and t6 (KTVFS and WTKVFS) = 19. 73. All these values are very large, and the differences between these variables are significant at the level of p <. 000. The t-values between the variables in Group B are: t1 (KTVOC and WTKVOC) =40. 68, t2 (KTMPH and WTKMPH) =42. 58, t3 (KTFCT and WTKFCT) =7. 09, t4 (KTPRON and WTKPRON) =− 9. 83, t5 (KTCONT and WTKCONT) = 17. 66, and t6 (KTVFS and WTKVFS) =19. 92. The differences between the variables in this group are also statistically significant at the level of p < . 000. The t-values for the differences between these variables in Group C are: t1 (KTVOC and WTKVOC) =20. 28, t2 (KTMPH and WTKMPH) =21. 04, t3 (KTFCT and WTKFCT) =7. 63, t4 (KTPRON and WTKPRON) =− 3. 74, t5 (KTCONT and WTKCONT) =11. 83, and t6 (KTVFS and WTKVFS) = 12. 35. The differences between the variables in this group are also significant at the level of p <. 000.

Table 6 – 22 Paired samples t-test results for Groups A, Group B, and Group C on variables of KTTOTL and WTKTOTL and WTTOTL

				Paired Differences					
Variables	Means	SDs	SEof Mean	Mean Difference	SD	SEof Mean	t-value	df	2-tail* sig.
Group A.									
KTTOTL	77.0259	6.333	.832	34.6121	6.997	.919	37.67	57	.000
WTTOTL	42.4138	7.194	.945	95% CI (32.772, 36.452)					
KTTOTL	77.0259	6.333	.832	35.4397	6.952	.913	38.83	57	.000
WTKTOTL	41.5861	7.242	.951	95% CI (33.611, 37.268)					
Group B.									
KTTOTL	83.6565	4.547	.424	22.5500	5.212	.486	46.40	114	.000
WTTOTL	61.1065	4.334	.404	95% CI (21.587, 23.513)					
KTTOTL	83.6565	4.547	.424	29.0711	7.486	.698	41.64	114	.000
WTKTOTL	54.5854	6.915	.645	95% CI (27.688, 30.454)					
Group C.									
KTTOTL	89.1121	3.199	.420	15.1897	4.139	.544	27.95	57	.000
WTTOTL	73.9224	3.662	.481	95% CI (14.101, 16.278)					
KTTOTL	89.1121	3.199	.420	23.9034	8.509	1.117	21.39	57	.000
WTKTOTL	65.2087	8.556	1.123	95% CI (21.666, 26.141)					

* $p <= 0.05$

The above analyses demonstrate that in all the three groups, there is a significant difference between the students' two types of performance. In all the three groups, the means for the KT variables are higher than those for the WT variables. This suggests that whether the students are of the low, average or the top level in English, their tendency to perform well in the KT and poorly in the WT is not greatly changed. Correlation and Regression analyses were applied to the three groups respectively in order to find out whether there were any different relationships between the KT variables and the WT variables among the three groups. The correlation coefficients and the R Squares are displayed in the following tables with other values omitted here.

The three groups show a difference when correlation analysis was applied. The correlation coefficients in Table 6 - 23 indicate that in Group A, the total mean score variables in the KT and the WT (i.e. KTTOTL and WTKTOTL, KTTOTL and WTTOTL) are correlated moderately, while in Groups B and C, the correlation coefficients are rather low for these variables. For the subvariables in the KT and the WTK, in Group A, KTVOC and WTKVOC, KTMPH and WTKMPH are of significant relationship but with low correlation coefficients. In Group B, only one pair of subvariables — KTVOC and WTKVOC is of significant relationship with $p < .05$, but the correlation coefficient is too small, which implies a rather weak relationship. In Group C, only KTVFS and WTKVFS are significantly correlated at the level of $p < .01$, but the correlation coefficient is also very low which suggests a low relationship between these two variables. For most of the subvariables in all the three groups, the correlation coefficients are very low. It seems that the better the students perform in the WT, the lower the correlation is between the KT subvariables and the WTK subvariables. There is lower correlation between the KT subvariables and the WTK subvariables in Group C (the top level group) than in Group A (the low level group). Group C shows a rather different picture, i.e. the students' performance in VFS (verb forms in sentences) in the KT corresponds with their performance in this component in the WTK. It seems that this group of students is stronger at sentence level usage and use, while the other two groups are stronger at word level usage and use. The correlation coefficients of WTKTOTL and WTTOTL in the three groups show a similar tendency to the coefficients of the above-mentioned variables, i.e. the correlation coefficient of these two variables in Group A is higher than those in the other two groups. The correlation coefficients of WTKTOTL and WTTOTL for the three groups are respectively: $r = .6078$ ($p < .01$) for Group A, $r = .4278$ ($p < .01$) for Group B, and $r = .3065$ ($p < .05$) for Group C.

Table 6 – 23 Correlation coefficients for all variables in the KT and the WT for the three groups respectively

Group A								
Variables	WTTOTL	WTKTOTL	WTKVOC	WTKMPH	WTKFCT	WTKPRON	WTKCONT	WTKVFS
KTTOTL	.4706**	.4822**						
KTVOC			.3465**					
KTMPH				.3185*				
KTFCT					−.1730			
KTPRON						−.0694		
KTCONT							.0493	
KTVFS								.2542
Group B	WTTOTL	WTKTOTL	WTKVOC	WTKMPH	WTKFCT	WTKPRON	WTKCONT	WTKVFS
KTTOTL	.3120**	.1908*						
KTVOC			.1881*					
KTMPH				.0982				
KTFCT					.1245			
KTPRON						−.1084		
KTCONT							.0355	
KTVFS								.0864
Group C	WTTOTL	WTKTOTL	WTKVOC	WTKMPH	WTKFCT	WTKPRON	WTKCONT	WTKVFS
KTTOTL	.2777*	.2016						
KTVOC			.0906					
KTMPH				−.0073				
KTFCT					.2445			
KTPRON						.0492		
KTCONT							.0966	
KTVFS								.3864**

* $p < 0.05$ ** $p < 0.01$ (2-tailed)

Based on the correlation analysis, multiple regression analysis was also employed, and hence the R Squares for all variables in the KT and the WT, which can help us see the amount of the KT subvariables in accounting for the WTK subvariables. Table 6 – 24 demonstrates that the KT variables in Group A account for more of the WT variables than the KT variables in the other two groups. But holistically speaking, in all three groups, the KT variables do not account for much of the WT variables. This is rather different from the results obtained when all 231 cases were considered. Regression analysis for each group shows that most of the variables in the KT do not have a significant linear relationship with the variables in the WT. The total mean score variables in the KT and the WT are significantly correlated, but with low Sig. F values (see Appendix for the F-values). Table 6 – 24 seems to indicate that in the low level group the students' knowledge contributes more to their ability to use that knowledge in context, but the case is different in the higher level groups. The table also seems to indicate that the lower level students are stronger at discrete-point task performance while the higher level students are stronger at contextualized task performance.

Table 6 – 24 R squares for the KT variables on the WT variables for Groups A, B and C

Group A								
Variables	WTTOTL	WTKTOTL	WTKVOC	WTKMPH	WTKFCT	WTKPRON	WTKCONT	WTKVFS
KTTOTL	.22168	.23252						
KTVOC			.12005					
KTMPH				.10147				
KTFCT					.02993			
KTPRON						.00482		
KTCONT							.00243	
KTVFS								.06461
Group B	WTTOTL	WTKTOTL	WTKVOC	WTKMPH	WTKFCT	WTKPRON	WTKCONT	WTKVFS
KTTOTL	.09734	.03919						
KTVOC			.03540					

Continued

KTMPH				. 00964				
KTFCT					. 01550			
KTPRON						. 01176		
KTCONT							. 00126	
KTVFS								. 00747
Group C	WTTOTL	WTKTOTL	WTKVOC	WTKMPH	WTKFCT	WTKPRON	WTKCONT	WTKVFS
KTTOTL	. 07711	. 04062						
KTVOC			. 00821					
KTMPH				. 00005				
KTFCT					. 05976			
KTPRON						. 00242		
KTCONT							. 00933	
KTVFS								. 14931

The answers to the null hypotheses presented in Chapter 4:

(i) The t-test results in Tables 6-12, 6-13 and 6-14 indicate that all the means, both the means for the total scores and the means for the components, are different at the statistical significance level of $p < .000$. Thus, the first null hypothesis is rejected and one of the corresponding alternative hypotheses must be accepted. From the mean tables, it can be seen that the means in the KT are greater than those in the WTK except for the subvariable KTPRON. Thus the first alternative hypothesis is accepted, i. e. the students' performance in decontextualized situations is better than their performance on the same linguistic knowledge in contextualized situations. The t-test analyses of the variables for the three groups show a similar tendency. (ii) The correlation coefficients displayed in Table 6-15 indicate that there is significant relationship between the students' performance on the same linguistic forms in decontextualised situations and their performance in contextualised situations. The students' performance on the same linguistic forms in decontextualised situations (KTTOTL) correlates moderately with their performance in contextualised situations (WTKTOTL) ($r = .6408$, $p < 0.01$). The students' KTTOTL is of marked relationship with their holistic writing score WTTOTL ($r = .7260$, $p < 0.01$). Thus, the second null hypothesis is rejected and the first of the corresponding alternative hypotheses is accepted, i.e. there is a positive relationship between the learners' two types of performance. But correlation analyses of the total variables KTTOTL, WTKTOTL and WTTOTL among the three groups give different results which will be discussed in Chapter 7. (iii) The regression results displayed in Tables 6-16 and 6-17 demonstrate that KTTOTL can account for 40.8% of the variance of WTKTOTL and 52.5% of the variance of WTTOTL. The accountability of KTTOTL for WTKTOTL and WTTOTL is rather limited, i.e. these students' performance of the "tested" grammar and lexis in decontextualized situations can account for some of their performance on the same linguistic knowledge in contextualized situations, but not the whole of their performance in contextualised situations. Thus, the third null hypothesis is rejected and its alternative hypothesis is accepted, i.e. the students' success in the performance of the KT does not entail their success in the performance of the WT. The regression analyses of the variables in the three groups give further evidence to this statement.

6.3 Presentation of the results from the survey

The survey was carried out with the purpose of investigating the possible factors operating within the learner or in the environment which might contribute to or hinder effective learning and the relationships between these factors and the students' attainments. The findings will be presented in the order of questions and hypotheses presented in Chapter 4.

6.3.1 Presentation of the results concerning the questions

Question 1. Are the students in the three schools strongly motivated and of favorable attitudes towards English learning in general?

This question will be answered by examining the intensity of the students' motivations and attitudes towards English learning.

Table 6 - 25 Intensity of motivations and attitudes of all students (for all 231 cases)

Intensity of Motivations	N	%	Intensity of Attitudes	N	%
Strong	143	61.90	Very Favorable	144	62.34
Moderate	87	37.66	Mod. Favorable	78	33.77
Weak	1	0.43	Unfavorable	9	3.90
Total	231	100.00	Total	231	100.00

Notes: Mod. = moderately; Chi square for Intensity of Motivations with 2 d. f. = 132.8831, $p < .0000$; Chi square for Intensity of Attitudes with 2 d. f. = 118.3636, $p < .0000$.

Table 6 - 25 shows that more than 90 per cent of the students fall into the categories of "Strong" and "Moderate" motivations, and more than 90 per cent of students have "Very Favorable" or "Moderately Favorable" attitudes towards the learning of the English language. This indicates that most of the students were strongly motivated in English learning. Their attitudes towards English learning were also favorable. To answer the questions related to this one, the results for the three groups (i.e. the groups obtained in the experiment by sorting cases based on the students' performance in the WT reflected in the variable WTTOTL) are also displayed here to see whether different levels of students show different intensity of motivations and attitudes in English learning. The results in Table 6 - 26 and the chi-square tests indicate that there is little difference among students of different levels. For all the three groups, the percentages for both motivations and attitudes amount to 90.

Table 6 - 26 Intensity of motivations and attitudes of Groups A, B and C

Grp / Intensity	Group A		Group B		Group C	
Intensity of Motivations	N	%	N	%	N	%

Continued

Intensity \ Grp	Group	A	Group	B	Group	C
Strong	34	58.62	69	60.00	37	63.79
Moderate	24	41.38	45	39.13	21	36.21
Weak	0	0.00	1	0.87	0	0.00
Total	58	100.00	115	100.00	58	100.00
Intensity of Attitudes	N	%	N	%	N	%
Very Favorable	27	46.55	72	62.61	30	51.72
Mod. Favorable	26	44.83	38	33.04	24	41.38
Unfavorable	5	8.62	5	4.35	4	6.90
Total	58	100.00	115	100.00	58	00.00

Note: (1) Chi square for Intensity of Motivations with 4 d. f. = 1.351417, not significant at $p < = 0.05$; (2) Chi square for Intensity of Attitudes with 4 d. f. = 4.890855, not significant at $p < = 0.05$;

For the intensity of motivations and attitudes by sex, and by schools, the results turn out to be similar to the results when groups are concerned (see the Appendix).

Question 2. Do the students in the three schools experience a high degree of exposure to English after class?

Table 6 – 27 Degrees of exposure to English after class for all students and for the three groups

	For All Subjects		For Group A		For Group B		For Group C	
Intensity	N	%	N	%	N	%	N	%
High	0	0.00	0	0.00	0	0.00	0	0.00
Moderate	150	64.93	31	53.45	77	66.96	42	72.41
Low	81	35.06	27	46.55	38	33.04	16	27.59
Total	231	100.00	58	100.00	115	100.00	58	100.00

Note: (1) Chi square for all students with $p < = 0.05$ and 1 d. f. = 20.6104, significant at $p < .0000$; (2) Chi square for Groups with $p < = 0.05$ and 2 d. f. = 4.992143, significant at $p < .08$.

Table 6 - 27 demonstrates that most students have moderate contact with English after class, which is the usual phenomenon in FLL context. However, the three groups reflect a different picture. The higher the students' level is, the more exposure they have. In Group C (the top level group), the percentage for "Moderate" exposure goes up to over 72%, which is apparently higher than that of the other two groups. In Group A (the Low level group), the percentage for "Moderate" is only 53%. For those who have much contact with English after class, what they did for most of the time is doing exercises or reviewing lesson notes, but few opportunities to speak or listen, and relatively more opportunities to write and read after their choices are examined in detail. Chi-square test for the whole group among the three intensity levels indicates that the three levels are statistically significant at $p <= 0.05$, whereas the chi-square test for the three groups indicates that the difference exists at $p <= 0.1$.

Question 3. What kinds of strategies are more frequently used among the students?

Six types of strategies were investigated in the survey. Table 6 - 28 demonstrates that, for all the students, only three of the learning strategies listed were relatively more frequently employed, i.e. Meml, Compst2, and Metacog2, which respectively belong to the strategies of memorization, compensation and metacognitive planning. Among the three groups, the higher level students employed more strategies and more frequently than the lower level students when a cut-off line is drawn at the point of 50 per cent. Among the strategies usually employed by these learners, the strategies of "memorizing vocabulary" and "guessing meaning when failing to understand" were comparatively more often used. With respect to the six types of strategies (see the Appendix), Table 6 - 29 demonstrates that for the "Definitely use" category, only MEMORY covers a relatively higher percentage of students among the six types where all cases are concerned. As for the three groups, however, for the "Definitely use" category, the students in Group A apparently employed none of the six types of strategies if we make 50 percent as a cut-off point. But the students in Group B and Group C were found to have employed the MEMORY strategies definitely in their learning. For the "Probably use" category, it seems that five of the six types of strategies were sometimes used when all cases are considered. When the three groups are considered respectively, it was found that in Group A, the former five types of strategies except for the last one (SOCIAL) were sometimes employed by these subjects, while in Group B and Group C, the latter five types of strategies except for the first one (MEMORY) were sometimes employed. Besides, the percentage for SOCIAL in Group C is relatively higher than those in the other groups.

Table 6 - 28 Frequency and percentage distribution of learning strategies[①] and techniques for the students who chose "Very Often" or "Always"

	For All Subjects (231)		Group A (58)		Group B (115)		Group C (58)	
Strategies	N	N/231 * 100%	N	N/58 * 100%	N	N/115 * 100%	N	N/58 * 100%
Mem1	160	69.3#	31	53.4#	80	69.5#	49	84.5#
Mem2	81	35.0	9	15.5	43	37.4	29	50.0#
Cogn1	15	6.5	2	3.4	9	7.9	4	6.9
Cogn2	103	44.6	13	22.4	53	46.1	37	63.8#
Compst1	54	23.4	17	29.3	23	20.0	14	24.1
Compst2	167	72.3#	46	79.3#	77	67.0#	44	75.9#
Metacog1	32	13.9	7	12.0	13	11.3	12	20.7

① Mem1 = memorizing vocabulary by means of association with sounds; Mem2 = memorizing vocabulary by associating the old with the new; Cogn1 = training mental processes by summarizing ideas in reading; Cogn2 = training mental processes by direct understanding in English; Compst1 = compensating with gestures when failing to converse; Compst2 = compensating by guessing when failing to understand; Metacog1 = trying to arrange more time to learn English; Metacog2 = paying attention to one's own progress; Affect1 = talking with others about one's own feeling in learning; Affect2 = encouraging oneself in learning English; Social1 = speaking with others; Social2 = learning with others and asking questions.

Continued

Metacog2	152	65. 8#	33	56. 9#	80	69. 5#	39	67. 2#
Strategies	N	N/231 * 100%	N	N/58 * 100%	N	N/115 * 100%	N	N/58 * 100%
Affect1	19	8. 3	5	8. 6	9	7. 8	5	8. 6
Affect2	85	36. 8	17	29. 3	43	37. 4	25	43. 1
Social1	5	2. 1	1	1. 7	2	1. 8	2	3. 4
Social2	72	31. 2	8	13. 8	37	32. 2	27	46. 5

Notes: 1. # = relatively higher percentage (over 50%); 2. The total number of each strategy for all subjects is 231, and for Group A, 58; for Group B, 115; and for Group C, 58.

Table 6 - 29 The students' use of the six types of learning strategies

	For All Subjects		Group A		Group B		Group C	
Memory	N	%	N	%	N	%	N	%
Definitely used	101	43. 7	9	15. 5	58	50. 4	34	58. 6
Probably used	111	48. 1	38	65. 6	52	45. 3	21	36. 2
Not used	19	8. 2	11	18. 9	5	4. 4	3	5. 2
Total	231	100. 0	58	100. 0	115	100. 0	58	100. 0
Chi-square test	2 d. f. **		4 d. f. **					
Cognitive								
Definitely used	14	6. 1	1	1. 7	9	7. 8	4	6. 8
Probably used	169	73. 2	36	62. 0	84	73. 0	49	84. 5
Not used	48	20. 8	21	36. 2	22	19. 2	5	8. 6
Total	231	100. 0	58	100. 0	115	100. 0	58	100. 0
Chi-test	2 d. f. **		4 d. f. **					
Compensation								
Definitely used	52	22. 5	14	24. 2	23	20. 1	15	25. 8
Probably used	163	70. 6	40	68. 9	81	70. 5	42	72. 4
Not used	16	6. 9	4	6. 9	11	9. 6	1	1. 7
Total	231	100. 0	58	100. 0	115	100. 0	58	100. 0

Continued

	For All Subjects		Group A		Group B		Group C	
Chi-test	2 d. f. **		4 d. f.		N. S.			
Memory	N	%	N	%	N	%	N	%
Metacognitive								
Definitely used	49	21.2	14	24.1	21	18.2	14	24.1
Probably used	154	66.7	33	56.9	85	74.0	36	62.1
Not used	28	12.1	11	19.0	9	7.9	8	13.7
Total	231	100.0	58	100.0	115	100.0	58	100.0
Chi-test	2 d. f. **		4 d. f.		N. S.			
Affective								
Definitely used	22	9.5	4	6.9	11	9.6	7	12.0
Probably used	153	66.2	32	55.2	80	69.6	41	70.7
Not used	56	24.2	22	37.9	24	20.8	10	17.1
Total	231	100.0	58	100.0	115	100.0	58	100.0
Chi-test	2 d. f. **		4 d. f.		N. S.			
Social								
Definitely used	10	4.3	0	0.0	6	5.2	4	6.9
Probably used	143	61.9	24	41.4	76	66.1	43	74.2
Not used	78	33.8	34	58.6	33	28.6	11	18.9
Total	231	100.0	58	100.0	115	100.0	58	100.0
Chi-test	2 d. f. **		4 d. f.		**			

Notes: ** significant at $p < .01$; d. f. = degree of freedom; N. S. = non-significant ($p > .05$)

Question 4. What kinds of methods do the students usually use after class to consolidate their learning in class?

This question is similar to the last one in nature, but it is dealt with from a more specific perspective. Table 6 – 30 manifests that for all students, whether their level is low, average or high, the methods they usually employed after class to consolidate their learning in class are not very different. The first four methods are common to all the students, which are fact-oriented rather than meaning-oriented.

Table 6 – 30 Frequency and percentage distribution of the methods the students used after class to consolidate their English learning in class (for all students and the three groups)

	For All Subjects (231)		Group A (58)		Group B (115)		Group C (58)	
Methods	N	N/231 * 100%	N	N/58 * 100%	N	N/115 * 100%	N	N/58 * 100%
M1	170	73.6#	44	75.9#	86	74.8#	40	69.0#
M2	99	42.9	19	32.8	41	35.7	39	67.2#
M3	181	78.4#	38	65.5#	96	83.5#	47	81.0#
M4	141	61.0#	33	56.9#	65	56.5#	43	74.1#
M5	26	11.3	10	17.2	8	7.0	8	13.8
M6	18	7.8	3	5.2	9	7.8	6	10.3
M7	9	3.9	3	5.2	4	3.5	2	3.4

Notes: # = relatively higher percentage (over 50%); The total number of each item for all subjects is 231, and for Group A, 58; for Group B, 115; and for Group C, 58. M1 = Memorize words and learn grammar; M2 = Read the text; M3 = Do exercises; M4 = Review lesson notes; M5 = Listen to tapes; M6 = Write compositions or diaries; M7 = Practise speaking with classmates

Question 5. What do the students think they are strong at in English learning?

In order to investigate the effect of the focus of classroom teaching on the students' attainments, one question was devised in the survey to request the students to evaluate themselves. The following results are rather discrete in percentage distribution. Most students were not sure about which aspect they were strong at. However, if we draw a line at the point of 30%, we can see that the learners tended to report that they were mainly good at certain aspects of language or single skills rather than comprehensive skills. One particular phenomenon is that 44.8% of the students in Group A (the low level group) reported that they were good at none of the listed aspects of language, while 55.2% of the students in Group C (the top level group) reported that they were good at grammar. This indicates that the students in Group

A are less confident in themselves, and the students in Group C focus more on grammar learning rather than on comprehensive skill learning. This may explain why Group C performed generally better in the aspect of "accuracy".

Table 6 - 31 Frequency and percentage distribution of the students' reports of their self-evaluation in English language competence

	For All Subjects (231)		Group A (58)		Group B (115)		Group C (58)	
Items	N	N/231 * 100%	N	N/58 * 100%	N	N/115 * 100%	N	N/58 * 100%
None	47	20.3	26	44.8#	17	14.8	4	6.9
Pronunciation	92	39.8#	12	20.7	54	47.0#	26	44.8#
Vocabulary	55	23.8	10	17.2	27	23.5	18	31.0#
Grammar rules	81	35.1#	12	20.7	37	32.2#	32	55.2#
Sent. Analysis	70	30.3#	12	20.7	37	32.2#	21	36.2#
Speaking	50	21.6	9	15.5	24	20.9	17	29.3
Reading Comp.	67	29.0	14	24.1	35	30.4	18	31.0#
Composition	38	16.5	8	13.8	17	14.8	13	22.4

Notes: # = relatively higher percentage (over 30%); For each item, the total number for the frequency in 'For All Subjects' is 231, and the percentage is 100%. For each item, the total numbers of the frequency of the three groups are: Group A = 58, 100%; Group B = 115, 100%; Group C = 58, 100%.

Question 6. Which of the class activities do the students prefer?

This question was administered to investigate whether the students' preference for the activities in class accords with their teachers' use of activities in class. The results will be considered with other questions. Table 6-32 shows that most students have a preference for the activity of "Conducting realistic and meaningful conversations" and "Reading aloud" in class.

Table 6 - 32 Frequency and percentage distribution of the students' responses indicating their preferences for activities in class

	For All Subjects (231)		Group A (58)		Group B (115)		Group C (58)	
Activities	N	N/231 * 100%	N	N/58 * 100%	N	N/115 * 100%	N	N/58 * 100%
Reading Aloud	94	40.7#	25	43.1#	43	37.4#	26	44.8#

Continued

Activities	N	N/231 * 100%	N	N/58 * 100%	N	N/115 * 100%	N	N/58 * 100%
Sent. Transf.	42	18.2	8	13.8	21	18.3	13	22.4
Recite Text	22	9.5	7	12.1	12	10.4	3	5.2
Recite Gram. Rules	24	10.4	8	13.8	13	11.3	3	5.2
Do MC Exercis.	57	24.7	21	36.2#	23	20.0	13	22.4
Dictation	27	11.7	8	13.8	13	11.3	6	10.3
Translation	57	24.7	12	20.7	31	27.0	14	24.1
Conduct Convs.	112	48.5#	25	43.1#	56	48.7#	31	53.4#
Listen to Tape	80	34.6#	19	32.8	37	32.2#	24	41.4#
Timed Writing	56	24.2	14	24.1	28	24.3	14	24.1

Notes: # = relatively higher percentage (over 30%); MC = Multiple Choice; The total number of each item for all subjects is 231, and for Group A, 58; for Group B, 115; and for Group C, 58.

Question 7. What kinds of activities do the teachers usually use in class in the three schools?

The items for choice for this question are the same as those in Table 6 – 32. The results in Table 6 – 33 are different from those in Table 6 – 32, which shows that the teachers' use of activities does not accord with the students' preferences.

Table 6 – 33 Frequency and percentage distribution of the students' reports on their teachers' use of activities in class

	For All Subjects (231)		No. 2 (57)		No. 28 (84)		No. 11 (90)	
Activities	N	N/231 * 100%	N	N/57 * 100%	N	N/84 * 100%	N	N/90 * 100%
Reading Aloud	171	74.0#	38	66.7#	62	73.8#	71	78.9#
Sent. Transf.	101	43.7#	34	59.6#	35	41.7#	32	35.6
Recite Text	58	25.1	6	10.5	30	35.7	22	24.4
Recite G. Rules	30	13.0	5	8.8	16	19.0	9	10.0
Do MC Exercis.	115	49.8#	28	49.1#	51	60.7#	36	40.0#

Continued

Activities	N	N/231 * 100%	N	N/57 * 100%	N	N/84 * 100%	N	N/90 * 100%
Dictation	109	47.2#	23	40.4#	33	39.3	53	58.9#
Translation	90	42.4#	36	63.2#	48	57.1#	14	15.6
Conduct Convs.	7	3.0	3	5.3	3	3.6	1	1.1
Listen to Tape	8	3.5	4	7.0	3	3.6	1	1.1
Timed Writing	118	51.1#	31	54.4#	32	38.1	55	61.1#

Notes: # = relatively higher percentage (over 40%); The total number of each item for all subjects is 231, and for Group A, 58; for Group B, 115; and for Group C, 58.

The activities that the teachers usually used in class are mainly "Reading aloud", "Sentence transformation", "Doing MC exercises", "Dictation", "Translation", and "Timed writing". These activities show a mixed nature.

Question 8. What kinds of homework do the teachers usually assign to their students?

Table 6 - 34 shows that the homework types that the teachers usually assigned to these students are "Memorizing vocabulary", "Reviewing rules", "Doing MC exercises", "Reading aloud", "Supplementary reading" and "Timed writing". The three schools do not show much difference in this respect.

Table 6 - 34 Frequency and percentage distribution of homework types for the students

	For All Subjects (231)		No. 2 (57)		No. 28 (84)		No. 11 (90)	
Homework Types	N	N/231 * 100%	N	N/57 * 100%	N	N/84 * 100%	N	N/90 * 100%
Memorize Voc.	159	68.8#	25	43.9	49	58.3#	85	94.4#
Review Rules	120	51.9#	24	42.1	33	39.3	63	70.0#
Do MC Exercis.	180	77.9#	43	75.4#	68	81.0#	69	76.7#
Recite Text	104	45.0	12	21.1	48	57.1#	44	48.9
Recite Pattern	53	22.9	16	28.1	28	33.3	9	10.0
Reading aloud	123	53.2#	39	68.4#	54	64.3#	30	33.3

Continued

Homework Types	N	N/231 * 100%	N	N/57 * 100%	N	N/84 * 100%	N	N/90 * 100%
Translation	96	41. 6	19	33. 3	51	60. 7#	26	28. 9
Supplmt. Read	148	64. 1#	43	75. 4#	47	56. 0#	58	64. 4#
Make dialogue	18	7. 9	6	10. 5	11	13. 1	1	1. 1
Timed Writing	155	67. 1#	40	70. 2#	60	71. 4#	55	61. 1#

Notes: # = relatively higher percentage (over 50%); The total number of each item for all subjects is 231, and for Group A, 58; for Group B, 115; and for Group C, 58.

Question 9. What are the foci of these teachers' teaching in class in these schools?

Table 6 – 35 Frequency and percentage distribution of the students' reports on their teachers' foci in teaching

	For All Subjects (231)		No. 2 (57)		No. 28 (84)		No. 11 (90)	
Items	N	N/231 * 100%	N	N/57 * 100%	N	N/84 * 100%	N	N/90 * 100%
Pronunciation	45	19. 5	12	21. 1	18	21. 4	15	16. 7
Vocabulary	157	68. 0#	32	56. 1#	46	54. 8#	79	87. 8#
Explain Rules	192	83. 1#	48	84. 2#	68	81. 0#	76	84. 4#
Listen. Comp.	14	6. 1	5	8. 8	5	6. 0	4	4. 4
Reading Comp.	138	59. 7#	36	63. 2#	57	67. 9#	45	50. 0#
Oral product.	47	20. 3	21	36. 8	20	23. 8	6	6. 7
Writing	112	48. 5	22	38. 6	48	57. 1#	42	46. 7

Notes: # = relatively higher percentage (over 50%); The total number of each item for all subjects is 231, and for Group A, 58; for Group B, 115; and for Group C, 58.

Generally speaking, the students believed that their teachers paid more attention to the teaching of vocabulary and grammatical rules and the training of reading skill. Writing seems to be given some attention, too.

Question 10. How do the teachers in these schools handle the errors their students made in class and in homework?

Table 6 – 36 Frequency and percentage distribution of the students' reports on their teachers' ways in handling the errors they make in class and in homework

	For All Students (231)		No. 2 (57)		No. 28 (84)		No. 11 (90)	
Items	N	%	N	%	N	%	N	%
In Class								
1	96	41.6#	26	45.6#	34	40.5#	36	40.0#
2	45	19.5	7	12.3	19	22.6	19	21.1
3	63	27.3	20	35.1#	17	20.2	26	28.9
4	26	11.3	3	5.3	14	16.7	9	10.0
5	1	0.4	1	1.8	0	0.0	0	0.0
Chi-test	4 d. f. **		8 d. f. N. S.					
In Homework								
1	91	39.4#	32	56.1#	30	35.7#	29	32.2#
2	70	30.3#	18	31.6#	22	26.2	30	33.3#
3	6	2.6	0	0.0	5	6.0	1	1.1
4	63	27.3	7	12.3	26	31.0#	30	33.3#
5	1	0.4	0	0.0	1	1.2	0	0.0
Chi-test	4 d. f. **		8 d. f. **					

Notes: The percentage here is based on the total of 100 for all students. d. f. = degree of freedom; # = relatively higher percentage (over 30%); ** $p < .01$; N. S. = non-significant ($p > .05$);
1 = Correct immediately; 2 = Point out but do not correct;
3 = Provide correct answers, and leave the correction to the students;
4 = Sometimes point out and correct, sometimes not;
5 = Not point out, leave it for students to discover and correct

From the table, it can be seen that the teachers in these schools tended to correct or at least pointed out the errors their students made in class and in homework.

Question 11. What language do the teachers and the students usually use in English class?

The results show that 69.3% of the students reported that their teachers used English and Chinese interchangeably in their teaching, i.e. "Sometimes in Chinese, sometimes in English", whereas 49.4% of the students reported that they usually used

Chinese to ask questions in class. Different schools do not show great differences in the use of Chinese.

Table 6 – 37 Frequency and percentage distribution of the students' reports on the languages they and their teachers most frequently used in class

	For All Students (231)		No. 2 (57)		No. 28 (84)		No. 11 (90)	
Items	N	%	N	%	N	%	N	%
For Teachers:								
Chinese	55	23. 8	5	8. 8	17	20. 3	33	36. 7
English	16	6. 9	9	15. 8	3	3. 6	4	4. 4
Eng. &Chinese	160	69. 3#	43	75. 4#	64	76. 2#	53	58. 9#
Chi-test	2 d. f. **		4 d. f. **					
For Students:								
Chinese	114	49. 4#	23	40. 4#	34	40. 5#	57	63. 3#
English	37	16. 0	17	29. 8	12	14. 3	8	8. 9
Eng. &Chinese	80	34. 6	17	29. 8	38	45. 2#	25	27. 8
Chi-test	2 d. f. **		4 d. f. **					

Notes: # = relatively higher percentage (over 40%); ** significant at p <. 01; d. f. = degree of freedom

Question 12. How do the teachers in these schools allot their time in class?

Table 6 – 38 Frequency and percentage distribution of the students' reports on their teachers' allocation of time in class in these schools

	For All Students (231)		No. 2 (57)		No. 28 (84)		No. 11 (90)	
Items	N	%	N	%	N	%	N	%
1	212	91. 9#	54	94. 7#	74	88. 1#	84	93. 3#
2	19	8. 2	3	5. 3	10	11. 9	6	6. 7
Chi-test	1 d. f. **		2 d. f. N. S.					

Notes: # = relatively higher percentage (over 50%); ** significantat p < . 01; N. S. = non-significant (p >. 05);

1 = more time for explaining vocabulary and rules

2 = more time for students to practise using the target language

The results indicate that the teachers usually spent most of the time in explaining vocabulary and grammatical rules in class. The three schools are not very different in this respect.

Question 13. Do the students have opportunities to interact with each other and with their teachers in class in English?

Table 6 - 39 Frequency and percentage distribution of the students' reports on the opportunities of interaction in class between teachers and students and among students

	For All Students (231)		No. 2 (57)		No. 28 (84)		No. 11 (90)	
Items	N	%	N	%	N	%	N	%
Never	23	10.0	2	3.5	3	3.6	18	20.0
Seldom	96	41.6	22	38.6	34	40.5	40	44.4
Sometimes	76	32.9	20	35.1	32	38.1	24	26.7
Often	33	14.3	11	19.3	14	16.7	8	8.9
Always	3	1.3	2	3.5	1	1.2	0	0.0
Chi-test	4 d.f. **				8 d.f. **			

Note: ** significant at $p < .01$ d.f. = degree of freedom

Table 6 - 39 indicates that the students did not feel that they had many opportunities for interaction in class. The sum of "Never" and "Seldom" makes up about 51.6%, which means that more than half of the students thought that they did not have many opportunities to speak with their teachers and their classmates in class.

6.3.2 Presentation of the results concerning the hypotheses in the investigation

The results of the following part provide evidence for the hypotheses relating to the variables of *motivations, attitudes, outside class language exposure and learning strategies* corresponding to the results in the experiment.

1. The students' attainments correlate with their strong motivations in learning and favorable attitudes towards the learning of the target language.

Factor analysis was applied first to examine whether the items about motivations did consist of two factors (i.e. the instrumental and integrative motivations). The results (Table 6 – 40) indicate that the two factors are different, although somehow Mintg3 belongs to both factors. This research does not attempt to provide a detailed study of the nature of motivations, but only inquire into the general state of the students' motivations in EFL learning and how their motivations were channelled in relation to their choice of learning strategies and accordingly how their motivations indirectly influence the nature of their final attainments. To spare space, among all the data from the experiment that enter into the analyses, only three total scores (variables) were chosen for the analyses here with the variables in the survey. They are KTTOTL, WTKTOTL, and WTTOTL. The Pearson Product-Movement correlation analysis results are displayed in Table 6 – 41.

Table 6 – 40 Rotated factor matrix by varimax for motivations (for 231 cases)

Variables	Factor 1	Factor 2
Minst1	.75958 *	.00002
Minst2	.77046 *	.11582
Minst3	.56274 *	.24789
Mintg1	.07651	.82607 *
Mintg2	.12426	.79053 *
Mintg3	.38504 *	.39445 *

Notes: Minst = items for instrumental motivations;
Mintg = items for integrative motivations.

Table 6 - 41 Correlation coefficients between the students' attainments in the experiment and their motivations① (for 231 students)

Variables	KTTOTL	WTKTOTL	WTTOTL
MINST1	.0181	-.0223	.0003
MINST2	-.0757	-.0477	-.0332
MINST3	.0928	.0382	.0633
MINTG1	.1935 **	.0473	.1202
MINTG2	.1495 *	.0273	.1029
MINTG3	.0473	-.0036	.0357
MINSTTL	-.0063	-.0234	.0030
MINTGTL	.1620 *	.0268	.1084
MOTL	.0979	.0032	.0697

Notes: * $p < .05$, ** $P < .01$.
MINST = items for instrumental motivations;
MINTG = items for integrative motivations;
MINSTTL = the total of instrumental motivations;
MINTGTL = the total of integrative motivations;
MOTL = the total of all kinds of motivations.

Table 6 - 41 indicates that there is not a significant relationship between the students' motivations as a whole and their attainments (for MOTL and KTTOTL, $r = .0979$; for MOTL and WTKTOTL, $r = .0032$; for MOTL and WTTOTL, $r = .0697$). When different orientations of motivations are considered, it is found that the integrative motivations significantly correlate with KTTOTL (the total score in the KT). However, the coefficient is rather small. Two of the integrative motivations (MINTG1 and MINTG2) significantly correlate with KTTOTL, but the coefficients for both are not very high. This

① MINST1 = Learning English helps me find a good job; MINST2 = Learning Engllish helps me raise my social status; MINST3 = Learning English helps me pass the MET to universities and colleges; MINTG1 = Learning English helps me understand the people and their life in other countries; MINTG2 = Learning English helps me contact with different people and talk with them; MINTG3 = Learning English helps me act and think as people in other countries.

seems to indicate that integrative motivations are also a drive to make learners pay attention to explicit knowledge learning, and also tells us something about what this group of learners' belief in learning a language.

Statistical analysis for the three groups was also conducted. The results in Table 6 – 42 show that in Group A (the low level group), motivations as a whole are found to correlate significantly with WTTOTL (the holistic score of the two writing tasks) with $r = 0.3066$, $p < 0.05$. When each item is analyzed, the item MINST3 is found to correlate significantly with both KTTOTL and WTTOTL of this group. This means that the students' motivation of learning for going to colleges or universities might have a direct influence on their final attainments. The first item in integrative motivations (MINTGl) also significantly correlates with KTTOTL of Group A. In Group B (the average level group), no significant correlation is found between motivations as a whole and the students' scores in the experiment. In Group C (the top level group), the results show that there is no significant correlation between MOTL and the students' attainments in the experiment. But significant relationship is found between KTTOTL with the integrative motivations as a whole with $r = 0.4189$, $p < 0.01$, and a negative relationship is found between KTTOTL with one of the instrumental motivation items MINST2 with $r = -0.3019$, $p < 0.5$.

Table 6 – 42 Correlation analysis of the students' motivations with their achievements (For Groups A, Group B, and Group C respectively)

	Group A			Group B			Group C		
Variables	KTTOTL	WTKTOTL	WTTOTL	KTTOTL	WTKTOTL	WTTOTL	KTTOTL	WTKTOTL	WTTOTL
MINST1	.0408	-.0099	.1458	.0581	.1388	.1720	.2728*	-.0839	.1659
MINST2	-.0042	.0101	.1077	.0587	-.0078	.1411	-.3019*	.0911	.0282
MINST3	.2854*	.1921	.3173*	.0530	-.0017	.0449	.0614	.0544	.1558
MINTG1	.4273**	.1777	.2423	-.0262	-.0888	.1231	.4376**	-.0014	.0942
MINTG2	.1048	.0366	.2412	.0928	-.1072	.0590	.4077**	.0407	.0210

Continued

Variables	KTTOTL	WTKTOTL	WTTOTL	KTTOTL	WTKTOTL	WTTOTL	KTTOTL	WTKTOTL	WTTOTL
MINTG3	.0194	.1323	.1271	.0632	-.1619	.0568	.1317	.1145	-.1129
MINSTTL	.1130	.0724	.2366	.0747	.0437	.1590	-.0820	.0506	.1357
MINTGTL	.2309	.1692	.2738*	.0633	-.1722	.1029	.4189**	.0853	-.0228
MOTL	.2106	.1486	.3066*	.0817	-.0797	.1545	.2219	.0869	.0692

Notes: * p<.05 ** p<.01 (2-tailed) Generally speaking, there is not a very significant relationship between the students' motivations and their ability to use what they have learnt, but their motivations are found to be related to the students' achievements of discrete linguistic knowledge.

2. The students' attainments correlate with their attitudes to the target language learning.

Correlation analysis of the variables in attitudes and the students' attainments indicates that there exists a significant relationship between the learners' attitudes and their attainments. The correlation coefficients are displayed in Table 6-43.

Table 6 - 43 Correlation analysis of the learners' achievements in the experiment with their attitudes

Variables	Aexp	Alike	Aprepr	ATITD
KTTOTL	.2074**	.3325**	.1218	.2844**
WTKTOTL	.1868**	.2305**	.1706**	.2603**
WTTOTL	.2638**	.3186**	.1637*	.3257**

Notes: * P<.05, ** P<.01 (2-tailed)
Aexp = Expect to Learn English well; Alike = like English;
Aprepr = Prepare for English Class; ATITD = Total Attitude Score.

Table 6 - 43 demonstrates that there exists a significant relationship between the students' achievements in the experiment and their attitudes towards English learning. But the coefficients are not very high, either. Comparatively, however, it seems that these students' attitudes correlate more closely with WTTOTL, which might indicate that favorable attitudes do facilitate these students' final internalization of the target language or the learners' final achievements help them to develop a favourable attitude to the target language learning. In order to see how much the attitude variables could account for the students' competence, Regression analysis was also employed.

Table 6 - 44 shows that although the learners' attitudes significantly correlate with their achievements, the determination indices are not high, all around 10% or below (see the R Squares and the Adjted R Squares). This indicates that we should be very careful in drawing conclusions from these results.

Table 6 - 44 Enter multiple regression analysis by attitude variables on the learners' attainments

Dependent Variables	Indep. Var.	Mpl R	R Square	Adjted R Square	F	F*
WTTOTL	ATITD	.32569	.10608	.10217	27.17423	.0000
KTTOTL		.28438	.08087	.07686	20.14852	.0000
WTKTOTL		.26026	.06773	.06366	16.63804	.0001
WTTOTL	Aexp	.26376	.06957	.06551	17.12281	.0000
	Alike	.31855	.10148	.09755	25.86261	.0000
	Aprepr	.16367	.02679	.02254	6.30313	.0127
KTTOTL	Aexp	.20743	.04303	.03885	10.29608	.0015
	Alike	.33252	.11057	.10669	28.46840	.0000
	Aprepr	.12183	.01484	.01054	3.45041	.0645
WTKTOTL	Aexp	.18678	.03489	.03067	8.27815	.0044
	Alike	.23050	.05313	.04899	12.84940	.0004
	Aprepr	.17058	.02910	.02486	6.86277	.0094

$* p <= .05$

3. The students' attainments correlate with the intensity of their outside class exposure to the English language.

The answer to this question can be seen from the results in Table 6-45.

Table 6 - 45 Correlation analysis of the students' outside class language exposure in listening, speaking, reading and writing with their attainments (for 231 cases)

Variables	EXPTL	E1	E2	E3	E4
WTKTOTL	.2321**	.0815	.2562**	.1231	.2163**
WTTOTL	.3058**	.1248	.3438**	.1673*	.2553**
KTTOTL	.3285**	.1909**	.3467**	.2034**	.2157**

Notes: * P<.05, ** P<.01 (2-tailed)
E1 = exposure in listening; E2 = exposure in reading; E3 = exposure in speaking;
E4 = exposure in writing; EXPTL = exposure total score

Table 6 - 45 indicates that there is a significant relationship between the students' achievements and their outside class language exposure, but the coefficients are not very high. This manifests that the accountability of these variables for the students' achievements is weak. The previous frequency distribution table in this chapter about the intensity of these learners' outside class language exposure (Table 6 - 27) can also be used here to answer this question.

4. The students' motivations correlate with their choices of learning strategies.

Table 6 - 46 Correlation analysis of these learners' motivations with their use of learning strategies (for 231 students)

Variables	MOTL	MINST1	MINST2	MINST3	MINSTTL	MINTG1	MINTG2	MINTG3	MINTGTL
MEM1	.0556	.0629	-.0158	.0360	.0256	.1495*	1804**	-.1035	.0649
MEM2	.1665*	.0673	.0460	1909**	.1238	2553**	.1516*	-.0111	.1511*
COGN1	.1516*	.0245	.0749	.0423	.0713	.1397*	.1216	.1220	1759**
COGN2	.0162	.0401	-.0926	-.0251	-.0532	.1135	.1359*	-.0356	.0751
COMPST1	.1142	.1071	.0757	-.0549	.0643	.0524	.0908	.1099	.1227
COMPST2	.0661	.0551	.0752	-.0234	.0576	.0963	.1486*	-.0705	.0521
METCOG1	.1261	.0118	.0078	.0475	.0268	.1047	.1066	.1547*	1764**
METCOG2	1878**	.1204	.1029	.1208	.1517*	.1424*	.1407*	.0807	.1591*
AFFECT1	.0700	.0609	-.0204	.0174	.0151	.0700	.0827	.0630	.0977

Continued

Variables	MOTL	MINST1	MINST2	MINST3	MINSTTL	MINTG1	MINTG2	MINTG3	MINTGTL
AFFECT2	2325**	.0318	.1522*	.1221	.1520*	2362**	1742**	.1163	2301**
SOCIAL1	2354**	.0494	.1295*	.0364	.1119	2526**	1797**	1710**	2720**
SOCIAL2	.0626	-.0826	.0867	-.0598	.0029	.0723	.1106	.0429	.0972
MEMORY	.1256	.0765	.0149	.1265	.0834	2334**	1968**	-.0717	.1232
COGNITIVE	.1024	.0408	-.0144	.0095	.0088	.1581*	.1616*	.0510	.1552*
COMPST	.1303*	.1183	.1041	-.0579	.0849	.0971	.1578*	.0497	.1293*
METACOG	1906**	.0805	.0674	.1023	.1086	.1500*	.1502*	.1426*	2035**
AFFECT	2017**	.0547	.0971	.0957	.1157	2043**	.1671*	.1157	2147**
SOCIAL	.1639*	-.0353	.1282	-.0253	.0583	1795**	1708**	.1172	2075**

Notes: 1. * $p < .05$ ** $p < .01$ (2-tailed)

2. MEMORY (vocabulary learning strategies) = {(Mem1 + Mem2) /2}; COGNITIVE = mental training {(Cogn1 + Cogn2) /2}; COMPST = compensation {(Compst1 + Compst2) / 2}; METACOG = evaluation of one's own improvement {(Metacog1 + Metacog2) /2}; AFFECT = manage one's own feelings {(Affect 1 + Affect 2) /2}; SOCIAL = practice {(Social 1 + Social 2) /2}. See Footnote 14 for definitions of other variables.

Table 6 – 46 shows that four types of the learning strategies including five substrategies correlate with motivations as a whole (MOTL). When different orientations of motivations are considered, the table shows that the motivations with an integrative orientation (MINTG1, MINTG2, MINTG3, MINTGTL) correlate with some of the learning strategies. No significant relationship was found between the six types of learning strategies with motivations of an instrumental orientation (MINST1, MINST2, MINST3, MINSTTL). Correlation analyses were also carried out among the three groups (see Appendix 4). It was found that in Group A, the motivations with an instrumental orientation significantly correlate with the MEMORY strategy with the coefficient of .3043 at the level of $p < .05$. One of the motivations with an integrative orientation (MINTG3) was found to correlate with the MEMORY strategy negatively. This indicates that more use of MEMORY strategy induces low interest in target language. Only one of the learning strategies (METACOGNITIVE) was found to correlate with motivations as a whole (MOTL). In Group B, the

AFFECTIVE strategy significantly correlates with MOTL, and two of the motivations with an integrative orientation (MINTG1, MINTG3) significantly correlate respectively with the strategies of MEMORY, METACOGNITIVE and AFFECTIVE. The motivations with an integrative orientation as a whole (MINTGTL) were found to significantly correlate with three of the learning strategies (METACOGNITIVE, AFFECTIVE and SOCIAL). The motivations with an instrumental orientation do not correlate with any of the six types of learning strategies. In Group C (the top level students in the experiment), three types of the learning strategies (COMPENSATION, AFFECTIVE and SOCIAL) were found to correlate with MOTL, and the motivations with an integrative orientation as a whole (MINTGTL) were found to significantly correlate with the three types of learning strategies (COMPENSATION, AFFECTIVE and SOCIAL). The coefficients are not very high for all those correlated variables, yet the analyses suggest that these subjects' frequency in employing the six types of learning strategies is somewhat influenced by their motivations. The low level subjects' choice of these strategies seemed to be influenced by their motivations with an instrumental orientation while the average and the top level subjects' employment of these strategies seemed to be more influenced by their motivations with an integrative orientation. The low level students appeared to be influenced by their motivations to employ the types of learning strategies like MEMORY and METACOGNITIVE, while the average and the top level students appeared to be influenced by their motivations to employ strategies like COMPENSATION, METACOGNITIVE, AFFECTIVE and SOCIAL. It seems that the higher level the students are at, the higher correlation coefficient can be obtained for the variables of MINTGTL and SOCIAL.

5. The students' attainments correlate with their language learning strategies.

Six large types of second language learning strategies which consist of twelve sub-strategies entered into the statistical analyses. Table 6 – 47 shows that most of the learners' learning strategies significantly correlate with their achievements except for the compensation strategy in speaking and reading. Among the six types of learning strategies, four of them correlate significantly with the students' WTKTOTL and WTTOTL, and five of them correlate significantly with the students' KTTOTL. This seems to indicate that the students' final attainments are somewhat influenced by their frequent use of learning strategies.

Table 6 − 47 Correlation analyses of the students' SLL strategies with their attainments (for 231 students)

Variables	KTTOTL	WTKTOTL	WTTOTL
Mem1	.2983**	.2364**	.3067**
Mem2	.4090**	.2595**	.3585**
Cogn1	.2505**	.1588*	.2179**
Cogn2	.3299**	.2844**	.3759**
Compst1	.0852	.0742	.0525
Compst2	.0639	−.0081	.0058
Metacog1	.1144	.0775	.0447
Metacog2	.1961**	.1036	.1614*
Affect1	.1561*	.0783	.1252
Affect2	.2595**	.1255	.2403**
Social1	.1978**	.1778**	.2125**
Social2	.3017**	.3020**	.3062**
MEMORY	.4113**	.2909**	.3892**
COGNITIVE	.3652**	.2801**	.3751**
COMPST	.1055	.0559	.0461
METACOG	.1886**	.1100	.1253
AFFECT	.2663**	.1303*	.2364**
SOCIAL	.3192**	.3093**	.3298**

* $P < .05$, ** $P < .01$ (2-tailed)

Notes: For the meaning of each variable of learning strategies, see the notes below Table 6 − 28.

What is more interesting to us is whether there are different relationships between learning strategies and the students' achievements among the three levels of groups. Thus, correlation analysis was further applied and the results in Table 6 – 48 were obtained.

The results show that the higher the students' level is, the more frequently they used these strategies, and the closer relationship there is between the frequency of the students' choice of strategies and the students' final attainments. In Group A, only one strategy (Mem2) significantly correlates with the students' KTTOTL. But in Group B (the average level), seven of the twelve sub-strategies significantly correlate with KTTOTL, while six of the sub-strategies significantly correlate with WTTOTL. In Group C (the top level group), two of the twelve sub-strategies significantly correlate with KTTOTL, and Cogn2 and Social 2 significantly correlate with WTTOTL.

Table 6 – 48 Correlation coefficients for Groups A, B, and C between the students' learning strategies and their achievements

	Group A			Group B			Group C		
Variables	KTTOTL	WTKTOTL	WTTOTL	KTTOTL	WTKTOTL	WTTOTL	KTTOTL	WTKTOTL	WTTOTL
Mem1	.0460	.0080	.1007	.1907*	.0655	.1940*	.3588**	.0762	.1689
Mem2	.3866**	−.0034	.1479	.2714**	.0429	.2236*	.2104	.0748	.1861
Cogn1	.0515	.0122	.0019	.3170**	.1105	.2466**	.0289	−.0860	.0168
Cogn2	.1148	−.0099	.0578	.1873*	.0743	.1877*	.0450	.0127	.2760*
Compst1	−.0447	.1063	.0308	.1828	.0133	.0565	.0153	.0897	−.0125
Compst2	.0135	.1050	.0389	.1744	−.0781	.0750	.1140	.1755	.2242
Metacog1	.0088	−.0223	−.1468	.1615	.0205	.0347	.0841	.1196	.0109
Metacog2	.1671	.0307	.2192	.2231*	.1303	.2464**	.2233	.0238	.1956
Affect1	−.0919	−.2300	−.1690	.2312*	.1409	.1098	.0633	−.1477	.0690
Affect2	.1125	−.1196	.0843	.2697**	−.0461	.2644**	.1384	.1127	.1910
Social1	.0116	.0239	−.1496	.1140	.0509	.0758	−.0404	−.1157	−.0026
Social2	.1104	.0425	.0831	.1438	.1005	.0555	.2667*	.2487	.2626*

Continued

Variables	KTTOTL	WTKTOTL	WTTOTL	KTTOTL	WTKTOTL	WTTOTL	KTTOTL	WTKTOTL	WTTOTL
MEMORY	.2276	.0034	.1405	.2808**	.0684	.2562**	.3367**	.0884	.2073
COGNITIVE	.1041	.0011	.0379	.3175**	.1166	.2743**	.0497	-.0526	.1908
COMPST	-.0342	.1476	.0468	.2420**	-.0368	.0874	.0794	.1775	.1205
METACOG	.1079	.0060	.0501	.2363*	.0908	.1691	.1872	.0838	.1277
AFFECT	.0302	-.2039	-.0298	.3210**	.0410	.2526**	.1293	-.0042	.1683
SOCIAL	.0922	.0463	-.0191	.1569	.0954	.0764	.1923	.1385	.2088

* $P<.05$, ** $P<.01$ (2-tailed)

Generally speaking, for the six types of strategies, in Group A, since most students seldom employed the learning strategies, little relationship could be found between these learners' attainments and their use of the learning strategies. But in Group B and Group C, some strategies were found to correlate with the students' final attainments. However, on further examination, it was found that the use of the strategies by the students in Group B and Group C seemed to emphasize the learning of discrete linguistic knowledge rather than the use of that knowledge. The strategy SOCIAL has no relationship with WTKTOTL and WTTOTL in all three groups. Yet, for those correlated variables, all the correlation coefficients are not very high. This indicates that the explanatory power of these strategies for the learners' attainments should be treated carefully.

6.4 Summary

In short, this chapter has provided the results from the experiment and the investigation. It includes three sections: the sorting and trimming of the data before statistical analyses, the presentation of the results from the experiment, and the presentation of the findings from the investigation.

The results of the analyses in the experiment reject the Null Hypothesis that the students' performance in the decontextualized task (KT) does not differ from that in the contextualized task

(WT). Therefore, the alternative hypothesis is accepted, i.e. the learners' performance on the same linguistic forms in the KT is better than that in the WT. Statistical tests indicate that the differences between KTTOTL and WTKTOTL and WTTOTL are significant at the level of $p < .000$. For the subvariables in the KT and the WTK, the differences are also significant at the level of $p < .000$. Correlation analysis indicates that there is significant positive relationship between the students' two types of performance. Regression analysis indicates that all those determination indices, which indicate the accountability of the KT variables for the WT variables, are not over 55 per cent.

The findings from the investigation and the analyses of the findings with the results from the experiment demonstrate that factors like *motivations, attitudes, learning strategies, outside class language exposure and classroom instruction methods* have some effect on the students' EFL learning process and their final attainments. Most students were found to have strong motivations in English learning, yet, their motivations as a whole did not significantly correlate with their achievements. The students' motivations were also found to correlate with their choice of the learning strategies. Favourable attitudes were found to significantly correlate with the students' achievements in the experiment. The students' outside class language exposure significantly correlates with their achievements. The second language learning strategies were mostly used by the students. Generally speaking, the higher level the students were at, the more strategies were found to be used. The results regarding the factors involved in classroom instruction demonstrate that the instruction methods might have an impact on the learners' learning process and hence the learners' final attainments. Detailed discussion of the results and findings will be given in Chapter 7.

Chapter 7 Discussion of the Results from the Experiment and the Investigation

In this chapter, the results presented in Chapter 6 will be discussed on the basis of the two objectives of this research, viz. (1) to explore the nature of the students' final attainment, and (2) to find out the possible factors that influence this group of learners' EFL learning process and their relationships with these learners' attainment.

7.1 Discussion of the results from the experiment

7.1.1 Summary of the results from the experiment

Tables 6 – 6 and 6 – 7 in Chapter 6 indicate that the students performed rather well in the decontextualized task (KT). For most of the sub-variables in the KT, the average scores are over 70% except for the KTPRONP. While in the contextualized task (WT), both the means in the WTK and the holistic mean (WTTOTL) are disproportionately lower than the scores in the KT. The mean percentage for each variable in the WT is not over 60% except for the variable WTKPRONP with the percentage of about 76%. The percentage of one of the variables WTKMPHP in the WTK does not even reach 40%. Statistical analyses manifest that the differences between the means in the KT and the means in the WT are significant at the level of $p < .000$. Correlation and Multiple Regression Analyses indicate that the KT variables significantly correlate with the WT variables, but the coefficients are not very high. The accountability of the KT variables for the WT variables is limited to a certain extent. Results of the analyses of the different levels of students are in accordance with the results of the analyses of the students as a whole.

7.1.2 Discussion of the results from the experiment

The rejection of the three null hypotheses (see the hypotheses in Chapter 4) lays the foundation for the following discussion.

(1) What have the participants gained after their learning of English for six years in schools?

As has been stated in Chapter 1, English as a foreign language is registered as a compulsory course from junior secondary schools. The students in this experiment belonged to the group of post-adolescents with the average age of 18 years old. Most of them started their first English learning at the age around 12 or 13[①]. This period gave them the advantage over adults in learning a second/foreign language. However, the results indicate that six years of formal learning in secondary schools cannot ensure that they could express simple ideas in the language they had been worked so hard at.

In the experiment, two tasks were devised — the KT and the WT. The KT was the controlled task, which consists of the grammar and lexis that was needed to encode the essential ideas for the WT (i.e. GL). The controlled GL in the KT were arranged from simple to complex, from word to sentences. It was assumed that the cognitive resources needed for the KT were mainly recognition, recalling and simple judgment. The whole experiment was so designed that the GL "tested" in the KT were those that presumably were to be used by the students in their accomplishment of the WT to convey the essential ideas contained therein.

The items in the KT are mostly discrete in nature, and are

---

① Since 2003, the local government has issued a policy stipulating that children in primary schools in Guangzhou are required to start English learning from Grade 1, which means that the early starters' age may range from 6 to 7 years old now.

basically a measurement of learners' receptive metalanguage. They are directed to testing the learners' knowledge about the GL. To accomplish the KT involves the employment of grammatical competence mainly or explicit linguistic knowledge (see Bialystok, 1981b). This kind of knowledge is usually abstract and out of context, and can be employed to verbalize by itself and to monitor language use when sufficient time is provided. The WT tasks, however, are orientated to measuring the learners' ability to use the GL in discourse. This kind of task is holistic in nature. Obviously, to accomplish the WT requires more cognitive resources than to accomplish the KT. It has been assumed that the performance of this kind of task involves the employment of implicit linguistic knowledge when time is limited together with other kinds of competence, such as discourse competence, sociolinguistic competence, strategic competence and cognitive and affective capacity, i. e., with the nature of communicative competence; while the accomplishment of the KT requires knowledge mainly of a grammatical nature. The experiment attempted to conduct a comparison between the students' performance on the same GL in decontextualized situations and in contextualized situations.

The results indicate that the students found it much easier to accomplish the KT but more difficult to accomplish the WT. The mean for KTTOTL for the 231 students is as high as 83. 36%, while the mean for WTKTOTL (the total mean score of the learners' appropriate linguistic production in the WT) is as low as 53. 99%. The approximate mean ratio between KTTOTL and WTKTOTL is about 1. 544: 1, i.e. for every 1. 544 grammatical forms and lexical items the students knew, they could only produce one of them correctly in contextualized situations. However, these linguistic features were the basic elements for encoding the essential ideas entailed in the two writing tasks. Thus, failure to produce them or to employ them correctly would certainly affect the successful conveyance of the stipulated ideas. The results reveal that the students could cope with the GL easily when they were presented in discrete forms, but when the GL were needed in meaningful contextualized tasks, the students were simply at a loss. A picture emerges from the above results: the students might have different types of representations of knowledge in their minds. If we follow the understandings of Bialystok (1978, 1994) and N. Ellis (2004), two types of knowledge are represented in language users' mind, i.e. explicit knowledge and implicit knowledge, of which explicit knowledge refers to that kind of declarative knowledge which is held consciously and is accessed through controlled processing, and implicit knowledge refers to that kind of proceduralized knowledge which is held unconsciously and is accessed through automatic processing, then, the results here provide the evidence for the distinctive nature of these two types of knowledge in general, and the results also accord with Bialystok (1982) 's assumption that in performing different tasks, learners are likely to draw differentially on both knowledge sources.

As has been discussed above, the tasks of KT and the WT are of different kinds in nature. They require competence of different types. Communicative competence is an interaction of many types of competencies, while grammatical competence is only one necessary component of CC. The working conceptual framework in Chapter 4 postulates that the learners' different kinds of language performance are undergirded by the above mentioned types of competencies. From the framework, we can see that CCP is undergirded by CC in which GC is integrated with other kinds of competence, and language learning and use occur in discourse. Thus we infer that the students could not use the requisite GL correctly in the WT probably because of the fact that the competence required by the WT does not match with that which is represented in the students' minds, but the competence required by the KT matches with that which is represented in the learners' minds. Thus, comparing the two mean scores of KTTOTL and WTKTOTL, and taking into consideration the nature of the two kinds of tasks, it may be inferred that what the students have attained might be in fact the discrete facts or rules of the target language rather than an established system. Most of the knowledge of the target language the students have attained might not have been internalized into a system which can be easily accessed, but have been in the state of moving towards the mastered stage. In other words, the forms or rules that the learners have attained have not been well mapped with their corresponding meanings yet. The experiment indicates that for the total "tested" GL, the students knew explicitly 83.36% of them, but could only implicitly produce correctly 53.99% of them. This leads us to the inquiry into the possible existence of that part of the knowledge that had not been emergent in the production. Do they still exist in the students' minds or are they simply lost? This urges us to go further to ask what stage these students are at, which will be dealt with later.

As far as the nature of knowledge is concerned, available theories as Krashen's and Bialystok's cognitive models in the field of SLA also provide basic frames for this kind of research. According to Krashen (1981) and Bialystok (1981b), only acquired or implicit linguistic knowledge can contribute to communicative tasks performance. Besides, Bialystok and other researchers believe that judgment tasks involve knowledge of a more implicit nature than knowledge of an explicit nature (Bialystok, 1981b). If so, the KT task also involves certain employment of some implicit linguistic knowledge. Bialystok (1981b) also argues that writing tasks involve mainly the use of explicit linguistic knowledge, for learners have time to think and thus have time to monitor their work. It is true that some explicit linguistic knowledge can also contribute to communication, especially when sufficient time is allowed. But to accomplish communicative tasks like the WT in the experiment within limited time, explicit linguistic knowledge only is definitlely not enough. Learners might use explicit linguistic knowledge to monitor their output in the process, but the employment of this type of knowledge cannot guarantee the successful accomplishment of such kind of communicative tasks, for communication-oriented tasks within limited time involve automatic processing of different types of competence. Thus, we believe that to accomplish writing tasks within limited time involves mainly the employment of implicit linguistic knowledge, while explicit knowledge only plays a very limited role. Writing certainly involves the monitoring process, but without sufficient amount of implicit linguistic knowledge, it cannot be fully accomplished. Based on this thinking, the author holds that there is in fact no strict distinction in the employment of these kinds of knowledge in accomplishing language related tasks. Different tasks might involve relatively different amount of these kinds of knowledge, which is actually a matter of degree rather than distinct types. This understanding on the basis of this study can further support Rod Ellis (2004)'s identification of the relativeness of pure measurement of explicit knowledge, while at the same time admitting the findings that there does exist two types of knowledge of distinct nature.

Taking into consideration the KT and the WT task form and content, we conclude that the accomplishment of the KT requires more explicit knowledge than implicit knowledge, whereas WT, a task of production within limited time, although it also involves the use of explicit knowledge for monitoring, involves mainly implicit linguistic knowledge, and a large amount probably. Hence, we conclude that the knowledge these students have attained is mainly a type of knowledge which is composed of more explicit knowledge and less implicit knowledge. This group of students seems to have quite a large amount of knowledge *about* the target language required by the secondary school syllabus, but their ability to automatically access that knowledge in context is limited. According to Bialystok (1981b), "A grammar task, ... relies primarily on knowledge of the formal features of language, while a communicative task can incorporate formal, rhetorical and instrumental aspects in various degrees" (p. 33). The results of our experiment accord with this statement. We thus have the same conclusion as Bialystok's (1981b, p. 43), viz. knowing a form does not ensure that the form will be used in free situations. To put it another way, learners cannot be guranteed the ability to employ the form freely in communicative situations unless they have established the relationship between the form and its functions or meanings in their minds.

This result does not suggest that the students have not learnt anything. They do have learnt a great deal of vocabulary and grammatical facts. The problem is not the quantity, but the quality, as Li (1993) has pointed out. The final question that is left to us might not be the one to ask how much the students have learnt, but how they were learning and what made them attain the type of knowledge they have now.

The results of the analyses of the sub-variables in the KT and the WTK correspond with the results of the analyses of the total variables except for the sub-variables KTPRON and WTKPRON. Two factors might cause the students' lower scores in KTPRON and their relatively higher scores in WTKPRON in the WTK. One of them might be that in the KT the students were requested to identify the functions of the pronouns in addition to the identification of pronouns. It might be due to the fact that these students had not obtained sufficient metalinguistic knowledge about sentences. This result accords with Bialystok's experiment (From Odlin, 1986, p. 130) in which her students were less successful in identifying the parts of speech in sentences than in making grammaticality judgments. Bialystok explained that it was because her subjects had not obtained enough metalinguistic knowledge and they were not given enough time, for later on, given enough time, her subjects' performance was improved. For this experiment, the same reason might also exist, but it seems that time was enough for the students' performance. Another factor might be that these learners employed fewer pronouns than the writing tasks required actually. This can be seen from the further check on these students' papers. The pronouns listed in the KT are the essential ones for the accurate expression of the ideas contained in the WT. "Each other", for instance, should be used together with the verb "exchange" when expressing the idea "to exchange the stamps with each other" in the first task. In the WT, the students were found to avoid using some pronouns such as "each other". Thus the conveying of the ideas in the writing tasks was affected. In most cases, the students were found to use simple personal pronouns frequently, such as the pronouns of "he, I, you, me". Therefore the mean score in the KT for KTPRON is relatively lower than that in the WTK. This result indicates another finding, i.e. these learners apparently employed the "avoidance" strategy in communication. The finding in this research concerning pronouns is different from other research results. Seliger (1979), for instance, in his experiment to testify Krashen's monitor theory, finds that the learner can produce the language of which the rules he cannot tell. But the analysis of the learners' writing papers in this research shows that the learners did not use the language correctly of which the rules they in fact knew. This indicates that learners' explicit knowledge about that rule has not been transferred into implicit knowledge yet, or they have not established the relationship between the form and its functions in their minds around this phenomenon. In terms of the pronouns in this experiment, the learners did not even know the rules of the pronouns in addition to their inability to use these pronouns. Therefore, they chose to use those they were familiar with instead, which certainly affects the accurate and appropriate expression of the essential ideas entailed in the WT.

As to the other components in the KT, the students performed particularly well. The mean scores are over 85%. But, for the same GL in the WT, most of the students did not choose them correctly. Generally speaking, the students could identify and gave the meanings explicitly nearly all the vocabulary items in the writing tasks (92. 93%), but could only produce 61% of them correctly. They could recognize or recall 86% of the rules of KTCONT but could only produce 67% of the basic grammatical concepts correctly. They were able to recognize and recall 89% of the morphological rules about noun plurals, verb forms, and the forms of the superlative and comparative degrees of adjectives and adverbs (KTMPH), but could only use 34% of the rules correctly in the contextualized task. Function words and verb tenses and voices are usually considered as more difficult elements in EFL learning than other units of the English language. However, for those function words and the rules concerning verb tenses and voices "tested" in the KT, the students could recognize or recall 71 to 74 per cent of them, whereas in the WT, the students could only use 59 to 42 per cent of them correctly.

It may be taken as granted in language learning that learners usually produce less than they in fact know, but as Li (1992) has pointed out when referring to the problem of the relationship between quantity and quality in secondary school language teaching in China,

> There is no denying that the quantity of input is important, but is it not more a matter of quality than quantity that we are facing now? Granted that you can never expect students to take in as much as you put in, but when the intake rate is disgracefully low after time and effort has been unsparingly spent, I would think it is time we looked into the quality of the input (Li, 1992, p. 11).

Therefore, we cannot but ask the whys behind when finding the unacceptable gap between the learners' knowledge about the same linguistic knowledge in decontextualized situations and their ability to access that knowledge in contextualized situations.

(2) **Does the students' lack of writing proficiency result from their lack of grammatical competence**?

The above analyses indicate that the learners performed better in the decontextualized task than they did in the contextualized task. Besides, the mean for the holistic score WTTOTL (the total score of the learners' linguistic production in the WT) is only 59.99%. When relating these results to the writing task itself, it indicates that these learners are poor at writing skill. The question arises then, "Does the learners' lack of writing proficiency result from their lack of grammatical competence?"

In SLA writing research, efforts have been made to explore the reasons for learners' success or failure in achieving the expected level of writing. The problem considered here is of wide interest and of first importance. It is still too early to write out a prescription without a good understanding of the causes behind. To start the exploration of the problem, generally accepted beliefs should be considered first.

It is generally believed in EFL instruction and learning in China that all skills in language are based first on the mastery of linguistic knowledge of the target language. It seems that this general belief is not problematic from the surface. But when applying it to EFL practice, careful consideration is required. In terms of the role of grammatical competence, different teaching approaches hold different principles. As the discussion in Chapters 2 and 3 indicates, too much emphasis has been given to grammatical competence development in the Traditional Approach (TA) by which learners develop a good knowledge of the rules of the target language, and are good at sentence analysis, translation, etc. but feel embarrassed in language use. The Structuralist Approach (SA), on the other hand, attempting to avoid the undesired consequences brought about by the TA, suggests that more attention be given to listening and speaking, which leads to the mechanical training of sentence patterns and detailed learning of sentence structures. Learners by this approach could produce single structures correctly but feel embarrassed in contextualized situations. The extremists in the Communicative Approach emphasize the social functions of language and meaning transfer, but pay little attention to accuracy development. Where should teachers and learners go? Should they only learn grammatical rules by sacrificing the social and cultural functions of language or should they just pay attention to the appropriacy effect without any consideration of the linguistic component? This is the "Balance Problem" in SLA or FLL studies. Canale and Swain's model is inspiring, and research of developmental and cognitive psycholinguists is thought-provoking. But let's not answer this question at the moment and go to find the possible answer from the fact. The results of the correlation and regression analyses in this research might help us see through the fog.

Table 6 - 15 in Chapter 6 demonstrates that the correlation coefficient between KTTOTL and WTKTOTL is 0.6408, while the coefficient between KTTOTL and WTTOTL is 0.7260. With these significant correlation coefficients as the basis, Multiple Regression method was employed to examine how much KTTOTL could account for WTKTOTL and WTTOTL. Tables 6 - 16 and 6 - 17 show that the R Square for KTTOTL on WTKTOTL is 0.4169, which means that KTTOTL could explain 41.69% of WTKTOTL in the WT. When the results entered into the equation which was obtained from the analyses, the predicted results were also obtained for WTKTOTL, i.e. when WTKTOTL was zero, KTTOTL was 35.1 per cent. When KTTOTL was 100 per cent, WTKTOTL was only 72.6 per cent. Thus we get the following figure:

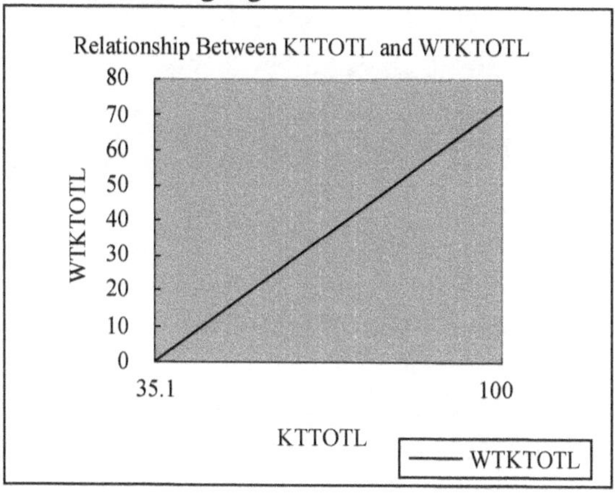

Figure 7-1 Relationship between KTTOTL and WTKTOTL (for 231 cases)

For KTTOTL on WTTOTL, the R Square is 0.52701, which means that KTTOTL could account for 52.70% of WTTOTL. The same results were also obtained for KTTOTL on WTTOTL. That is, KTTOTL was 40.69% when WTTOTL was zero. When KTTOTL was 100 per cent, WTTOTL was 82.9%. Thus, we get Figure 7-2 based on the equations obtained from the regression analyses.

We can see from the R Squares that the determination indices of KTTOTL on the WT variables are not very high. The figures demonstrate further that writing and the use of the linguistic knowledge in writing can only start with minimum accumulation of rudimentary linguistic knowledge, which is in accordance with our common sense. But the problem is that the high accumulation of linguistic knowledge does not guarantee the learners' ability to use the linguistic knowledge correctly in context. The increase of linguistic knowledge in quantity does not guarantee the increase of linguistic knowledge in quality. This

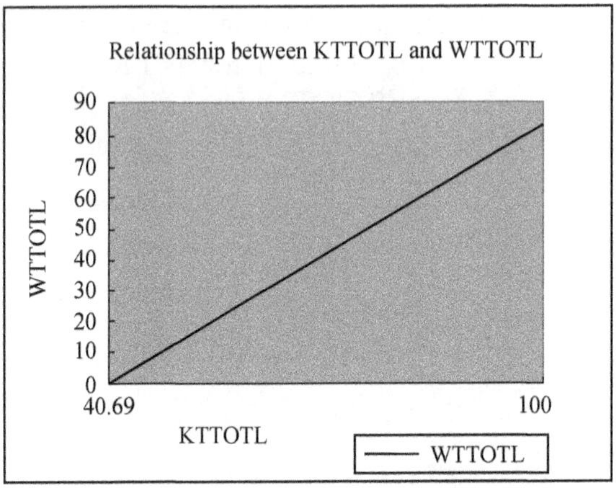

Figure 7 - 2 Relationship between KTTOTL and WTTOTL (for 231 cases)

phenomenon can be clearly observed from the following figures when the students were grouped according to their holistic scores in the WT.

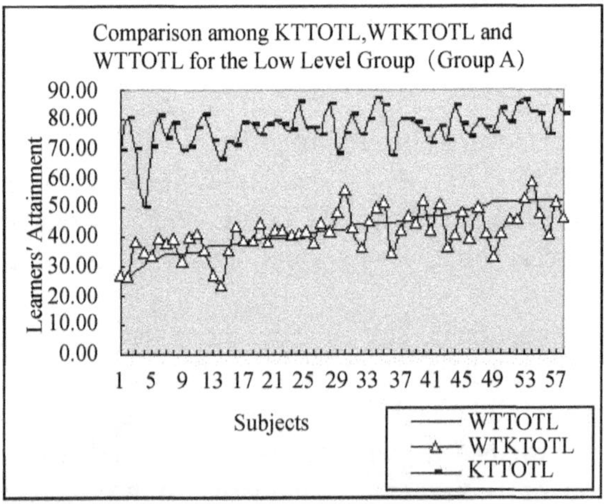

Figure 7 - 3 Comparison between KTTOTL, WTKTOTL and WTTOTL in Group A

In all the three figures Figure 7 - 3, Figure 7 - 4 and Figure 7 - 5, the learners' writing performance (WTTOTL) does not correspond well with their knowledge of the required GL

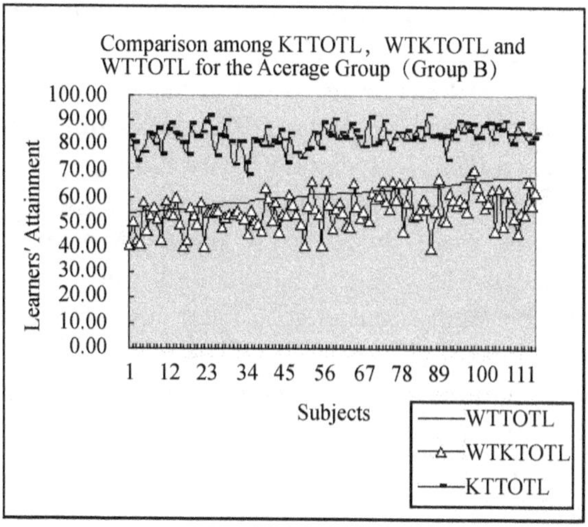

Figure 7 - 4 Comparison between KTTOTL, WTKTOTL and WTTOTL in Group B

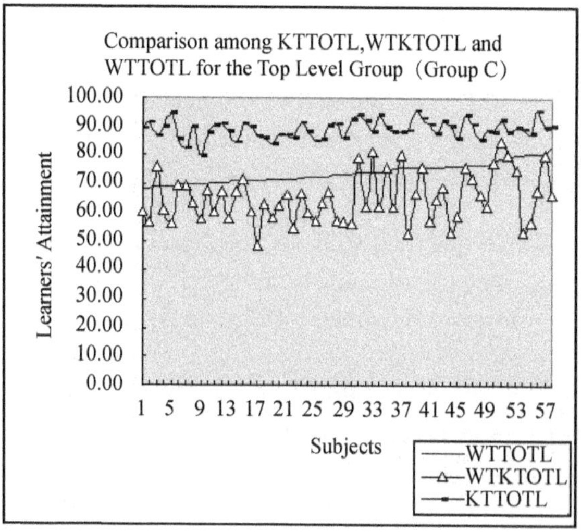

Figure 7 - 5 Comparison between KTTOTL, WTKTOTL and WTTOTL in Group C

(KTTOTL) and their use of the GL in context (WTKTOTL). The learners stored more knowledge about the target language in their minds than they could actually use that knowledge to accomplish communication-oriented tasks. This result is in accordance with the research results in SLL writing. In Krapels (1993)'s review of SLA writing research, he mentioned three studies on this problem, i.e. Jones (1982 cited from Krapels, 1993), Zamel (1982 cited from Krapels, 1993) and Raimes (1985 cited from Krapels, 1993) who studied this problem from different angles with different research methods. All three researchers conducted their studies in a second language situation and used the "composing aloud" or test methods together with interviews, observations, and questionnaires to find out the writing processes and the relationship between linguistic competence and writing proficiency. Krapels summarized each of the three researchers' findings as follows:

> Jones concluded that the poor writer had never learned how to compose, and this general lack of competence in composing, rather than a specific lack in L2 linguistic competence, was the source of her difficulty in L2 writing (Krapels, 1993, p. 40).

> Zamel (1982) also found that competence in the composing process was more important than linguistic competence in the ability to write proficiently in English... (Krapels, 1993, p. 40).

> Raimes found that her students' composing competence did not correspond with their linguistic competence, a recurrent finding in L2 writing research (Krapels, 1993, p. 44).

Correlation and regression analyses for the sub-variables in the KT on the sub-variables in the WTK demonstrate a clearer picture for us. All the KT sub-variables on the WTK sub-variables except for the pronouns show a significant relationship at the level of $F < .0000$. But the R Squares are very low. KTVOC, KTMPH in the KT could account for 20 to 26 per cent of WTKVOC and WTKMPH in the WTK, but other variables such as KTCONT, KTVFS in the KT could only account for about 10 per cent of WTKCONT and WTKVFS in the WTK. The percentage for KTFCT in the KT in explaining WTKFCT in the

WTK is as low as 0.2%. Apart from the differences among the three variables (KTTOTL, WTKTOTL and WTTOTL) that have been discussed in (1), another kind of difference is found, i.e. the higher level the students are at, the greater variation is found in these learners' scores in WTKTOTL. It can be seen from the above three figures that as the learners' writing proficiency increases, the gap between their KTTOTL and WTKTOTL is narrowed as the learners' writing proficiency increases, yet the difference between their WTKTOTL and WTTOTL increases. This indicates that when the learners devoted more of their attention to the conveying of meaning, their attention to the formal features of language was somewhat lessened, which also gives further support to the hypothesis about learners' limited processing capacity. The R-squares indicate further that the better these students performed in the WT, the lower the determination indices of the KT variables on the WT variables were. This result seems to support Bialystok's (1981b, p. 41) model, which points out the decreasing role of linguistic information in instrumental tasks. According to Bialystok (1981b, p. 41), the decreasing role of linguistic information in instrumental tasks is compensated by an increasing involvement of conceptual information. Figure 7-5 for Group C (the top level group) demonstrates this point obviously. In Figure 7-5, most of the mean scores of the students' WTKTOTL are lower than the mean scores of their WTTOTL. The results of the correlation and regression analyses help us draw the conclusion that the learners' grammatical competence can only explain part, *but not the whole*, of their writing proficiency, for grammatical competence is only one necessary component of CC. In this experiment, obviously, the learners' performance of the WT not only involves the formal aspect of language, but also the rhetorical aspect (i.e. rules of discourse) and the instrumental aspect (i.e. the ability to express the conceptual meaning appropriately in a given context).

The findings in this research, although with different methods, correspond with the findings of research in second language learning, i.e. learners' linguistic competence does not correspond with their writing proficiency. Learners' failure in writing does not mainly result from their lack in linguistic competence. Linguistic competence only plays a moderate role in writing. Cases in foreign language learning conditions seem to have the same problem as those in SLL conditions in this respect. Thus, the solution to the balance problem in teaching methodology may be easier if we consider the research findings about the contribution of linguistic competence to learners' communicative language competence.

The discussion about questions (1) and (2) provides evidence for the assumptions made in the working conceptual framework in Chapter 4, i.e. different types of knowledge lead to different types of performance. Most learners in this study failed to express the simple ideas contained in the writing tasks which involve knowledge of a holistic and communicative nature. This indicates that most of the learners lack this kind of holistic knowledge. But their good performance in the KT reflects that they have quite a large amount of explicit knowledge about the elements of the target language for these kinds of tasks. What they lack is the ability to organize the elements in their syntactic combinations according to their pragmatic functional applications.

(3) **Which aspects of the linguistic knowledge are more difficult for these secondary school EFL learners?**

With the above discussion covering mainly holistic problems, the discussion about this question will be focused on local areas which concern the relatively difficult aspects for the students' linguistic performance in decontextualized and contextualized situations.

From the mean tables in Chapter 6, we find that KTFCT, KTPRON, KTVFS in the KT and WTKMPH, WTKFCT and WTKVFS in the WTK are relatively more difficult components for these students. As has been stated previously, the KTPRON in the KT is difficult, for learners were requested to recognize the pronouns and recall their functions in the KT, while in the WT, learners tended to avoid using them, which should not mean that they can use pronouns better when expressing ideas.

Function words, verb tenses and voices in sentences are

always considered as more difficult than others for EFL learners. The results in this experiment have provided evidence for this point. What merits particular attention are the morphological forms in the KT and the WTK. These forms turned out to be very easy for this group of learners when they were presented in the tasks for the learners to recognize and recall the rules concerning noun plurals, verb conjugations and the forms of comparative and superlative degrees for adjectives and adverbs. However, when these forms were employed to accomplish the two writing tasks, the mean percentage for correct choice of WTKMPH in the WTK drops to the lowest among all the sub-variables in the WTK with only 33.77%. This finding also accords with the findings in SLL research. Silva (1993a) reviewed 72 reports of empirical research comparing L1 and L2 writing processes. When discussing errors easily committed by L2 writers, those reviewed research findings show that L2 learners make more morphosyntactic errors, and more errors with verbs, prepositions, articles and nouns, which are similar to the findings in this experiment. A list of example sentences with errors committed by these learners can be referred to in Appendix 5.

Generally speaking, with respect to the vocabulary required by the two writing tasks, most learners could recall the forms and the basic meanings of the words but were unable to apply them appropriately to the required contexts. For instance, "to welcome" is usually used when one person meets another one in a particular place, as in the airport, one may say "Welcome to China". But, when writing to a friend, if the same idea is expressed, this pattern is seldom used. In the students' papers, however, most of them used this sentence in writing their letters to their penpals. Another example indicates the same phenomenon. When expressing the idea "Huang Hua told me that you liked collecting stamps, too.", many students expressed this idea by writing "Huang Hua talked about you with me." which conveys a different meaning in effect.

Most of the students' errors in their writings are related to morphological forms, verb tenses, and verb voices. This group of learners seemed to be baffled when they were grappling with the expression of the essential ideas contained in the WT. The third person singular form of the present tense of verbs after the subjective pronoun "I" was chosen, as in the sentence "I likes to collect stamps very much.", which is obviously an error committed by overgeneralization of rules. Active voice was chosen when a passive voice was needed, as "He born in 1963." They opted for the present perfect aspect when a present progressive tense was needed, as in the sentence "I've sent several Chinese stamps for you."

There are also errors about verb or sentence patterns. This can be seen from the above two example sentences, too. The students were found to have much difficulty in dealing with tenses and basic patterns in clauses. They were also found to have much difficulty in coping with some of the parts of speech. The verb "like", for instance, was not used as it should be by most of the students, as it was used in the sentence "I am like collecting stamps very much." — a reflection of the mismatch between word function and form, which is a stage most learners were at.

Diversity of sources is another feature of this group of learners' errors in production. In the field of SLA, two types of errors have been identified, i.e. *interlingual errors* and *intralingual errors* (Richards, 1971). Interlingual errors refer to second language learners' errors that could be traced to L1 interference, and intralingual errors refer to errors that could be traced to different strategies in the target language learning, such as "overgeneralization", "simplification", "communication-based" errors and "induced" errors that are caused by teachers' instruction. Applying this classification to this study, it was found that most errors committed by these students were intralingual errors, such as "I likes collecting stamps.", "He play matches", "He born in 1993.", and so on. This further indicates the dynamic nature of this group of learners' second language development. There were also some errors that could be traced to L1 interference. For instance, in the sentence "I very like to collect stamps", the learners obviously applied the Chinese structure of "henxihuan" (很喜欢) here to express the idea of "I like collecting stamps very much" in English. There are many other sentences of this kind, which can be seen from Appendix 5.

In short, the use of such language elements as function words, pronouns, verb tenses and voices, and noun plurals, which is found to be difficult for second language learners, is also difficult for the students in this experiment. The difficult components in both the KT and the WT are mainly at the sentence level.

(4) **Which stage are the students at?**

In designing the experiment, one component in the KT was deliberately devised with corresponding sections for comparison, i.e. the morphological forms. It was devised on the basis of the degree of the involvement of cognitive resource for the accomplishment of the tasks. Thus it was arranged in the KT from recognizing to recalling and from word level to sentence level. The results were compared with the corresponding components in the WTK. The equivalent component in the WTK is the application level. Thus we obtain the results in the following tables.

Table 7-1 Distribution of means for different levels of MPH variables in the KT and the WTK

Variables	Means	SDs	Mini.	Maxi.	ValidN	Labels
NPLRCG	4.52	.63	.00	5.00	231	recognize-Npls.
VCRCG	8.33	.70	3.50	9.00	231	recognize-Vconju.
ADJRCG	2.92	.23	1.50	3.00	231	recognize-adj&adv
NPLRCL	2.30	.30	1.00	2.50	231	recall-Nplurals
VCRCL	4.13	1.01	.00	5.00	231	recall-Vconju.
ADJRCL	2.27	.49	.00	3.00	231	recall-adj&adv
KRCGTL	15.77	1.15	9.00	17.00	231	total-for-recgn.
KRCLTL	8.71	1.38	2.00	10.50	231	total-for-recall.
KTMPHTL	24.47	2.23	12.5	27.5	231	KTMPH-total
WTKMPHTL	9.29	4.89	.81	22.65	231	WTKMPH-total
In-per-cent-form:						
NPLRCGP	90.39	12.56	.00	100.00	231	(var. * %/5)
VCJRCGP	92.57	7.79	38.89	100.00	231	(var. * %/9)

Continued

Variables	Means	SDs	Mini.	Maxi.	ValidN	Labels
ADJRCGP	97. 33	7. 54	50. 00	100. 00	231	(var. * %/3)
NPLRCLP	92. 03	11. 90	40. 00	100. 00	231	(var. * %/2. 5)
VCJRCLP	82. 60	20. 16	. 00	100. 00	231	(var. * %/5)
ADJRCLP	75. 83	16. 20	. 00	100. 00	231	(var. * %/3)
KRCGTLP	92. 77	6. 79	52. 94	100. 00	231	(var. * %/17)
KRCLTLP	82. 91	13. 11	19. 05	100. 00	231	(var. * %/10. 5)
KTMPHTLP	88. 97	8. 10	45. 45	100. 00	231	KTMPH-in-100
WTKMPHTLP	33. 77	17. 79	2. 94	82. 35	231	WTKMPH-in-100

Notes: var. * %/5 = variable score multiplied by 100 and the result is then divided by the total score of that variable

Three levels were compared in Tables 7 - 1 and 7 - 2. From the mean distribution in Table 7 - 1, it can be seen that the means for KRCGTLP, KRCLTLP and WTKMPHTLP decreases from high to low. The mean for the recognition level (KRCGTLP) is apparently much higher than the mean for the recalling level (KRCLTLP), while the mean for the application level (WTKMPHP) is much lower than it is expected. The paired t-test results indicate that the differences among all these variables are significant at the level of p <. 00.

Table 7 - 2 Paired samples t-tests among the KT recognition variables, recall variables and WTKMPH

Variables	Mean	SD	SE of Mean	t-value	df	2-tail Sig. *
KREGTLP	92. 7680	6. 789	. 447	13. 65	230	. 000
KRCLTLP	82. 9107	13. 112	. 863	95% CI (8. 434, 11. 281)		
KRCLTLP	82. 9107	13. 112	. 863	43. 33	230	. 000
WTKMPHTLP	33. 7662	17. 787	1. 170	95% CI (46. 909, 51. 380)		
KREGTLP	92. 7680	6. 789	. 447	54. 60	230	. 000
WTKMPHTLP	33. 7662	17. 787	1. 170	95% CI (56. 872, 61. 131)		
WTKMPHTLP	33. 7662	17. 787	1. 170	-53. 07	230	. 000
KTMPHTLP	88. 9728	8. 099	. 533	95% CI (-57. 257, -53. 156)		

* p< =0. 05

It does not surprise us to obtain this result, because the requirement for cognitive resource at each level is different. What attracts us is that the mean score for the application level is too low, which indicates something about the students' linguistic attainment. The data demonstrate that the students were able to recognize correctly 92.77% of the "tested" morphological forms and recall 82.91% of them, but were only able to employ 33.77% of these forms correctly in sentences. This makes it reasonable to conclude that most of the students failed to achieve the expected writing proficiency probably not only because they lack the composing competence, but also because they lack the expected linguistic competence. They are still at the stage of recalling discrete and isolated rules rather than at the stage for real contextualized language application. Further analyses of the different groups of the students divided by WTTOTL show a similar tendency.

At the level of recognition in the KT, the comparison between morphological forms and verb forms in sentences (here the VFS—verb tenses, voices) was also conducted. The results are displayed in Table 7 - 3.

Table 7 - 3 Distribution of means for MPH and VFS in the KT

Variables	Mean	SD	Mini.	Maxi.	ValidN	Label
KRCGTL	15.77	1.15	9.00	17.00	231	total-for-recgn.
KTVFS	7.76	1.38	1.0	10.0	231	KT-vforms-in-sent.
KRCGTLP	92.77	6.79	52.94	100.00	231	var. * %/17
KTVFSP	73.87	13.16	9.52	95.24	231	KT-vfs-in-100

Notes: var. * %/17 = variable score multiplied by 100 and the result is then divided by the total score of that variable

It can be seen clearly that the mean percentage score for recognition at word level is higher than that for recognition at sentence level. Paired samples t-test results indicate that this difference is significant at the level of $p < .000$. This indicates that the students performed better at the word level than at the sentence level at the recognition stage. This illustrates further the fact that the learners had a better grasp of isolated linguistic knowledge than sentence or discourse level linguistic knowledge. Nonetheless, at the application level (WTK), the students seemed to perform better in WTKVFS than in WTKMPH (see Table 6 – 10). Even so, the difference between the two mean percentages is only 8. It seemed that the students tended to use tenses or voices correctly in production but failed to use the correct conjugations of the verbs. But holistically speaking, the learners found it difficult to use the rules of verbs in contextualized situations both at the word level and at the sentence level (WTKMPH and WTKVFS). Table 6 – 10 shows that the mean percentages for both WTKMPHP and WTKVFSP are disproportionately lower than all other sub-variables in the WTK.

(5) Findings about the writing processes as a byproduct of the experiment

The goal of the experiment is not process-oriented initially, but it is interesting to examine a little bit the process of the students' performance by the way. In the implementation of the experiment, a guideline sheet together with a blank piece of paper was delivered to every invigilator. The invigilators were asked to observe and write down the students' general performance behavior in composing. The notes taken by the invigilators in each class attracted the researcher's attention during the data processing. It was found that most of the students in School No. 2 (i.e. the first-class school which is supposed to be one of the best secondary schools by the City Education Bureau in Guangzhou) did some planning before they wrote and read again or revised their writings afterwards. Some students even wrote it first in their self-prepared pieces of paper and quickly copied it down on the "examination paper". But in School No. 28 and School No. 11, no such process was found. Most of the students in these two schools wrote their first drafts on the "examination paper" immediately when they saw the topics. They did little planning and revising. They were found to be always murmuring some of the words they could not recall correctly.

When assessing the papers of each school, the two raters

including the researcher found that the papers from School No. 2 were better organized and more appropriate in expressing the essential ideas than those from the other two schools. Papers from the other two schools seemed to state the facts in the order listed in the tasks. Little readjustment of the facts or reorganization of the ideas occurred. Obviously, the students in School No. 2 were employing their composing competence and their explicit linguistic knowledge to monitor their composing process and products while the students in the other two schools did not.

This result from the simple observation seems to accord with the SLL research result as can be seen from the summary by Krapels (1993) that learners' lack of composing competence also plays a role in explaining learners' poor performance in their writings. And it also reminded us of Bialystok (1978) 's statement about the monitoring role of explicit linguistic knowledge in language use.

7.2 Discussion of the findings from the survey

The investigation was carried out after the experiment with the aim to find out the possible factors that contribute to or hinder effective EFL learning, i.e. to attempt to find out the causes underlying the results obtained from the experiment both from the learning process and the teaching process. Questionnaires were employed as the instrument for the investigation. The major factors covered in this research were (1) motivations, (2) attitudes, (3) outside class language exposure, (4) SLL learning strategies, and (5) classroom instruction. The results were displayed in Chapter 6 in the order of the research questions and hypotheses under two objectives: (1) the general findings about the factors under consideration; (2) the relationship between these factors and the experimental results. The following discussion will focus on four aspects: (1) the relationship between motivation-attitudinal variables and the experimental results, (2) the relationship between outside class language exposure and the experimental results, (3) the relationship between learning strategies and the experimental results, and (4) the relationship between classroom instruction (the nature of input) and the experimental results. Finally, the results of a case analysis will be provided together with a brief discussion on the results from the questionnaire for the teachers.

7.2.1 Findings from the QL and their relationships with the experimental results

(1) The Motivation-attitudinal variables

Motivation-attitudinal variables have been widely discussed in the field of SLA. Results showing that motivations correlate with language competence are mainly concerned with learners in a bilingual situation. As has been reviewed in Chapter 3, there are also studies that show weak correlations between motivation-attitudinal variables and learners' language competence in foreign language situations (Carroll, 1962; Savignon, 1972; Chandrasegaran, 1981). These different findings indicate the complex nature of the relationship between motivational-attitudinal variables and learners' achievements. What about the situations in Chinese secondary schools?

The analyses in Chapter 6 indicate that there is not a significant relationship between the motivations as a whole and the students' achievements either in the decontextualized task or the contextualized task, although the learners are found to be mostly strongly motivated (see Table 6 – 25). It was expected that in Chinese situations, instrumental motivations would strongly correlate with learners' grammatical competence or communicative language competence development. However, when different orientations of motivations were analyzed, it was found that the students' integrative motivations significantly correlated with their performance in the decontextualized task, i.e. the KTTOTL in the KT with $r = 0.1620$, $p < .05$, while their instrumental motivations did not significantly correlate with any of their scores in the experiment. This seems to indicate that this group of learners ave interested in the target language culture, but their interest seems to be channelled to the learning of linguistic facts.

The motivations of the three levels of students divided by the writing proficiency (WTTOTL) were also analyzed and it was found that for the motivations as a whole, in Group A (the low level group), the students' motivations significantly correlated with the holistic writing score (WTTOTL in the WT) with $r = 0.2727$, $p < .05$. Further analyses manifested that the motivation (one of the motivations with an instrumental orientation) of "Learning English helps me to pass the National Entrance Examinations" significantly correlated with both KTTOTL and WTTOTL in Group A with $r = 0.2854$ and $p < .05$ for the former and $r = 0.2986$ and $p < .05$ for the latter. This agrees with the researcher's assumption. The NEE for Chinese secondary school students performs the role of a promoter in EFL learning. However, the correlation coefficients are too low to be regarded as an important factor for these students. But, it does indicate that the NEE has its effect on EFL learning in secondary schools.

In Group B (the average level group), however, there was no significant correlation between the students' motivations and their performance in either task (the KT and the WT). Inverse relationship was found in this group between the motivations and WTKTOTL— the use of the linguistic knowledge in the WT. This result is strange. It seems to indicate that the stronger the learners' motivations were in EFL learning, the poorer performance they gave in applying the grammatical knowledge in contextualized situations, or vice versa. It might also indicate that the learners' motivations had been channelled to other kinds of learning instead of learning how to use the linguistic knowledge in context.

In Group C (the top level group), the students' motivations on the whole did not correlate with any of the three variables. But detailed analyses demonstrated that the students' integrative motivations significantly correlated with KTTOTL.

Inverse relationship was found in this group between one of the instrumental motivations and KTTOTL. Generally speaking, although these learners' motivations did not seem to have a direct influence on their attainments. The relationship that has been found is between these learners' motivations and their KTTOTL, which indicates that these learners' strong motivations seemed to be channelled to the learning of linguistic knowledge in decontextualized situations. This is in accordance with this group of students' situation, i. e. their goal for learning English is directed to the preparation of the NMET, and their understanding of the preparation means to memorize discrete linguistic items.

In order to examine more clearly how the learners' motivations influence their EFL learning, correlation analysis between the motivations and the learning strategies was also conducted. The results demonstrate that the motivations as a whole (MOTL) significantly correlate with most of the learning strategies. This indicates that these learners' motivations are facilitative in their choice of learning strategies (for details, see Table 6 - 46 and Appendix 4). The students' different kinds of motivations influence their choice of different learning strategies, which in turn influences the learners' final attainment. The results in Table 6 - 46 and Appendix 4 seem to indicate that the higher level students were somewhat influenced by their motivations with an integrative orientation, while the lower level students were somewhat influenced by their motivations with an instrumental orientation in their choice of the six types of the strategies. However, the coefficients are not so high as to be decisive for interpretation.

The students' attitudes were found to significantly correlate with their achievements in the experiment, as can be seen from Table 6 - 43. But regression analysis indicates that the explanatory power of the attitudes for WTTOTL is not very high (R Square =. 10608). Further analysis of each group of students demonstrates that in Group A there is a significant correlation between the students' attitudes and their WTTOTL with $r = .2659$, $p < .05$, while in Group B the attitudes were found to significantly correlate with WTTOTL with $r = 0.3048$, $p < .01$, and in Group C significant correlation was found between the attitudes and KTTOTL with $r = 0.3081$, $p < .05$. This indicates that the more favorable attitudes the learners have, the higher achievements they obtain, which is in accordance with Gardner & Lambert (1972) 's findings.

When the motivation variables and the attitude variables are put together, the results are different. It was found that the motivation-attitudinal variables (MAV) as a whole significantly correlated with the learners' performance results both in the KT and the WT. The correlation coefficients between MAV and KTTOTL, MAV and WTKTOTL, and MAV and WTTOTL are respectively 0.2240^{**}, 0.1439^{*}, 0.2265^{**} (Notes: * * $p < .01$, * $p < .05$). This indicates that learners' affcts do play a role in their learning although the coefficients are not very high.

The analyses of the motivation-attitudinal variables do not completely accord with any of the studies reviewed in Chapter 3. The results concerning the relationship between the learners' motivations and the learners' attainments are consistent with Carroll (1962) 's and Savignon (1972) 's studies, and partially consistent with Gardner and Lambert's (1972) findings. The results regarding the relationship between the learners' attitudes and their attainments are contrary to Chandrasegaran (1981) 's findings about her Group A, but accord with her findings about her Group B. Analysis by groups indicates a roughly similar result to Chandrasegaran's findings about her Group B, i.e. more competent students tend to have more favorable attitudes. But, the correlation between the attitudes and KTTOTL in Group C (the top group) needs to be carefully considered as far as communicative language competence is concerned. It was found that in the top level group, the students' writing proficiency did not significantly correlate with their attitudes.

The analyses of motivation-attitudinal variables tend to indicate that the learners' CC development does not mainly rely on the intensity of their motivations and attitudes, but mainly rely on how their motivations and attitudes work together and how their motivations and attitudes are guided to facilitate these learners' choice of learning strategies and then indirectly influence their final internalization of the target language system.

(2) Outside class language exposure

Research in SLA indicates that high exposure contributes to successful second language learning. Hypothesis about the relationship between exposure and second language learning was also made earlier in Krashen's work. Krashen's theory involves much of the discussion about the subconscious process of language acquisition. Bialystok, based on the exposure hypothesis, put forward her well-known second language acquisition model (Bialystok, 1978). Language exposure is considered to be closely related to second language learning. Chandrasegaran (1981) researched cases in foreign language situations in Malaysian schools and concluded that "There is a definite link between degree of exposure to English and competence in the language." What about the cases in Chinese secondary schools? Does outside class language contact influence learners' attainment of their linguistic and communicative language competence?

Results from this investigation accord with Chandrasegaran's findings, i. e. there is a significant correlation between the learners' outside class language exposure to English and their achievements in the experiment (see Table 6 – 45). The correlation coefficients show that the correlation reaches a moderate level. The frequency table (Table 6 – 27), however, illustrates another point, i. e. in EFL learning situation, high exposure outside the classroom seldom occurs. It can also be seen clearly from Table 6 – 27 that the top level students have more language exposure after class than the low level or average level students. This indicates that the learners' communicative language competence development is influenced by the degree of outside class exposure. As has been pointed out in Chapter 5, the students are in Guangzhou, which is one of the more developed cities in China; hence, they have more opportunities to be exposed to English. This might be different from the case in other places in China. Generally speaking, this research further testifies that more exposure does play a role in facilitating learners' CC development, and also finds out that the secondary school EFL learners are exposed to English to some extent, although the degree of exposure is not high.

(3) **Learning strategies**

There are different ways in classifying learning strategies in

SLA studies. The strategies investigated here are from Oxford's list (1990), which mainly concerns the cognitive and psychological processes in SLL. There are six types of strategies chosen for this investigation. They are: (1) memorization of vocabulary, (2) cognitive learning strategies, (3) compensation strategies, (4) metacognitive learning strategies, (5) affective learning strategies, and (6) social learning strategies. In each strategy, two sub-strategies are included (see Chapter 3 and Appendix 4). Table 6 - 28 gives the results concerning all the strategies.

Tables 6 - 47 and 6 - 48 display the correlation coefficients between these strategies and the learners' achievements in the experiment. It was found that for all 231 students, five out of the six types of strategies significantly correlated with KTTOTL, and four out of the six types of strategies significantly correlated with WTTOTL and WTKTOTL. When different levels of the students were analyzed, it was found that only one sub-strategy significantly correlated with KTTOTL in Group A. None of the six types of strategies correlated with either KTTOTL or WTTOTL in Group A. But in Group B, five out of the six types of strategies significantly correlated with KTTOTL, and three out of the six types of strategies correlated with WTTOTL. Group C showed a different picture, in which one out of the six types of strategies correlated with KTTOTL, while two of the sub-strategies correlated with WTTOTL. In all three groups, no significant correlations were found between WTKTOTL and the learning strategies. Based on these results, two tentative conclusions are then drawn about the relationship between the learning strategies and the learners' attainment. First, the results indicate that the more proficient the learners were in English, the more strategies they employed in their EFL learning. Second, the results also imply that the learners seemed to employ most of the strategies to help them learn the discrete units of the target language rather than develop their communicative competence. Among the six types of strategies, the Memory Strategies have the closest relationship with the learners' KTTOTL and WTTOTL, while the correlation coefficients between other types of strategies (which focus mainly on mental training, practice and compensation) and the learners' achievements are around 0.3 or below. Among the six types of strategies, the former three (Memory, Cognitive, Compst) are defined as direct strategies by Oxford (1990) which involve the direct target language learning, while the latter three (Metacog, Affect and Social) are defined as indirect strategies, which involve the planning of learning, the controlling of emotions and the using of the target language. However, the "Social" strategy was found to have no significant relationship with these students' attainments in the KT and the WT. This indicates that these students seldom chose to use this strategy to practise using what they learnt. This might have affected the development of their communicative competence in their EFL learning, and helps us explain why these learners performed better in the KT than in the WT. The data presented in the frequency tables further illustrated this point. It was found that the higher level students employed more strategies while the lower level students employed fewer strategies in learning. The strategies employed by the higher level students are mainly those concerning the planning of learning, the controlling of emotions, and the using of the target language, while the main strategy employed by the lower level students is mainly concerned with memorizing vocabulary.

Table 6 – 28 (the frequency table) also helps us see one very subtle difference between the students in Group A and in Group C. In addition to the strategies which the students in Group A usually employed (Mem1, Compst2, and Metacog2), the students in Group C also frequently employed strategies as Mem2 and Cogn2. This indicates that the higher level students pay more attention to their mental training than the lower level students.

We can now conclude from the above discussion that this group of students' second language development is somewhat affected by the above-mentioned factors. It was found that the learners' favorable attitudes towards the learning of the target language, large amount of exposure to the target language , and more and frequent employment of the learning strategies contribute to their success in fostering their communicative competence. It was also found that the learners' attention was mainly directed to the learning of the discrete units of the target language rather than the learning of the combinations of those units and the applications of the combinations in pragmatic contexts.

Although all the correlation coefficients and the R Square coefficients in the above analyses are not very high, which may affect the explanatory power of the factors on this group of learners' second language development, nonetheless, the analyses do sketch a general picture of EFL learners' learning processes in secondary schools in China.

The factors under discussion up to now are mainly from the angle of the learners themselves. The results help us infer the learning process of the learners, but we still cannot offer a satisfactory explanation to the experimental result as to why these learners achieved higher scores in the KT and disproportionately lower scores in the WT. It has been hypothesized at the beginning of this study that in China factors from the teaching processes might have greater impact on learners' final achievements than learners' individual factors. Thus we attempted to look into the same problem from another side — the teaching processes in Chinese secondary schools.

(4) Classroom instruction

As Saleemi (1989) pointed out, "One's view of input is inevitably circumscribed by one's view of language..." (p174), the different kinds of classroom input are actually the materialization of related understandings of the nature of language and what should be learnt. The teachers' views in the three schools (School No. 2, School No. 28, and School No. 11) can be deduced from what they did. Then the nature of input can also be inferred.

In order to explore the causes underlying the learners' achievements from an angle of the teaching process, a set of questions were designed in the QL. The questions mainly cover the following aspects: (1) *the learners' reports of the methods they used after class to consolidate their learning in class*, (2) *the learners' evaluation of their strong and weak aspects in their language competence*, (3) *the learners' reports of their preference for the listed activities in class,* (4) *the learners' reports of their teachers' employment of activities in class*, (5) *the learners' reports of the homework types assigned by their teachers*, (6) *the learners' reports of their teachers' foci in teaching in class*, (7) *the learners' reports of their teachers' ways in handling the errors they made in class and in homework*, (8) *the learners' reports of their use of language for communication and their teachers' use of language for teaching in class*, (9) *the learners' reports of their teachers' allocation of time in class*, and (10) *the learners' reports of their opportunities for interaction in class between teachers and students and among students themselves.* These ten factors are certainly not sufficient for fully understanding the teaching processes in Chinese secondary schools, but a general picture can be drawn about the possible effect of teaching processes on the learners' achievements in the KT and the WT in the experiment.

As for (1), it can be seen from Table 6 – 30 that these students tended to use M1, M3 and M4 more frequently than other methods whether they are of the top level, average or low levels. These three methods are respectively *memorizing vocabulary*, *doing grammatical exercises*, and *reviewing lesson notes.* These methods are mainly orienting to the learning of the discrete elements of the target language. The other three methods which are meaning-oriented were not frequently employed by these students. This indicates that these students' attention was on the learning of the knowledge about the target language or facts about English rather than on the use of the knowledge. The answer to (2) can be obtained from Table 6 – 31. Although the percentage distribution is not discriminating, relatively higher percentages for *Grammar*, *Pronunciation* and *Sentence analysis* were found. The learners tended to believe that they were stronger in these three aspects compared with the other aspects. As for the three groups, the item that was chosen by relatively more students in Group A is *None,* which covers 44.8% of the students in this group. In Group B, the item that was mostly chosen is *Pronunciation* and in Group C, the item covering the highest percentage is *Grammar.* Among the three groups, only in Group

C, one of the more comprehensive skills *Reading comprehension* was chosen by comparatively more students. The percentage of this item is over 30 percent. Thus we conclude that most students believed that they were strong in linguistic knowledge. This accords with their focus in EFL learning as can be seen from (1). With regard to (3), whether the students are of the top, average or low level, most of them had a preference for the activities of *Reading aloud, Conducting realistic conversations* (CRC) and *Listening to tapes* (LT). Of the three, the percentage of CRC is the highest. But in Table 6 - 33 with respect to the teachers' employment of activities in class (for (4)), it can be seen that the activities the teachers usually implemented in class are not consistent with the students' preferences. The teachers employed activities like *Sentence transformation*, *Doing MC exercises*, *Dictation*, *Translation*, *Timed writing* (TW) and *Reading aloud* rather than the activities most students liked. The teachers' employment of activities is more consistent with some of the sub-tests in the NMET. Activities like CRC and LT (*Listening to tapes*) are more authentic and communicative in nature, but were seldom employed in class. What is interesting here is that when we give a close examination of the percentage distribution in the three schools, it is found that more than half of the students in School No. 2 and School No. 11 reported that their teachers usually employed the activity of TW, while in School No. 28, only 38.1% of the students reported that their teachers applied the activity of TW in class. This is in accordance with the distribution of the writing proficiency scores in the three schools. Although School No. 11 is considered to be the school of the lowest level in the city, some of the students' scores in this school appeared in the upper part of the list when all scores were sorted by WTTOTL after the experiment, which indicates that timed writing may play a facilitative role in the development of writing skill.

With regard to (5), the homework types, the students' reports indicate that their teachers usually asked them to *memorize words*, to *do MC exercises*, to *read supplementary materials* and to *write compositions*. The three schools, however, show different tendencies. In School No. 2 and School No. 28, the teachers tended to assign homework types of a more comprehensive nature, while in School No. 11, the teachers tended to emphasize the learning of rules and vocabulary in addition to assigning supplementary readings and compositions. This helps to explain the relative better performance of the students in Schools No. 2 and No. 28 in their writing. In regard to (6), the teachers' foci in teaching in class, most learners seem to agree on that their teachers focused mainly on *Vocabulary*, *Rules explanation* and *Reading comprehension*. But in School No. 28, the students reported that their teachers also focused on *Writing*.

As for (7), most learners reported that their teachers usually handled their errors in two ways: *correct errors immediately* or *point them out without correction*. The teachers in the three schools showed the same tendency in handling the errors made by the learners in class, but they were different in handling the errors in the learners' homework. On the whole, the students' report indicates that their teachers usually corrected their errors or at least pointed them out. These methods might be suitable for Chinese EFL learners, for most Chinese secondary school learners believed that they could only learn the right things from their teachers, which is in line with the basic understanding of classroom culture in China. But another conclusion can also be drawn that perhaps just because of the teachers' attitudes of this type to the learners' errors, the learners gradually develop a kind of unwillingness to use the target language and they are afraid of answering questions in class. This may explain partially the silence problem in Chinese classrooms. Does this indicate that the students are mentally blocked, passive and dare not express their own ideas frankly in class? Can we further infer that the students try to avoid being corrected and find safer ways for EFL learning, i.e. learning by comprehension but not by production? This still needs to be further explored.

As far as (8) is concerned, Table 6 – 37 demonstrates that in all the three schools, the learners reported that their teachers sometimes spoke in English, sometimes in Chinese, but never totally in English or in Chinese. But as to the students, over 49%

of them reported that they asked questions in Chinese. 16% of the students tried to ask questions in English and 34.6% of the students asked questions in class sometimes in English and sometimes in Chinese. The tendency in the three schools is more or less the same. This shows that Chinese was still the main language for communication in English class in these schools. Admittedly, the use of the mother tongue for beginners might be necessary and helpful, yet for the students in this experiment, who were middle school students in their sixth year of English learning, too frequent use of the mother tongue in the EFL class may not be as helpful as expected. When assessing and analyzing the writing papers, the author found that most students were in fact doing translations. Their sentence structures are based on Chinese, which can be seen from the discussion of the errors in the experiment. Studies have shown that too much dependence on the mother tongue causes negative transfer. Early contrastive analysis on learners' errors in SLL and FLL has testified this point. This does not mean that it is better to discard the use of the mother tongue in learning a foreign language. In fact, appropriate use may speed up EFL learning, especially when a new concept is introduced. Learners can also make use of mother language structures to learn English. In fact in this investigation, learners have been found to employ their native language as a kind of learning strategy. The problem is that when adequate linguistic knowledge has been introduced, learners should be encouraged to produce the target language and communicate in this language, which might result in faster intake of the target language system.

As for (9), the teachers' allocation of time in class, Table 6 – 38 demonstrates that most students reported that their teachers spent most of the time in explaining words and rules. The students had few opportunities to practise using English. This finding is consistent with the findings about (10). Table 6 – 39 (for (10)) shows that more than half of the students reported that they *Seldom* or *Never* had opportunities to interact with each other or with their teachers in English in Class. This is what most EFL classes are usually like in Chinese secondary schools. Learners are crammed with linguistic knowledge but have few opportunities to use what they have learnt.

The investigation of the teaching process in these schools provides for us what teachers and learners were doing in their English classes in these schools. Taking all the above-mentioned points into consideration, an inference of the current state of the nature of input can be drawn.

It can be seen from all the investigation results that EFL learning and instruction in Chinese secondary schools are heavily influenced by the NMET, hence the advocacy of doing *MC exercises*, *timed writing* and *supplementary reading* in and out of class. This is clearly a strong backwash effect of the NMET, as has been discussed by Li (1993). However, the excessive advocacy of doing MC exercises brings about problems. For a test, the use of MC format increases the reliability, especially for a large-scale test in China. However, the MC format has its own limitations in the coverage of language samples. The test of linguistic forms in single sentences which are decontextualized in nature can easily lead teachers and students astray. Teachers in secondary schools spend little time in thinking over how to improve the MC exercises to make them more contextualized. Most of them just take books with MC exercises advertising a good and faster way for the preparation of the NMET and assign the exercises as homework to their students. However, as has been stated above, the reform of the NMET does show its positive effect. This can be seen from the survey results that there was a tendency to advocate the exercises of *timed writing* and *supplementary reading* in the investigated schools.

Results about the other factors in the investigation of the teaching process are also impressive if we examine them from another angle. The activities these teachers usually employed, the teachers' attitudes to the learners' errors, the homework types the teachers usually assigned to their students, the opportunities for interaction in class, the frequent use of Chinese in class, the time spent on words and rules explanation, the focus of these teachers in their teaching, and the learners' self evaluation of their strong and weak aspects in language competence indicate that the emphasis of EFL learning in secondary schools is mainly on the learning of linguistic knowledge in decontextualized situations. Some attention has also been given to the training of more comprehensive skills like reading comprehension and writing. This could partly be the effect of the NMET, and partly the effect of the Traditional Approach in EFL teaching. We cannot simply conclude that the teaching approach in secondary schools are on the traditional side, but at least in these schools, it can be seen clearly that the teachers' techniques and methods show the tendency of more a Grammar-Translation Methodology (GTM) than of a Structuralist Approach (SA) or a Communicative Approach in nature (CA). Nonetheless, it is still too absolute to conclude that the teaching approaches that are prevailing in these schools are purely the GTM. It seems that all these approaches are mixed together, but with the emphasis on the former two. The frequent use of MC exercises by teachers and learners in EFL teaching and learning reminds us of the SA. The use of translation, sentence analysis, writing and reading reminds us of the TA. Besides, the explanation of words and rules for most of the time in class by teachers, few chances of interaction for the learners, the particular attention to vocabulary and grammar learning, and most of the homework types all remind us of the TA. One may argue, perhaps, that the employment of different activities is not important, for any kind of activities can be made meaningful, such as the activities of *Translation*, *Dictation*, etc. This is true. The point is what lies in the teachers' minds. If these teachers had no clear understandings of when, how and why to intervene the learners' learning process, they would simply teach by their intuitions. Translation and dictation might have been carried out at word or sentence level rather than at discourse level. Learners under this instruction would certainly feel baffled when they were put in realistic language contexts. In fact, the results from the questionnaire for the teachers have demonstrated that most of the teachers in these schools were only familiar with the TA. This helps us conclude that in these secondary schools, the TA still plays an important role.

The investigation results also indicate that most teachers and learners in these schools paid much attention to the reception of linguistic knowledge and little attention to production. This can be drawn from the great amount of time spent by teachers for the explanation of rules and words, the requirement for the students to review rules after class, the few chances for in-class interaction, the supply of a great deal of supplementary readings, and so on. Although attempts have been made to pay attention to writing, most learners do not like it very much. Learners' affective factors may work to inhibit their real learning under such circumstances.

To conclude, the discussion above helps us infer that the classroom instruction in these secondary schools is mainly form-based instruction, hence the form-based input. Most learners, heavily influenced by this kind of instruction, chose form-based learning strategies, such as memorizing vocabulary, doing MC exercises, etc. Most of the linguistic knowledge might have been imparted in decontextualized situations. Since these EFL learners were seldom exposed to the target language in communicative situations, it was impossible for them to apply what they have learnt to contextualized situations. Thus, the linguistic knowledge they have learnt could only be a kind of *fragmented declarative knowledge* stored in the mind as any other kinds of encyclopedic knowledge picked up here and there. This kind of knowledge is easily forgotten after a short period of time if it is not consolidated, for it is not systematic and not associated with its relevant contexts. Learning under such circumstances is not a voluntary act, rather a process of passively receiving knowledge, which can easily raise learners' affective filter to the unfavorable high level to function, and inhibit learners from voluntarily noticing the relationship between the forms they learnt and their meanings in relevant contexts. Hence, favorable conditions for the mapping of the forms with their meanings cannot be satisfied, conceptual links cannot be established, and therefore, learning does not actually take place. This explains why so many secondary school graduates are unable to carry out simple communicative tasks in English after time and effort has been spent. Many adult EFL learners have to start from the very beginning when they go to night schools or colleges to consolidate their English, for they have forgotten most of the linguistic knowledge they have learnt in their secondary schools. This also helps us explain the learners' differences in their performance of the KT and the WT. Since the linguistic knowledge in the KT was put in decontextualized situations, and was in discrete forms, most learners found it easy to accomplish the KT. But to accomplish the WT, the required linguistic knowledge needed to be retrieved, rearranged, and put into contextualized situations. Tasks of this kind require knowledge of a communicative nature. Learners, who have not been given this kind of training, will certainly find it difficult. But the final aim for any foreign language learning should be communication. If the EFL learners cannot apply what they have learnt to realistic communication, these learners cannot be considered to have mastered the English language system. The nature of classroom instruction determines the nature of the input. In naturalistic second language acquisition situations, if instruction cannot provide learners with favourable input, learners, with strong motivations, can still find opportunities to be exposed to the target language. But in foreign language learning situations, the input of a foreign language comes mainly from classroom, therefore, the quantity and the quality of input are both crucially important. This brings us to the question again: "What kinds of knowledge should we aim at in EFL learning?", which is a question we need to ask again and again whenever we start learning or teaching a language.

However, there are no "good" or "bad" language teaching techniques. Any language teaching techniques can help to produce the best language user if they are adjusted well to the learner, the social needs, the learning process, and the final goal of learning. The problem does not lie in the techniques employed by the teachers, but the principles that guide the use of these techniques. The TA has been criticized for producing learners who know about the target language but cannot use it, because the TA-based class is characterized by the explanation of rules and new words in a given text, and learners have few opportunities to participate in meaningful and realistic communicative interaction. The SA has been severely attacked for its view of language learning as a kind of mechanical training or a habit formation process. Learners are then trained to do all kinds of pattern drills which focus on isolated linguistic features. This kind of learning, on the one hand, strangles the learner's creativity, and on the other hand, deprives the language of its value, for it simply takes the language out of its context. Thus, the knowledge the learner attains in the end is discrete and unsystematic. Hence, it is not the teaching techniques under the TA or SA that are criticized, rather the principles behind. Language learning is conducted among human beings, which should never be ignored. Compared with the previous two approaches, the communicative approach embodies more of the development of such modern sciences as psychology, linguistics, cognitive psycholinguistics, anthropology, educational linguistics, etc. whose principles are also good reflections of SLA research findings. In line with this inquiry, language is then acquired as a system, a mapping of form and meaning, and an integration of different conpetencies. Language learner is regarded as intelligent beings who have the ability to manage the business of language learning. Thus, when a learner learns a language, he is at the same time developing his whole-person competence, and hence, developing the ability to communicate in the target language. A language learner grows with his learning. The CA advocates a quite different learning process from the TA and the SA. Although the CA also encounters challenges from different aspects, its basic dynamic, integrative and holistic view of language, language learning and the language learner is still very powerful and enlightening.

7.2.2 Case analysis

In order to gain a deeper understanding of the EFL learning situations in these secondary schools, a case analysis for the students was also conducted.

Ten students were randomly sampled from the 231 students, i.e. one from every 23 students. For each student, his scores in the KT and the WT and his responses to the QL were put together to see how he performed in the KT and the WT and whether his/

her answers to the items in the QL corresponded with his performance. Among the ten students, three were from the low level group, four from the average level group and three from the top level group. They were sampled according to their position in the list ordered by their scores. Since the analysis about the performance of the total number of students in the KT and the WT has been conducted, the analysis here was only considered as a piece of supporting evidence for group analysis. Thus, to spare space, only the results of three of the ten students were presented. Each of the three students was the first of that sampled group. In order to see clearly, all the data were displayed in table form for the three students, and the scores for the sub-variables in the KT and the WT were in percentage form. The data for the three students are displayed in Appendix 5.

The results of the three students' performance in the KT and the WT and their responses to the QL accord with the results that have been discussed when all students were taken into consideration. Student No. 1 (from the low level group) performed rather poorly in the WT compared with the other two students. For the GL, he knew 82.00 per cent, but he could only use correctly 35.04 per cent of them. For the other 64.96% of the GL, he was either unable to recall them when needed, or unable to use them correctly, or even had no idea about them although it was certain that his teachers had imparted these elements in class all through his EFL learning period. When the sub-variables were examined, it was found that this student could recognize or recall 89.09% and 80.95% of the rules of morphological forms and verb forms in sentences respectively. When expressing the ideas contained in the writing tasks, however, he could only produce correctly 14.71 and 11.11 per cent of them respectively. The apparent disproportion between these scores indicates that this student acquired little of the grammatical knowledge his teachers had imparted to him. For the two writing tasks, many of the messages were lost. For Task One (about Jordan) in the WT, he could only convey one of the eleven ideas correctly. For the other ideas, he conveyed them either inappropriately or wrongly. For Task Two (the letter), he could only convey one of the ideas completely and accurately, while other ideas were either lost or conveyed wrongly. It was obvious that this student had a lot of difficulty in producing and organsing his ideas. He produced sentences like "Though Jordan don't play gram, he still is the greatly basketball player.", or "But when Michael Jordan have got what he wanted." But the same student in the KT could recall very well the rule of the superlative degree of adjectives and the third person singular form of the simple present tense of verbs. Student No. 2 (from the average level group) and Student No. 3 (from the top level group) show similar tendencies but with relatively a narrower gap between her KT scores and WT scores. Student No. 2 conveyed three of the eleven ideas completely and correctly for Task One and one of the eight ideas correctly for Task Two. But he produced sentences like "I heard my friend you like to collect stamps." and "I am like to collect stamps, too.", etc. This student could recognize well the gerund form after the verb "like" in sentences in the KT. The third student (Student No. 3) could convey six of the eleven ideas correctly for Task One and two of the eight ideas correctly for Task Two. But she was unable to tell the difference between the pronoun "they" and the pronoun "them" in use. Thus, she produced a sentence like "I hope you will like they."

When we probed into the students' responses to the QL, a subtle difference was found among the three students' learning processes.

Student No. 1 and Student No. 2 started learning English later than Student 3, and they did not obtain any help from their parents. Student No. 3, however, had the opportunity to learn English from her parents before she entered school. It is still uncertain whether early learning is better than later learning in theory, but research in second language acquisition indicates that children do acquire a second language faster and easier than adult beginners (White, 1989).

The three students also differ in the degree of outside class language exposure. Student No. 1 had little language exposure after class. Student No. 2 attempted to read some English readers or speak to his sister. Student No. 3 managed to listen, speak, read and write in English after class sometimes. She was moderately exposed. Her responses show that she attempted to listen to "American Oral English" (a textbook), to speak to her parents in English, and to write letters in English.

The difference among the three students can also be seen in their employment of learning strategies. Among the six types of learning strategies, Student No. 1 only definitely used *metacognitive strategies*, Student No. 2 only definitely used *memory strategies*, while Student No. 3 definitely employed five of the learning strategies. The frequent use of learning strategies has been pointed out to be a feature of good language learner (Oxford, 1990; Stern 1983).

When the students were required to evaluate themselves in English learning, Student No. 1 did not seem to have any confidence in himself. His answer is "None is good". Students No. 2 and No. 3, however, believed that they were strong in *Pronunciation*, *Vocabulary*, *Grammar* and *Reading comprehension*. Students No. 2 and No. 3's responses correspond with their teachers' evaluation and their performance in the KT and the WT.

The three students show similar tendencies in the methods they used after class to consolidate their learning, i.e. *memorizing new words and grammatical rules* and *reviewing lesson notes and doing exercises.* Student No. 3 did something more, i.e. *keeping a diary and doing some controlled writing exercises.* In general, these students mainly learn their English in the way they learn other subjects.

Generally speaking, although the three students of different levels do not show great differences in their learning processes, it can be seen, however, that Student No. 3 had paid more attention to meaning-oriented learning and had attempted to use what she had learnt, while Students No. 1 and No. 2 had few chances to use what they had learnt and their learning processes showed a form-based tendency. This might help us to explain why Student No. 3 performed better than Students No. 1 and No. 2 in the WT although her KT total score was not so different from theirs.

7.2.3 Analysis of the questionnaire for the teachers (QT)

The questionnaire for the teachers (QT) is mainly concerned with background information with a purpose to gain a general picture of what these teachers think and do in their teaching.

Three sections (II, III, IV) were particularly written to help us to infer the teaching approaches these teachers might apply, i.e. the teachers' general knowledge of teaching approaches, the teachers' views about language competence and what they actually did in their teaching. The frequency results show that in Section I, 56.1% of the teachers in these schools heard of Grammar-Translation Method (GTM or TA) and 41.5% of them responded that they were familiar with GTM. For the other seven approaches, the percentage of the teachers who selected "Yes" is not over 40. Section II is about the teachers' views of language competence. The teachers were asked about the relatively important aspects in their teaching. Frequency results show that more than 60% of the teachers selected *Pronunciation*, *Vocabulary*, *Listening*, and *Speaking*. As to the aim in teaching, 65.9% of the teachers responded that they aimed at preparing students for the NEE. More than 50% of the teachers believed that a good learner meant that he could easily accomplish simple communicative tasks. About 61% of the teachers responded that the focus of testing should be on language use.

Frequency results for Section III demonstrate that activities which are advocated by Grammar-Translation Method were generally used by these teachers. Over 50% of the teachers selected the activities like *Reading Aloud*, *Sentence Transformation*, *Reciting Sentence Patterns*, and *Doing Multiple Choice Exercises*. Few teachers selected the other activities like *Listening Comprehension*, *Conducting Realistic Conversations*, *Guided Writing*, etc. As for the homework types, over 60% of the teachers reported that they often assigned the following types of homework: *Memorizing Vocabulary*, *Doing Supplementary MC Exercises*, *Reciting Text*, and *Making Sentences with New Words and Phrases*. Around 40 to 50% of the teachers usually assigned students the types of homework like *Reading Aloud*, *Translation*

Exercises, and *Reading Supplementary Materials*. Over 55% of the teachers responded that the test methods which were frequently used in class were *Multiple Choice Items*, *Sentence Transformation*, *Asking Questions on the Underlined Parts*, *Translating Sentences*, *Sentence Completion*, *Reading Comprehension* and *Cloze*. These teachers were also requested to evaluate their students' strong aspects in English. Over 61% of the teachers believed that their students were strong in *Pronunciation*. Around 40% to 50% of the teachers believed that their students were strong in *Vocabulary*, *Grammar* and *Reading comprehension*. These results agree with the learners' responses.

The results demonstrate that these teachers' views about EFL competence do not accord with their practice in teaching. It seems that these teachers were partially accepting the idea that EFL teaching should aim at the successful use of the target language. Nevertheless, they have not made an attempt to make changes in their teaching practice yet. The teachers in these schools generally employed the Traditional Approach which emphasizes grammar learning and the training of reading skill which were receptive basically. Opportunities were also given to the students for practising using the language, but these practices were mainly meant for the practising of discrete units of the target language than to practise using the combinations of those units in situated contexts. The heavy influence of the NMET in these schools can be seen from the frequent use of *Cloze* test format and *Multiple Choice* test format. The results in the QL and the QT all indicate that exercises of the MC format are one of the major activities and homework types in EFL learning and teaching.

The discussions about the experimental results and the investigation results demonstrate that the students in this study were strong in grammatical competence and weak in communicative competence. They were strong in discrete linguistic knowledge, but weak in discourse linguistic knowledge. The investigation about the learning process and the teachers' teaching process shows that the students spent more time in learning discrete language units than in fostering the ability to combine larger units in contextual situations. The role of output has not been identified yet, hence few productive classroom activities were assigned to the students. Most of the students failed to express the essential ideas contained in the writing tasks which involve knowledge of a holistic nature, but performed very well in the KT which requires knowledge of a grammatical nature. The learning process of the students in the low level group (the low score holders in WTTOTL) shows a tendency of a more form-based nature, while the learning process of the students in the top level group (the high score holders in WTTOTL) shows a tendency of a more meaning-based nature. This implies that the learners' different kinds of performance in the devised tasks mainly come from their employment of different types of knowledge represented in their minds. To accomplish communication-oriented tasks involves the calling for acquired proceduralized knowledge system, while to accomplish fact-oriented tasks involves the activating of declarative knowledge mainly.

In short, the investigation of the teaching process in these schools indicates that in the EFL learning classes in these schools, the quantity of declarative linguistic knowledge input seems to be adequate, but the quality of the input does not seem to satisfy the needs for EFL development. We thus conclude that the nature of the input in these schools is in general of a more discrete nature than of a holistic nature, of a more decontextualized nature than of a contextualized nature, of a more explicit nature than of an implicit nature although some exercises are comprehensive in nature (e. g. reading comprehension, timed writing) which explains the relative better performance of some students in the top level group. Most of the knowledge represented in the learners' minds are discrete declarative facts rather than interconnected proceduralized system. The input of these schools is form-based rather than meaning-based. The effect of this kind of instruction on learners, which can be seen from the learners' responses in the questionnaire about their learning methods and strategies, results in a more form-based learning than a meaning-based learning. Learners' passive role in learning may also be considered as a debilitating factor to prevent real learning from taking place.

7.2.4 Summary of the discussion in relation to the conceptual framework

Taking into consideration all the factors discussed above and the experimental results, it can be found that the learners are taking a road of form-oriented learning rather than a meaning-oriented one although the investigation also shows that the learners have a preference for activities of a meaning-oriented nature. The understandings of language competence by the learners and the teachers in these schools are mainly "mastery" of discrete linguistic knowledge and good performance in grammatical exercises, although they claimed that they were more concerned with language use in real life. This brings us to the conceptual framework put forward in Chapter 4.

In the framework, two learning approaches are represented. Once the learner obtains the input, there will be internal processing of the input. If the nature of the input is form-based and learners employ form-based learning strategies, with favorable attitudes towards English learning and strong motivations in EFL learning, learners finally devote much time to the learning of linguistic knowledge. With hard work, learners finally could develop a kind of competence — which is grammatical competence mainly. To put it in another way, if learners have few opportunities to practise using this grammatical knowledge, the linguistic knowledge they learnt will be mostly turned into explicit knowledge. This kind of knowledge is declarative in nature, i.e. it is mainly about facts of the language. Little knowledge they learnt can be converted to implicit knowledge, i.e. knowledge that can be automatically employed for communication immediately when needed. The explicit linguistic knowledge, however, can be converted to implicit knwoledge when learners are conscious of what they are learning, and are given opportunities to practise using that knowledge in contextualized situations and voluntarily make use of the opportunities.

The other approach, however, is meaning-based learning,

which occurs in contextualized situations. That is, to learn linguistic knowledge in the environment of discoursal and social-cultural contexts. Learners by this road vuluntarily apply EFL learning strategies of a functional nature and pay attention to the understanding of meaning rather than forms.

The results have provided evidence for the assumption that "a single ability is inadequate to account for the development of language proficiency" (Bialystok, 1981b, p39). EFL learners' communicative competence consists of different aspects of language. Mastery of one does not entail mastery of the other.

The experimental results and the investigation support the framework. Most of the learners in this experiment take the form-based road and hence better achievements in the KT and poor performance in the WT. Most of the students in this experiment have stored in their minds a great deal of linguistic knowledge about English, but acquired only little of it.

The findings are significant in that on the one hand they have provided evidence for some of the existing theories about the role of linguistic knowledge in use, the statement about EFL learners' limited processing capacity, the relationship between linguistic knowledge and composing ability, the possible causes for failed mapping between form and meaning in second langauge development, the difficult aspects for learning for EFL learners the role and the effect of different types of classroom instruction, and sources of error; on the other hand, they have diagnosed the problems in EFL learning and teaching in Chinese secondary schools, and thus they have provided evidence to help us determine the status quo of EFL learning in Chinese secondary schools.

Although direct cause-and-effect relationship between the factors under consideration and the learners' attainments cannot be drawn, the analysis of this investigation does set us thinking about the situation and help us explain the inefficiency of SLL in these classrooms.

7.3 Summary

This chapter provides a detailed discussion of the results presented in Chapter 6. The discussion consists of two large sections: the discussion of the results from the experiment and the discussion of the results from the investigation. The findings correspond with the working framework proposed in Chapter 4, i.e. different types of knowledge representation result in different kinds of language performance, and different learning processes result in different types of knowledge. The knowledge these learners have attained is mainly declarative explicit knowledge which is mainly discrete in nature, and thus undergirds these learners' salient performance in the decontextualized task. The students found it hard to accomplish the writing tasks not because they lack grammatical knowledge, but because they lack integrative communicative competence. These results are closely related to the learners' learning process. This leads us to the final chapter — Chapter 8.

Chapter 8 Conclusion

8.1 Overview

This book was motivated by the fascinating complexity of second language learning process which often perplexes both language-related researchers and practitioners with such daunting questions as "Why do some learners succeed while others fail with the same amount of effort and time?", "What is the nature of the knowledge that is required for a successful SLLner?", "What factors are working behind the second language learning process?" and so on. Attracted by this complexity, an attempt was made to scratch a little of this field by focusing its attention on the final attainment and the learning process of one group of Chinese EFL learners, i. e. Chinese secondary school EFL learners, with the purpose of exploring the possible relationship among the participant factors in second language learning process.

Why do most secondary school EFL learners fail to achieve the expected level of English proficiency after six or more years' hard work? Based on a working conceptual framework, an experiment was conducted and a follow-up investigation was carried out. The experiment was to explore the nature of the knowledge the secondary school EFL learners had "mastered", and the investigation was to act as an aid to find out the underlying factors that might contribute to or hinder effective EFL learning. The findings are mainly concerned with two aspects: the nature of the knowledge attained by the secondary school EFL learners, and the learners' learning process.

8.2 Summary of the findings in this research

8.2.1 The nature of the EFL learners' attainment

The nature of the students' final attainment was coped with by conducting an experiment which consists of two types of tasks, i.e. the decontextualized language task (KT) and the contextualized language task (WT). By controlling the GL, the students' two types of performance were compared. The study was carried out on the basis of a working conceptual framework which assumes the relationships between the different kinds of knowledge and the corresponding performance. The analyses of the variables in both types of performance and the follow-up case analyses help us draw the following conclusions about the status quo of the secondary school EFL learners' final attainment:

(1) The knowledge "mastered" by the secondary school EFL learners under this study is, on all evidence, not that kind of knowledge which is proceduralized as a system, but the type of knowledge that is discrete and explicit in nature and is made up of mainly isolated linguistic units which can be easily accessed only in decontextualized situations, but does not favor free and automatic access in time-constrained communicative tasks.

(2) The results of the statistical analyses indicate that the learners' performance on the linguistic knowledge in the KT can account for 41.1% of the learners' linguistic production in the WT (WTK) and 52.7% of their writing performance. This implies that lexico-grammatical knowledge does play a role in learners' communicative language production. Nonetheless, attention only to the development of forms does not provide sufficient conditions for the full development of the secnod language system, i.e. grammatical competence is only one necessary component in CC. Vocabulary and grammar learning may not work as expected unless it is situated in meaningful contexts so as to make it possible for the mapping between form and meaning to emerge. The learners' poor composing ability cannot only be attributed to their lack of grammatical

competence, but also some other competencies.

(3) Detailed analyses indicate that these learners are now at the stage of isolated linguistic knowledge recall rather than free contextualized knowledge use. Most of the learners can only operate the target language at word or sentence level rather than at discourse level. In other words, this group of learners' knowledge representation is not as well interwoven with each other and systematic as to be able to be easily accessed for communicative use when in need.

(4) The regression analysis indicates that accumulation of grammatical knowledge only cannot guarantee successful language production in contextualized situations, because grammatical knowledge can only account for part of the appropriate production in the communicative tasks.

(5) The analysis of the higher level group's performance in both KT and WT provides further support for Bialystok (1981b, p41) 's statement about the decreasing role of linguistic knowledge information in instrumental tasks, i.e. the better learners perform in instrumental tasks, the less important role linguistic information plays because the decreasing role of linguistic information in instrumental tasks is compensated by an increasing involvement of conceptual information. From this perspective, learners' second language development should involve more information than linguistic information only.

(6) The analyses of the learners' linguistic performance in the productive tasks indicate that function words, verb tenses and voices at sentence level and above sentence level are more difficult than others for this group of EFL learners to acquire.

8.2.2 The learners' attainments and factors underpinning their learning process

The follow-up investigation aiming at the exploration of the causing factors behind was an attempted probe from a process perspective. The five factors under investigation, i.e. *motivations, attitudes, outside class language exposure, learning strategies,* and *classroom instruction* were approached by means of questionnaires. Statistical and qualitative analyses of the results help us draw the following conclusions:

(1) The factors of *attitudes*, *outside class language exposure*, and *learning strategies* were found to significantly correlate with the learners' performance both in isolated linguistic knowledge task and in holistic language use tasks. The learners' motivations as a whole, however, were not found to significantly correlate with their performance. However, when different orientations of motivations were analyzed, it was found that the students' integrative motivations significantly correlated with their performance in the decontextualized task, i.e. the KTTOTL in the KT with $r = 0.1620$, $p < .05$, while their instrumental motivations did not significantly correlate with any of their scores in the experiment. It indicates that these learners' integrative motivations were channeled to the learning of discrete linguistic rules. On the whole, the correlation coefficients are not so high as to help us draw any significant conclusions absolutely.

(2) Detailed analyses indicate that the factors under study were found to play a role in this group of learners' learning process. The learners with higher scores in the writing tasks (i.e. the top level students in this study) were found to be more integratively motivated, to have more outside class language exposure, to employ more learning strategies (Five of the six types are found to be employed by this group.), to pay more attention to meaning-oriented-learning (More indirect strategies are employed, such as Metacognitive strategies, Affective strategies and Social strategies.). Learners without the above-mentioned characteristics demonstrated comparatively poorer performance in the writing tasks.

(3) An in-depth analysis of the factors involved in classroom instruction sketches an outline of EFL instruction and learning processes in these schools. Neither the instructors nor the learners seemed to have developed a clear understanding of what EFL learning should target at. The frequency results indicate that these schools were heavily influenced and manipulated by the NMET, which can be evidenced by the chosen teaching and learning activities. It has been found that the NMET has had both positive and negative washback effect on these learners'

learning and the classroom instruction in these schools, which can be seen from the mixed choices of language instruction methods and form-based and meaning-based activities in these schools. However, as a whole, most teachers employed more activities of a form-based nature rather than of a meaning-based nature. Most learners employed learning strategies of a more form-based nature, too. Discrete linguistic units learning such as grammatical rules and vocabulary was of fucused attention in these schools while language production activities were seldom employed. This group of learners was also heavily influenced by their teachers' classroom instruction methods and their teachers' focus in teaching. The learners' strong motivations were channelled to the learning of discrete linguistic knowledge. The results indicate that form-based instruction played a major role in these schools; hence, form-based learning was induced.

(4) The results also indicate that classroom instruction did not match well with the learners' expectation, which might trigger learners' affective filter and prevent learning from taking place. Learners' factors were obviously not treated seriously in classroom instruction in these schools. The investigation of the classroom instruction indicates that the EFL classes were mainly teacher-centered, and the learners seldom had opportunities to demonstrate their initiatives. The EFL learning in these secondary schools was fully occupied by the preparation for the NMET, which might lead the EFL teaching and learning away from its supposed goal.

(5) An analysis of the observation notes of the learners' composing process indicates that proficient learners were found to have special habits in their composing process. They knew how to plan, organize and revise in the process of writing, while poor writers did not. This finding corresponds with Raimes (1985) 's finding.

The investigation from the process perspective manifests that the factors under discussion have effect on the learners' final attainment of different types of knowledge, and these types of knowledge representation in turn undergird learners' different kinds of performance.

8.3 Significance of the research and the discussions

In summary, this study has raised a number of issues, many of which need further exploration. On the whole, the research has achieved its goal in that it has diagnosed some of the problems in EFL teaching and learning in the secondary schools and laid a foundation for further studies. The methods are empirical in nature with a combination of experiment and survey, and the findings are inspiring. The contributions of this study lies in the following aspects:

(1) This study is the first of this type of large-scale comprehensive study targeting toward the exploration into the nature of the laerners' attainment and their learning processes in secondary schools in China, which provides us a basic sketch of what is going on in Chinese EFL secondary school classrooms. The findings will be useful not only for EFL practitioners, but also for EFL policy makers.

(2) This study has made an attempt to combine two lines of inquiry in the probe into EFL learning problems, i.e. the exploration of SLA process inquiry together with the competence inquiry in language instruction field; hence it is of methodological significance in this type of research.

(3) The findings in this research are significant in providing empirical evidence for quite a number of argumentative statements about second language development in a foreign language context, such as *the role of linguistic knowledge in communicative competence, the role of linguistic information in instrumental tasks, the relationship between explicit knowledge and implicit knowledge, the abilities involved in composition, the role of classroom instruction, the effect of classroom exercise types, the role of learning strategies, the role of learners' affects, the role of outside classroom exposure*, etc.

(4) The framework proposed in Chapter 4 is not only used for guiding this research, but can also work as a theoretical framework to guide EFL language instruction in classrooms, especially for those instructions which are biased in their

orientation toward rules learning only, and those which are on the way of form-based instruction but are intending to modify their instructional methodology. It is hoped that the contributions could inspire future in-depth research in this field on the one hand, and initiate action research for classroom instruction reform and attempts at new explorations on the other hand. However, given that we only studied one age group with limited linguistic features and delimited by the nature of this study and other factors, many aspects have not been discussed fully in this book. Much is left to be done in the future.

8.4 Implications of this study

With the purpose of this research in mind, the implications of this study will be discussed from the following aspects: (1) the typicality of the Chinese secondary school EFL learners, (2) the relationship between grammatical competence and communicative language competence, (3) the problem of the nature of input, and (4) the role of learner in EFL learning, (5) the role of language tests in China, and (6) what this research means for language pedagogy in classrooms.

(1) The Typicality of the EFL learners in These Secondary Schools

The results in this study indicate that the secondary school EFL learners in these schools do not differ significantly among themselves in their learning processes on the one hand, and they are typical of secondary school learners in China on the other hand. This may be related to the similarity in teaching syllabuses, textbooks, and even teaching approaches in Chinese secondary schools. EFL learning in secondary schools in China basically follows a roughly similar national syllabus and a guided list of textbooks. The unanimity of language teaching and learning processes is another feature of language instruction in China. All learners in Chinese secondary schools start English learning almost at the same time with little background differences in language exposure, which has been reflected in the investigation, although changes have taken place in recent years in big cities which require an earlier age of English learning now. The students in these schools show little difference in their learning conditions both at schools and at home. Most of the students find little help from their parents in their English learning. This similarity indicates that the problems found in this study are representative of most of the cases in most Chinese secondary schools, although it is also necessary that future studies concerning Chinese secondary school EFL learners should draw samples from different areas and with different educational backgrounds.

(2) Relationship between grammatical competence and communicative competence

The problem of the role of linguistic knowledge in second/foreign language learning is closely related to how people view the world and its relationship with language, how people view language and its functions in society, and how people view human beings as a distinct group from other kinds of animals, etc. Much has been discussed about the development of theories around the role of linguistic knowledge and communicative competence in Chapter 2. With the aforementioned theories as the basis and the results of this study as references, the author attempts to make the following statements.

Language is cognitively, culturally and socially rooted. Therefore, language, by nature, exists and develops in its dynatnic use. To learn a language, one should neither neglect the cognitive aspects nor the functional aspects of language. Language is mainly for communication. For most EFL learners, EFL is finally to be used as a language for communicating ideas. Therefore EFL learning should aim at communicative competence, i.e. the internalized integrated knowledge system that can be freely employed in real language communication. To learn a language involves more than studying one aspect of language. Grammatical competence is only one component of communicative competence, but not the whole for language learning. It should be given its proper role in the learning process, but should not be given so emphatic a position that other kinds of competence could not have the chances to be developed, especially in instructed classroom second language learning situations when learners have few opportunities to enjoy meaningful communication in authentic contexts. EFL learning might result in better achievements if formal intervention occurs in meaningful contexts and learners' conscious activity is activated so that the construction of form-meaning relationships and the transfer of explicit knowledge to implicit knowledge can be facilitated.

(3) The Problem of the Nature of Input

Among all the identified factors in SLA, the factor of input has attracted most of the attention in this field because of its significance in the SLA process. As has been identified and evidenced in this study, the nature of input plays a decisive role in channeling learners' attention and their choice of processing strategies, hence determining the construction of the internal knowledge structure. Different types of input learners receive and different processes through which learners receive input will determine the nature of the input learners receive. The results in this study indicate that in instructed classroom learning, when instructors' choice of classroom activities, homework assignments and instruction focus are targeted at discrete linguistic forms, learners' choice of processing strategies are also channeled to the form-based strategies such as memorizing rules and vocabulary and doing multiple choice exercises to consolidate the forms. As has been evidenced in this study, learners were found to excel in identifying and recalling explicit and discrete linguistic units like verb conjugations, declensions of nouns, adjectives and pronouns, and all the listed vocabulary, but they were disabled when they encountered more integrative tasks which require the knowledge of a more systematic and holistic nature to integrate those discrete units to accomplish communicative tasks.

Examination of those students who relatively performed better in both the KT and the WT and the investigation of their learning process factors indicate that even in form-based instruction, if learners oriented their attention to meaning, their choice of learning strategies were different from other learners who oriented themselves to forms only, and then their strategies of processing the input might also be different. In addition, implicit learning process was also found to occur in these learners. Thus we infer that the knowledge constructed by these learners must also be different.

Thus, we conclude that even if any learning really occurs in this process, explicit learning or form-based learning may still prolong the learning process, and cause a delayed emergence of the required knowledge system. The fact that a lot of Chinese students' complaint of the loss of what they learnt in their middle schools about English and having to go to training centers for help when they grow up is not without reason. However, although there is still not sufficient evidence to indicate whether explicit knowledge can be transferred to implicit knowledge, the good performance of some students in this study seems to indicate that this might be possible if sufficient conditions are provided, as we point out above that when the learners' attention is targeted at meaning, plus their personal effort and assistance from outside, they could manipulate the form-based input in a certain way to suit their own purpose. Even so, on the whole, formed-based input is still not recommended as the only way of learning a second language, because it is obvious that it twists the nature of the necessary input for real learning to occur. At this point, meaning-based input is recommended for instructed classroom second language learning, in which different components of communicative competence are integrated implicitly together with other subject knowledge in contextualized situations, and in which learner factors are treated seriously. Input with such nature is believed here to be able to facilitate language acquisition to occur faster.

(4) The role of learner in EFL learning

One of the features that distinguish SLA research from early applied linguistic research is that SLA research gives more attention to learners' role in second language learning process. However, most of the studies are from a linguistic perspective rather than from the perspective of the major participants of the process. External factors and learners' language are of more concern than the internal factors whereas learners as social agents and active intelligent growing beings are not given sufficient attention. It is here that Vygotsky's historical sociocultural theory glitters. According to Vygotsky (1981), "any function in the individual's cultural development appears twice, or on two planes. First it appears on the social plane and then on the psychological plane." Learners' development "does not proceed as the unfolding of inborn capacities, but as the transformation of innate capacities once they intertwine with socioculturally constructed mediational means" (Lantolf and Pavlenko, 1995, p. 109). Language is acquired through the revolutionary activity of making meaning (Newman and Holzman, 1993, p. 87), and in this process, "*second* language learners have a *second* chance of creating new tools and new ways of meaning" (Lantolf, 1998, p. 427). Thus, accents, (un)grammaticality, and pragmatic and lexical failures are not just flaws or signs of imperfect learning but ways in which learners attempt to establish (new) identities and gain self-regulation through linguistic means (ibid). Human mental activity, hence, is the consequence of the dialectic interaction between natural and cultural/historical forces. Learners' role as active agents in the learning process has been identified with this perspective.

To apply this perspective to instructed EFL learning, in SLLners' language development, the time and method of intervening should be well designed to match learners' cognitive style, and in-class language activities should be targeted at involving learners in meaningful interactive communicative tasks so as to arouse learners' interest and willingness to learn. Since late 1980s and early 1990s, researchers have noticed the role of learners' attention in learning and indicated that differential attention to different parts of language may result in different attainments, and learners' voluntary role in attending to different types of input should not be neglected (Alanen, 1995; Jourdenais, Ota, Stauffer, Boyson, & Doughty, 1995; Leow, 1997, 1998a, 1998b; Long, 1991; Robinson 1996a, 1996b; Schmidt & Frota, 1986;

VanPatten & Cadierno, 1993; White, 1998; Schmidt 1990, 1992, 1993a, 1993b, 1994, 2001; Gass 1988, 1997; Gass & Svetics, 2003; etc.). When learners' attention is directed to discrete linguistic facts learning, learners' meaning constructing ability will be inhibited, and the connection between form and meaning will be delayed. Learners, as major participants, should be treated as intelligent human beings whose higher abilities can be developed under guidance rather than treating them as machine-like passive receivers, as is reflected in the activities in these schools. This is of particular significance in the Chinese society of a very long history and priority of top-down relationship between teachers and learners. Learning cannot be guaranteed if learners' initiative is inhibited.

(5) The role of language tests in China

One of the impacting factors found in this research is that both teachers and learners in the investigated schools were heavily occupied with the preparation for the NMET, and exercises with multiple-choice format were the widely-chosen exercise type. This is a problem that cannot be eschewed in the future in a country like China with such a big population. The results warn us that EFL testing should not take the same format for too long in case of an induction of negative washback effect. With the reforms being carried on in instruction in recent years all over the country, more integrative tasks are recommended for the measurement in large-scale tests and computerized language testing can be adopted as an efficient means to assist in the measurement if possible. Policies should be made to divert students into different levels of higher or continuing education and give more independence to local educational institutions in their recruitment process. Varieties of assessment should also be recommended so as to relieve the NEE of the heavy responsibility and its decisive role in a student's life.

(6) What this research means for language pedagogy in classrooms

The findings warn us of a possible problematic orientation of language education prevailing in Chinese secondary schools, which may influence learners' whole person development, because facts-oriented learning can break down learners' development of creative thinking and disrupt learners' holistic language competence development.

Therefore, based on the working framework proposed in Chapter 4, and taking into consideration the current EFL teaching in China, the following teaching principles are suggested for possible reforms in second language classrooms:

1) Integrate skill training with culture learning so as to make learning content-based;

2) Contextualize skill and vocabulary development within discourses so as to make learning discourse-based;

3) Orient teaching to facilitative guiding so as to develop learners' autonomy in learning;

4) Channel learners' affects development toward a positive direction so as to arouse learners' learning interest;

5) Increase exposure to authentic language by all possible means with possible variety of modality so as to gurantee sufficient and authentic target language input;

6) Balance communication-oriented activities with necessary expertise guidance in language use so as to guarantee necessary explicit linguistic instruction in meaning-oriented learning;

7) Balance input with output in classroom instruction so as to give learners sufficient oppoutinities to try to produce the language they are learning;

8) Give students training on learning strategies when necessary and possible so as to facilitate learners' autonomy and learning efficiency;

Various classroom activities can be employed to practise the above-mentioned principles, such as *making mock phone calls, conducting surveys or interviews about a country to elicit information, a mock letter to look for a place to live in in a foreign country, writing emails to apply for scholarship of a foreign university, guided movie-watching to help learn about cuture and speech acts, guided reading and writing to summarize gist of discourses, dictation of cultural knowledge, role-playing a speech act*, *writing an advertisement*, *developing a report by a group*, etc.

Language learning will become more interesting when cultural content is embedded. Language learning process, to a certain extent, is a means to experience a new culture. Actitivies with an integrative nature and an explicit linguistic goal may help to facilitate learners' acquisition process.

8.5 Limitations and Future Studies

Like any other studies in this field, when the study was finished, regrets were also found. This study was an attempt to touch upon a problem with unexpected complexity. Although the study basically has achieved its goal and many factors were included in the experiemnt and the investigation, others were unable to be dealt with owing to the lack of time and personnel. At least two limitations were found in this study: (1) the lack of wide-ranging samples of secondary school EFL learners in China, and (2) the lack of detailed studies of the underlying factors. The first problem is foreseeable, yet it is hard to be surmounted. Statistically, EFL learners of different areas should be sampled since China is such a large country. The second limitation is caused partly by the researcher's lack of experience in this kind of research, and partly because of the lack of time and personnel. Thus methods of interview and classroom observation were not employed; hence the factors under study were not fully investigated as expected. Nonetheless, this study was designed to explore mainly the nature of Chinese secondary school EFL learners' final attainment, detailed studies of the interrelated underlying factors were therefore delimited to those that are supposed to be closely relevant to secondary school EFL learning in China. However, the deliberate exclusion of other factors from this study does not mean that they are unimportant. It is believed by the researcher that in fact more studies should be carried out later to find out the causes behind the current findings.

Many aspects concerning Chinese secondary school EFL learning deserve some in-depth investigation. It has been found out, for instance, by some scholars (Ahmad, 1982; Taborek and Adamouski, 1984; Wangsotorn, 1987; Melton, 1990; etc.) that Chinese learners have a different mode of thinking from second language learners in other countries, and thereby exhibit different behaviour from other second language learners in class. For instance, most Chinese learners are usually silent in class and have a preference for listening to teachers. Thus in class, influenced by the Chinese traditional culture which appreciates implicitness or reservation, learners often feel embarrassed when they are asked to answer questions by their teacher. It is still unknown whether these different kinds of behaviour are advantageous to EFL learning or not. Besides, there are few studies on Chinese secondary school EFL learners' learning styles, their performance on other skills, their writing processes, and on how their teachers' instruction influences their learning processes, etc. Longitudinal studies need to be conducted to collect more data about secondary school EFL learning processes. Studies on how to solve those problems discovered in this study need to be conducted, too.

In brief, this study is only an attempt in this field. It does not aim to answer all questions, but aims to delve into manageable problems that are of first importance to the study in this area, i.e. what should be learnt. It is limited in its findings, but inspires us to go further.

8.6 Remarks on language form, meaning and the language learner

The relationship among EFL form, meaning and the EFL learner as reflected through this study and the discussion throughout this book indicates that second language learning is not a matter of acquiring the knowledge pertaining to language forms only, but an interactive process of language form, its meaning and the learner in situated contexts.

Language is rooted in sociolcultural contexts, and gains its meaning in language users' communicative process. Language meaning, although intangible, is actually enclothed by language form, which is in fact a matierialization of meaning of different types. Meaning cannot find its existence without its form, but form becomes void when its content is gauged out. Taking into account this basic nature of language, therefore, a meaning-oriented and contextualized process with a focus on the whole system rather than on the discrete forms in instruction or learning is believed to be more facilitative than the opposite is. Too much focus on discrete facts learning may not only delay learners' development of holistic language system construction, but also does harm to learners' development of problem-solving ability with language. Yet, neither form nor meaning of a second language means anything when language learner is not in. Therefore, whatever language instruction approach an instructor employs, disappointment is bound to occur without being able to engage the learner in the process. By engaging the learner, we mean that the learner's consciousness needs to be aroused, adjusted and channeled to the right goal of learning which is set for and by him/her, his/her affective factors adjusted, his/her personality respected and its development embedded into the whole plan of his/her second language development, and hence his/her voluntary participation in the interactive process of learning, which then can make it possible for learning to take place. It is in this sense that we find that Li (1987) 's addition of learners' cognitive and affective capacity is worthy of particular attention in understanding learners' second language development.

As has been indicated throughout the book, to understand second language learning process, a good understanding of the nature of language, the participants and the interrelationship among all the factors is fundamentally important. We have made our attempts, and are still working on this complexity. Misty as it is in the front, but we are on the way.

REFERENCES

Ahmad, F. (1982). Teaching-Learning at the Basic Level. *TESOL TALK*, 1/13, pp. 8 – 12.

Alanen, R. (1995). Input enhancement and rule presentation in second language acquisition. In R. Schmidt (Ed.), *Attention and awareness in foreign language learning* (Tech. Rep. No. 9, pp. 259 – 302). Honolulu: University of Hawaii Press.

Aljaafreh, A., & Lantolf, J. P. (1994). Negative feedback as regulation and second language learning in the zone of proximal development. *Modern Language Journal,* 78, pp. 465 – 483.

Anderson, J. R. (1983). *The Architecture of Cognition.* Cambridge, MA: Harvard University Press.

Anderson, J. R. (1980). *Cognitive Psychology and Its Implications.* San Francisco: Freeman.

Anderson, J. R. (1985). *Cognitive Psychology and Its Implications* (2nd ed.). New York, Freeman.

Anderson, R. W. (1981). (ed.) *New Dimensions in Second Language Acquisition Research.* Rowley, Mass., USA: Newbury House.

Anderson, R. W. (1984). The one to one principle of interlanguage construction. *Language Learning,* 34 (4), pp. 77 – 95.

Arnold, J. (1999). *Affect in Language Learning.* Cambridge: Cambridge University Press.

Bachman, Lyle F. (1990). *Fundamental Considerations in Language Testing.* Oxford: Oxford University Press.

Bachman, L. F. & Palmer, A. S. (1996). *Language testing in practice.* Oxford: Oxford University Press.

Bardovi-Harlig, K. (2000). *Tense and Aspect in Second Language Acquisition: Form, Meaning, and Use.* Malden, MA: Blackwell.

Bardovi-Harlig, K. & Stringer, D. (2010). Variables in Second Language Attrition. *Studies in Second Language Acquisition*, 32, pp. 1 - 45.

Bialystok, E. (1978). A theoretical model of second language learning. *Language Learning,* 28 (1), pp. 69 - 83.

Bialystok, E. (1979). Explicit and implicit judgments of L2 grammaticality. *Language Learning,* 29, pp. 81 - 104.

Bialystok, E. (1981a). Some evidence for the integrity and interaction of two knowledge sources. In Anderson, R. W. (ed.) (1981), pp. 62 - 74.

Bialystok, E. (1981b). The role of linguistic knowledge in second language use. *Studies in Second Language Acquisition,* 4 (1): 31 - 45.

Bialystok, E. (1982). On the relationship between knowing and using linguistic forms. *Applied Linguistics,* 3, pp. 181 - 206.

Bialystok, E. (1983). Inferencing: Testing the 'hypothesis-testing' hypothesis. In W. Seliger and M. H. Long (1983), pp. 104 - 123.

Bialystok, E. (1988). Psycholinguistic dimensions of second language proficiency. In Rutherford, W. & Sharwood-Smith, M. (eds.), *Grammar and Second Language Teaching,* pp. 31 - 50. Rowley, Mass.: Newbury House.

Bialystok, E. (1994). Representation and ways of knowing: Three issues in second language acquisition. In N. Ellis (ed.), *Implicit and explicit learning of languages,* pp. 549 - 569. San Diego, CA: Academic Press.

Bialystok, E. & Sharwood-Smith, M. (1985). Interlangauge is not a state of mind: An evaluation of the construct for second-language acquisition. *Applied Linguistics,* 6, pp. 101 - 17.

Bialystok, E. & Frohlich, M. (1977). Aspects of Second Language Learning in Classroom Settings. *Working Papers on Bilingualism,* 13, pp. 1 - 26.

Bloomfield, L. (1933). *Language*. New York: Holt.

Brumfit, C. (1981). Teaching the ' general student '. In K. Johnson & K. Morrow (eds.), *Communication in the Classroom - Applications and Methods for a Communicative Approach*, pp. 46 – 51. Essex: Longman.

Brumfit, C. (1984). *Communicative Methodology in Language Teaching*. Cambridge: Cambridge University Press.

Bybee, J. & Scheibman, J. (1999). The effect of usage on degrees of constituency: The Reduction of *don't* in English. *Linguistics, 37, pp.* 575 – 596.

Bybee, J. & S. Thompson. (2000). Three frequency effects in syntax. *Berkeley Linguistic Society*, 23, pp. 65 – 85.

Cadierno, T. & Lund, C. (2004). Cognitive linguistics and second language acquisition: motion events in a typological framework. In B. Van Patten, J. Williams, S. Rott & M. Overstreet (eds.), 2004, pp. 139 – 154.

Canale, M. (1983). From communicative competence to communicative language pedagogy. In J. C. Richards and R. W. Schmidt (eds.): *Language and Communication,* pp. 2 – 28. London: Longman.

Canale, M. and Swain, M. (1980). Theoretical bases of communicative approaches to second language teaching and testing. *Applied Linguistics,* 1, pp. 1 – 47.

Carroll, J. (1962). The prediction of success in intensive foreign language training. In R. Glaser (ed.), *Training and research in education,* pp. 87 – 136. Pittsburgh, PA: University of Pittsburgh Press.

Carroll, J. B. (1966). Research in Foreign Language Teaching: The Last Five Years. In Robert G. Mead. (ed.) *Language Teaching: Broader Contexts.* North-East Conference on the Teaching of Foreign Languages, reports of the Working Committees, pp. 12 – 42. (mimeo).

Carroll, S. E. (2001). *Input and evidence: The raw material of second language acquisition.* Amsterdam: John Benjamins Publishing Company.

Celce-Murcia, M. (2008). Rethinking the role of communicative competence in language teaching. In E. Alcón Soler and

M. P. Safont Jordà (eds.), *Intercultural Language Use and Language Learning*, pp. 41 – 57. Springer Science + Business Media B. V.

Chandrasegaran, A. (1981). *Problems of Learning English As a Second Language*. (RELC: Monograph series, pp. 129 – 81). SEAMEO Regional Language Centre: Singapore University Press.

Chaudron, C. (1990). *Second Language Classrooms: Research on Teaching and Learning*. Cambridge: Cambridge University Press.

Chomsky, N. (1965). *Aspects of the Theory of Syntax*. Cambridge, Mass.: M. I. T. Press.

Chomsky, N. (1980). *Rules and representations*. Columbia University Press, New York.

Chomsky, N. (1981). *Lectures on Government and Binding*. Dordrecht: Foris Publications.

Christiansen, M. H. and Chater, N. (2001). Connectionist psycholinguistics: capturing the empirical data. *Trends in Cognitive Sciences*, 5, pp. 82 – 8.

Cook, V. J. (1996). Competence and multi-competence. In G. Brown, K. Malmkjaer, & J. Williams (eds.), *Performance and competence in second language acquisition*, pp. 57 – 69. Cambridge: Cambridge University Press.

Corder, S. P. (1967). The significance of learners' errors. *IRAL* 5, pp. 161 – 70.

Corder, S. P. (1973). *Introducing Applied Linguistics*. Harmondworth: Penguin.

Corder, S. P. (1981). *Error analysis and interlanguage*. Oxford: Oxford University Press.

Cummins, J. (1979). Cognitive/Academic language proficiency, linguistic interdependence, the optimal age question and some other matters. *Working Papers on Bilingualism*, 19, pp. 197 – 205.

Cummins, J. (1980). The cross-lingual dimensions of language proficiency: implications for bilingual education and the optimal age issue. *TESOL Quarterly*, 14, pp. 175 – 187.

Cziko, G. (1984). Some problems with empirically-based models of communicative competence. *Applied Linguistics,* 5 (1), pp. 23 – 38.

Doughty, C. J. (2004). Effects of instruction on learning a second language: a critique of instructed SLA research. In B. Van Patten, J. Williams, S. Rott & M. Overstreet, (eds.), pp. 181 – 202.

Doughty, C. J. & Long, M. H. (2003). *The Handbook of Second Language Acquisition.* Blackwell Publishing Ltd.

Donato, R. (2000). Sociocultural contributions to understanding the foreign and second language classroom. In J. P. Lantolf (ed.), *Sociocultural theory and second language learning,* pp. 27 – 50. Oxford: Oxford University Press.

Ellis, N. C. (1993). Rules and instances in foreign language learning: Interactions of explicit and implicit knowledge. *European Journal of Cognitive Psychology, 5,* pp. 289 – 318.

Ellis, N. C. (2002). Frequency effects in language processing. *SSLA,* 24, pp. 143 – 188

Ellis, N. (2003). Constructions, chunking, and connectionism: The emergence of second language structure. In C. Doughty & M. H. Long (eds.), *Handbook of second language acquisition* , pp. 33 – 68. Oxford: Blackwell.

Ellis, N. C. (2004). The processes of second language acquisition. In B. VanPatten, J. Williams, S. Rott, & M. Overstreet (eds.), pp. 49 – 76.

Ellis, N. C., O'Donnell, M. B. and Römer, U. (2013). Usage-Based Language: Investigating the Latent Structures That Underpin Acquisition. *Language Learning,* 63, Issue Supplement 1, pp. 25 – 51.

Ellis, R. (1984). Can Syntax Be Taught? A Study of the Effects of Formal Instruction on the Acquisition of WH Questions by Children. *Applied Linguistics,* Vol. 5/2, pp. 138 – 155.

Ellis, R. (1985). *Understanding Second Language Acquisition.* Oxford: Oxford University Press.

Ellis, R. (1990). *Instructed Second Language Acquisition.* Oxford: Basil Blackwell Ltd.

Ellis, R. (1991). *Second language acquisition and language pedagogy.* Clevedon: Multilingual Matters.

Ellis, R. (1994a). Implicit / Explicit Knowledge and Language Pedagogy. *TESOL Quarterly*, vol. 28, No. 1, Spring, pp. 166 – 172.

Ellis, R. (1994b). *The Study of Second Language Acquisition.* Oxford: Oxford University Press/上海：上海外语教育出版社.

Ellis, R. (2004). The Definition and Measurement of L2 Explicit Knowledge. *Language Learning*, 54 (2), pp. 227 – 275

Felix, S. W. (1981) . The Effect of Formal Instruction on Second Language Acquisition. *Language Learning,* 31 (1), pp. 87 – 112.

Firth, A., & Wagner, J. (1997). On discourse, communication, and (some) fundamental concepts in SLA research. *The Modern Language Journal*, 81, pp. 286 – 300.

Fishman, J. 1964. Language maintenance and language shift as fields of inquiry. *Linguistics,* 9, pp. 32 – 70.

Feuerstein, R., Falik, L., Rand, Y. & Feuerstein, R. S. (2006). *You love me! Don 't accept me as I am.* Jerusalem: ICELP Press.

Gardner, R. C., and Lambert, W. E. (1972). *Attitudes and Motivation in Second Language Learning.* Rowley, Mass: Newbury House.

Gass, S. M. (1993). Second Language Acquisition: Past, Present and Future. *Second Language Research,* 9 (2), pp. 99 – 117

Gass, S. M. (1988). Integrating research areas: A framework for second language studies. *Applied Linguistics*, 9, pp. 198 – 217.

Gass, S. M. (1997). *Input, interaction and the second language learner.* Mahwah, NJ: Erlbaum.

Gass, S. M. (1997). Comprehension, output, and the creation of learner systems. In Gass, S. M. *Input, Interaction, and the Second Language Learner*, pp. 134 – 149. Mahwah, NJ: Lawrence Erlbaum Associates, Publishers.

Gass, S. M. (2004). Context and second language acquisition. In B.

Van Patten, J. Williams, S. Rott & M. Overstreet (Eds.), pp. 77 – 90.

Gass, S. & Svetics, I. (2003). Differential Effects of Attention. *Language Learning*, 53 (3), September, pp. 497 – 545.

Giles, H., Taylor, D. and Bourhis, R. Y. (1973). Towards a Theory of Interpersonal Accommodation Through Language: Some Canadian Data. *Language in Society*, 2, pp. 177 – 192.

Givón, T. (1995). *Functionalism and grammar.* Amsterdam, Netherlands: John Benjamins.

Goldberg, A. E. (1995). *Constructions: A Construction Grammar Approach to Argument Structure.* Chicago: University of Chicago Press.

Goleman, D. (1995). *Emotional Intelligence.* New York: Bantam Books.

Goodluck, H. (1991). *Language Acquisition.* Oxford: Basil Blackwell Ltd.

Gregg, K. (1984). Krashen's monitor and Occam's razor. *Applied Linguistics*, 5, pp. 79 – 100.

Halliday, M. A. K. (1993). Towards a language-based theory of learning. *Linguistics and Education*, 5, pp. 93 – 116.

Hawkins, R. (2001). The theoretical significance of universal grammar in second language acquisition. *Second Language Research*, 17 (4), pp. 345 – 367.

Hulstijn, J. H. & Hulstijn, W. (1984). Grammatical errors as a function of processing constraints and explicit knowledge. *Language Learning*, 34/1, pp. 23 – 43.

Hymes, D. H. (1971). Competence and performance in linguistic theory. In R. Huxley and E. Ingram (eds.): *Language Acquisition: Models and Methods*, pp. 3 – 28. New York: Academic Press.

Hymes, D. H. (1972). On Communicative Competence. In J. B. Pride and J. Holmes (eds.): *Sociolinguistics*, pp. 269 – 293. Harmondsworth: Penguin.

Hymes, D. H. (1989). Postscript. *Applied Linguistics*, 10 (2), pp. 244 – 250.

Hymes, D. H. and J. Gumperz (eds.). (1964). *The Ethnography of*

Communication. Washington, DC: American Anthropological Association.

Hornberger, N. H. (1989). Tramites and Transportes: The Acquisition of Second Language Communicative Competence for One Speech Even in Puno, Peru. *Applied Linguistics,* 10 (2), pp. 214 – 230.

Hughes, A. and Proter, D. (eds.) (1983). *Current Developments in Language Testing.* London: Academic Press.

Jackendoff, R. (1983). *Semantics and Cognition.* Cambridge, Mass.: MIT Press.

Jones, S. (1982). Attention to rhetorical form while composing in a second language. In C. Campbell, V. Flashner, T. Hudson, and J. Lubin (eds.), *Proceedings of the Los Angeles Second Language Research Forum,* Vol. 2, pp. 130 – 143. Los Angeles: University of California at Los Angeles.

Jourdenais, R., Ota, M., Stauffer, S., Boyson, B., & Doughty, C. (1995). Does textual enhancement promote noticing? A think-aloud protocol analysis. In R. Schmidt (ed.), *Attention and awareness in foreign language learning,* 9, pp. 183 – 216. Honolulu: University of Hawaii Press.

Kaplan, R. (1967). Contrastive rhetoric and the teaching of composition. *TESOL Quarterly,* 1, pp. 10 – 16.

Kaplan, R. (1966). Cultural thought patterns in intercultural education. *Language Learning,* 16, pp. 1 – 20.

Krashen, S. (1981). *Second Language Acquisition and Second Language Learning.* Oxford, England: Pergammon.

Krashen, S. (1982). *Principles and practice in second language acquisition.* Pergamon.

Krashen, S. (1985). *The Input Hypothesis: Issues and Implications.* New York: Longman Group Limited.

Krapels, A. R. (1993). An Overview of Second Language Writing Process Research. In B. Kroll 1993 (ed.), pp. 37 – 56.

Kroll, B. (1993) (3rd.) (ed.). *Second Language Writing: Research Insights for the Classroom.* New York: Cambridge University Press.

Lakoff, G. (1987). *Women, Fire, and Dangerous Things: What*

Categories Reveal about the Mind. Chicago: University of Chicago Press.

Langacker, R. W. (1987). *Foundations of Cognitive Grammar. Vol. 1: Theoretical Prerequisites.* Stanford, CA: Stanford University Press.

Langacker, R. W. (1991). *Foundations of Cognitive Grammar. Vol. 2: Descriptive Application.* Stanford, CA: Stanford University Press.

Lantolf, J. p. (1993). Sociocultural theory and the second-language classroom: The lesson of strategic interaction. In J. A. Alatis (ed.), *Strategic interaction and language acquisition: Theory, practice, and research,* pp. 220 – 233. Washington: Georgetown University Press.

Lantolf, J. P. (1996). Second language acquisition theory building: " Letting all the flowers bloom!" *Language Learning,* 46, pp. 713 – 749.

Lantolf, J. P. (1998). Review Article: Vygotsky's Zone of Proximal Development and Krashen's *i + 1*: Incommensurable Constructs; Incommensurable Theories. *Language Learning,* 48: 3, pp. 411 – 442.

Lantolf, J. P. (2006). Sociocultural Theory and L2: State of the Art. *SSLA*, 28, pp. 67 – 109.

Lantolf, J. P., & Pavlenko, A. (1995). Sociocultural theory and second language acquisition. *Annual Review of Applied Linguistics,* 15, 108 – 124.

Lantolf, J. P. & S. Thorne. (2006). *Sociocultural Theory and the Genesis of Second Language Development.* New York: Oxford University Press.

Larsen-Freeman, D. (1997). Chaos/complexity science and second language acquisition. *Applied Linguistics,* 18, pp. 141 – 165.

Larsen-Freeman, D. (2004). Reflections on Form-Meaning Connection Research in Second Language Acquisition. In B. Van Patten, J. Williams, S. Rott & M. Overstreet (eds.), pp. 237 – 244.

Larsen-Freeman, D. and Long, M. H. (1991). *An Introduction to Second Language Acquisition Research.* England:

Longman Group UK Limited.

Leech, G. (2011). Why frequency can no longer be ignored in ELT?. *Foreign Language Teaching and Research (外语教学与研究)*, 43, 1, pp. 3 – 20.

Leow, R. (1997). Attention, awareness, and foreign language behavior. *Language Learning*, 47, pp. 467 – 505.

Leow, R. (1998a). The effects of amount and type of exposure on adult learners' L2 development in SLA. *Modern Language Journal*, 82, pp. 49 – 68.

Leow, R. (1998b). Toward operationalizing the process of attention in SLA: Evidence for Tomlin and Villa's (1994) fine-grained analysis of attention. *Applied Psycholinguistics*, 19, pp. 133 – 159.

Long, M. (1983). Does Second Language Instruction Make a Difference? A Review of Research. *TESOL Quarterly* 17 (3), pp. 359 – 382.

Long, M. (1991). Focus on form: A design feature in language teaching methodology. In K. de Bot, R. Ginsberg, & C. Kramsch (eds.), *Foreign Language Research in Cross Cultural Perspective*, pp. 39 – 52. Amsterdam: Benjamins.

Long, M. H. and Robinson, P. (1998). Focus on form: theory, research and practice. In C. Doughty and J. Williams (eds.). *Focus on Form in Classroom SLA*, pp. 15 – 63. Cambridge: Cambridge University Press.

Lyons, J. (1996). *Linguistic Semantics*. Cambridge: Cambridge University Press.

Lyster, R. (1994). The effect of functional-analytic teaching on aspects of French immersion students' sociolinguistic competence. *Applied Linguistics*, 15, pp. 264 – 87.

MacWhinney, B. (1999). (ed.) *The Emergence of Language*. Mahwah, NJ: Lawrence Erlbaum Associates.

Marsden, E. & Chen, Hsin-Ying. (2011). The Roles of Structured Input Activities in Processing Instruction and the Kinds of Knowledge They Promote. *Language Learning*, 61, 4, pp. 1058 – 1098.

McClelland, J., D. E. Rumelhart and the PDP Research Group (eds.). (1986). *Parallel Distributed Processing:*

Explorations in the Microstructure of Cognition. Two Volumes, Volume 2: Psychological and Biological Models. Cambridge, MA: MIT Press/Bradford Books.

Mclaughlin, B. (1980). Theory and Research in Second Language Learning: An Emerging Paradigm. *Language Learning,* 30 (2), pp. 331 – 350.

Mclaughlin, B. (1983). Second Language Learning: An Information-processing Perspective. *Language Learning,* 33 (2), pp. 135 – 158.

McLaughlin, B. (1987). *Theories of second-language learning.* London: Edward Arnold.

Mclaughlin, B., Rossman, T. and Mcleod, B. (1983). Second Language Learning: An Information-processing Perspective. *Language Learning,* 33 (2), pp. 135 – 158.

Melton, C. D. (1990). Bridging the Cultural Gap: A Study of Chinese Students' Learning Style Preferences. *RELC Journal,* 1/21, pp. 29 – 47.

Miller, G. A. (1956). The magic number seven, plus or minus two: some limits on our capacity for processing information. *Psychological Review,* 63, pp. 81 – 97.

Munby, J. (1978). *Communicative Syllabus Design.* Cambridge: Cambridge University Press.

Myles, F., Mitchell, R. & Hooper, J. (1999). Interrogative chunks in French L2: A basis for creative construction? *Studies in Second Language Acquisition,* 21, pp. 49 – 80.

Naiman, N., Frohlich, M., Stern, H. H., & Todesco, A. (1978). *The Good Language Learner.* Toronto: Ontario Institute for Studies in Education.

Newman, F., & Holzman, L. (1993). *Lev Vygotsky: Revolutionary scientist.* London: Routledge.

Norris, J., & Ortega, L. (2000). Effectiveness of L2 instruction: A research synthesis and quantitative meta-analysis. *Language Learning,* 50, pp. 417 – 528.

Nunan, D. (1992). *Research Methods in Language Learning.* Cambridge, UK: Cambridge University Press.

Odlin, T. (1986). On the nature and use of explicit knowledge. *IRAL,* 24 (2), pp. 123 – 144.

Odlin, T. (2008). Conceptual Transfer and Meaning Extensions. In Peter Robinson and Nick Ellis (eds.). *Handbook of Cognitive Linguistics and Second Language Acquisition*. New York: Routledge, pp. 306 – 340.

Oller, J. W. Jr. (1976). Evidence for a general proficiency factor: an expectancy grammar. *Die Neueren Sprachen*, 2, pp. 165 – 74.

Oller, John W., Jr. (1983). "g", What is it?. In Hughes, A. and Porter, D. (eds.) 1983, pp. 35 – 37.

Oxford, R. L. (1990). *Language Learning Strategies*. New York: Newbury House Publishers.

Pica, T. (1983). Adult acquisition of English as a second language under different conditions of exposure. *Language Learning*, 33 (4), pp. 465 – 97.

Pica, T. (1985). The selective impact of classroom instruction on second language acquisition. *Applied Linguistics*, 6 (3), pp. 214 – 22.

Pica, T. (1991). Input as a theoretical and research construct — From Corder's original definition to current views. *IRAL*, XXIX/3, pp. 185 – 196.

Pienemann, M. (1984). Psychological Constraints on the Teachability of Languages. *Studies in Second Language Acquisition*, 6 (2), pp. 186 – 214.

Pienemann, M. (1987). Determining the influence of instruction on L2 speech processing. *Australian Review of Applied Linguistics*, 10 (2), pp. 83 – 113.

Pienemann, M. (1989). Is language teachable? *Applied Linguistics*, 10 (1), pp. 52 – 79.

Pinker, S. D. (1994). *The Language Instinct*. New York: Harper Collins.

Punch, K. (1998). *Introduction to social research: Quantitative and qualitative approaches*. London: Sage.

Radford, A. (1997). *Syntax: a minimalist introduction*. Cambridge, England: Cambridge University Press.

Raimes, A. (1983). Anguish as a second language? Remedies for composition teachers. In A. Freeman, I. Pringle, and J. Yalden (eds.), *Learning to Write: First Language/*

Second Language. pp. 258 – 272. London: Longman.

Raimes, A. (1985). What unskilled ESL students do as they write: A classroom study of composing. *TESOL Quarterly, 19* (2), pp. 229 – 258.

Richards, J. (1971). Error analysis and second language strategies. *Language Sciences,* 17, pp. 12 – 22.

Rivers, W. (1968). *Teaching foreign language skills.* Chicago: University of Chicago Press.

Rivers, W. (1973). From linguistic competence to communicative competence. *TESOL Quarterly,* 7, pp. 25 – 34.

Robinson, P. (1994). Comments on Rod Ellis' s "The Structural Syllabus and Second Language Acquisition" — Implicit Knowledge, Second Language Learning, and Syllabus Construction. *TESOL Quarterly,* 28, 1, pp. 161 – 166.

Robinson, P. (1996). *Consciousness, Rules, and Instructed Second Language Acquisiton: Theoretical Studies in Second Language Acquisition.* New York: Peter Lang Publishing Inc.

Rubin, J. (1975). What the 'good language learner' can teach us. *TESOL Quarterly,* 9, pp. 41 – 51.

Saleemi, A. P. (1989). Inputs for L2 Acquisition. *IRAL,* 27 (3), pp. 173 – 191.

Saussure, F. (1964) [1916]. *Course in General Linguistics.* New York: McGraw-Hill.

Savignon, S. J. (1972). *Communicative Competence: An Experiment in Foreign-Language Teaching.* Philadelphia: Centre for Curriculum Development, Inc.

Savignon, S. J. (1983). *Communicative Competence: Theory and Classroom Practice.* Mass.: Addison-Wesley Publishing Company.

Schmidt, R. (1990). The role of consciousness in second language learning, *Applied Linguistics,* 11, pp. 129 – 158.

Schmidt, R. (1992). Psychological mechanisms underlying second language fluency. *Studies in Second Language Acquisition,* 14, pp. 357 – 385.

Schmidt, R. (1993a). Consciousness, learning and interlanguage pragmatics. In G. Kasper and S. Blum-Kulka (eds.),

Interlanguage pragmatics, pp. 21 – 42. New York: Oxford University Press.

Schmidt, R. (1993b). Awareness and second language acquisition. *Annual Review of Applied Linguistics*, 13, pp. 206 – 226.

Schmidt, R. (1994). Implicit learning and the cognitive unconscious. In N. Ellis (Ed.), *Implicit and explicit learning of languages*, pp. 165 – 209. London: Academic Press.

Schmidt, R. (1995). Consciousness and foreign language learning: A tutorial on the role of attention and awareness in learning. In R. Schmidt (Ed.), *Attention and awareness in foreign language learning*, pp. 1 – 63. Honolulu: University of Hawaii Press.

Schmidt, R. (2001). Attention. In P. Robinson (ed.), *Cognition and second language instruction*, pp. 3 – 32. Cambridge, England: Cambridge University Press.

Schmidt, R., & Frota, S. (1986). Developing basic conversational ability in a second language: a case study of an adult learner of Portuguese. In R. Day (ed.), *Talking to learn: Conversation in second language acquisition*, pp. 237 – 326. Rowley, MA: Newbury House.

Schumann, J. H. (1976). Second language acquisition research: getting a more global look at the learner. *Language Learning*, Special Issue, Number 4, pp. 15 – 28.

Schumann, J. H. (1978). The acculturation model for second language acquisition. In R. Gingras (ed.). *Second Language Acquisition and Foreign Language Teaching*, pp. 27 – 50 . Arlington, VA.: Center for Applied Linguistics.

Seliger, H. (1979). On the nature and function of language rules in language teaching. *TESOL Quarterly*, 13, pp. 359 – 70.

Seliger, H. and Long, M. (eds.) (1983). *Classroom Oriented Research in Second Language Acquisition.* Rowley, Mass.: Newbury House.

Selinker, L. (1972). Interlanguage. *International Review of Applied Linguistics* , 10, pp. 209 – 31.

Selinker, L., Swain, M. and Dumas, G. (1975). The interlanguage hypothesis extended to children. *Language Learning*, 25, pp. 139 – 52.

Silva, T. (1993a). Toward an Understanding of the Distinct Nature of L2 Writing: The ESL Research and Its Implications. *TESOL Quarterly*, 27 (4), pp. 655 – 677.

Silva, T. (1993b). Second Language Composition Instruction: Developments, Issues, and Directions in ESL. In B. Kroll, (1993), (ed.), pp. 11 – 23.

Skehan, P. (1998). *A Cognitive Approach to Language Learning*. Oxford: Oxford University Press.

Slabakova, R. (2010). Semantic Theory and Second Language Acquisition. *Annual Review of Applied Linguistics*, 30, pp. 249 – 265.

Sonbul, S. & Schmitt, N. (2012). Explicit and Implicit Lexical Knowledge: Acquisition of Collocations Under Different Input Conditions. *Language Learning*, 63 (1), pp. 121 – 159.

Spolsky, B. (1989). Communicative competence, language proficiency, and beyond. *Applied Linguistics*, 10 (2), pp. 138 – 155.

Stern, H. H. (1975). What can we learn from the good language learner? *Canadian Modern Language Review*, 31, pp. 304 – 18.

Stern, H. H. (1983). *Fundamental Concepts of Language Teaching*. Oxford: Oxford University Press.

Swain, M. (1981). Immersion education: applicability for nonvernacular teaching to vernacular speakers. *Studies in Second Language Acquisition*, 4 (1), pp. 1 – 17.

Swain, M. (1993). The output hypothesis: Just speaking and writing aren't enough. *Canadian Modern Language Review*, 50, pp. 158 – 64.

Swain, M. (1995). Three functions of output in second language learning. In G. Cook and B. Seidlhofer (eds). *Principle and Practice in Applied Linguistics: Studies in Honour of H. G. Widdowson*, pp. 125 – 44 . Oxford: Oxford University Press.

Swain, M. and Deters, P. (2007). " New" Mainstream SLA

Theory: Expanded and Enriched. *The Modern Language Journal*, 91, Focus Issue, pp. 820 – 836.

Taborek, E. and Adamouski, E. (1984). To seal up one's mouth three times. *TESOL TALK*, 3/15, pp. 88-55.

Talyor, D. S. (1988). The meaning and use of the term 'competence' in linguistics and applied linguistics. *Applied Linguistics*, 9 (2), pp. 148 – 168.

Tarone, E. (2007). Sociolinguistic Approaches to Second Language Acquisition Research — 1997 — 2007. *The Modern Language Journal*, 91, Focus Issue, pp. pp. 837 – 848.

Tomasello, M. (ed.) . (2003). *The new psychology of language : cognitive and functional approaches to language structure* (vol. 2). Mahwah, New Jersey: Lawrence Erlbaum Associates, Publishers.

Toth, P. D. (2006). Processing Instruction and a Role for Output in Second Language Acquisition. *Language Learning*, 56 (2), pp. 319 – 385.

van Lier, L. (1996). *Interaction in the language curriculum: Awareness, autonomy and authenticity.* London: Longman.

VanPatten, B. (1990). Attending to form and content in the input: An experiment in consciousness. *Studies in Second Language Acquisition*, 12, pp. 287 – 301.

VanPatten, B. (1994). Evaluating the role of consciousness in second language acquisition: Terms, linguistic features and research methodology. *AILA Review*, 11, pp. 27 – 36.

VanPatten, B. (1996). *Input processing and grammar instruction.* Norwood, NJ: Ablex.

VanPatten, B., & Cadierno, T. (1993). Explicit instruction and input processing. *Studies in Second Language Acquisition*, 15, pp. 225 – 243.

VanPatten, B. (2004). Input and output in establishing form-meaning connections. In B. VanPatten, J. Williams, S. Rott & M. Overstreet (eds.), pp. 29 – 48.

VanPatten, B. & Benati, A. (2010). *Key terms in second language acquisition.* London: Continuum.

VanPatten, B., Williams, J., Rott, S. and Overstreet, M. (2004). *Form-Meaning Connections in Second Language Acquisition.* Mahwah, New Jersey, USA: Lawrence Erlbaum Associates, Inc., Publishers.

Vollmer, H. J. (1983). The Structure of Foreign Language Competence. In Hughes, A. & Proter, D. (eds.), pp. 3 – 34.

Vygotsky, L. S. (1978). *Mind in society: The development of higher psychological processes.* Cambridge, MA: Harvard University Press.

Vygotsky, L. S. (1981). The genesis of higher mental functions. In J. V. Wertsch (ed.), *The concept of activity in Soviet psychology,* pp. 144 – 188. Armonk: Sharpe.

Wangsotorn, Achara. (1987). Relationship between Learning Modes and the Beginners' Success in English. *RELC Journal,* 1/18, pp. 31 – 45.

White, L. (1989). *Universal Grammar and Second Language Acquisition.* Amsterdam: John Benjamins.

White, J. (1998). Getting the learners' attention: A typographical input enhancement study. In C. Doughty & J. Williams (eds.), *Focus on form in classroom second language acquisition,* pp. 85 – 113 . New York: Cambridge University Press.

White, L. (2003). *Second language acquisition and Universal Grammar.* Cambridge: Cambridge University Press.

Widdowson, H. G. (1978). *Teaching Language as Communication.* Oxford: Oxford University Press.

Widdowson, H. G. (1983). *Learning Purpose and Language Use.* Oxford: Oxford University Press.

Widdowson, H. G. (1989). Knowledge of language and ability for use. *Applied Linguistics,* 10 (2), pp. 128 – 137.

William, J. N. (2004). Implicit learning of form-meaning connections. In B. VanPatten, J. Williams, S. Rott & M. Overstreet (eds.), pp. 203 – 218. .

Willis, D. (1990). *The Lexical Syllabus.* London: William Collins Sons & Co Ltd.

Young, Richard. 1987. 'The Cultural Context of TESOL —A Review of Research into Chinese Classrooms'. *RELC Journal*, 18 (2), pp. 15-30.

Zuengler, J. & Miller, E. R. (2006). Cognitive and Sociocultural Perspectives: Two Parallel SLA World. *TESOL Quarterly*, 40 (1), pp. 35-58.

常新萍 (Chang, Xinping). (1996). *Research on EFL Learning in Chinese Secondary Schools.* Ph. D. dissertation. Guangdong University of Foreign Studies, Guangzhou.

桂诗春 (Gui, Shichun). (1986).《标准化考试：理论、原则与方法》. 广州市：广东高等教育出版社. (*Standardized Test —Theory, Principles and Techniques.* Guangzhou: Guangdong Tertiary Education Press).

桂诗春 (Gui, Shichun). (1988).《应用语言学与中国英语教学》. 济南市：山东教育出版社. (*Applied Linguistics and English Teaching in China.* Jinan: Shandong Education Publishing House.)

桂诗春 (Gui, Shichun). (1990). Social Psychological Aspects of English Language Learning in China. *ELT in China: Papers Presented at the International Symposium on Teaching English in the Chinese Context,* pp. 115 - 137. Beijing: Foreign Language Teaching and Research Press. (《中国英语教学》. 北京：外语教学与研究出版社.)

桂诗春 (Gui, Shichun). (1992) (ed.).《中国学生英语学习心理》. 长沙市：湖南教育出版社. (*The Psychology of Chinese Learners of English.* Changsha: Hunan Education Press.)

桂诗春 (Gui, Shichun). (1993). 语言使用的研究方法.《现代外语》, 3, 1 - 6 页. (Language in Use and Its Research Methods. *Modern Foreign Languages*, 3, pp. 1 - 6.)

李良佑, 张日昇, 刘犁 (Li, Liangyou, Zhang, Risheng, and Liu, Li). (1988).《中国英语教学史》. 上海: 上海外语教育出版社. (*The History of English Language Teaching in China.* Shanghai: Shanghai Foreign Language Education Publishing House.)

李筱菊 (Li, Xiaoju.). (1984). In Defence of the Communicative

Approach. *ELT Journal,* 38 (1), pp. 2 – 13.

李筱菊 (Li, Xiaoju). (1987).《交际英语教程》. 上海：上海外语教育出版社. (*CECL-Communicative English for Chinese Learners.* Shanghai: Shanghai Foreign Languages Education Publishing House.)

李筱菊 (Li, Xiaoju). (1990a). CECL: Towards a more holistic view of language, language learning, and the learner. *ELT in China: Papers Presented at the International Symposium on Teaching English in the Chinese Context,* pp. 47 – 62. Beijing: Foreign Language Teaching and Research Press.

李筱菊 (Li, Xiaoju). (1990b). How Powerful Can a Language Test Be? The MET in China. *Journal of Multilingual and Multilingual Development,* 11 (3), pp . 393 – 404.

李筱菊 (Li, Xiaoju). (1992). How Much English Do Our School-leaving Students Have? —Feedback from a National EFL Test in China. *ELT in China 1992,* pp. 657 – 674. Beijing: Foreign Language Teaching and Research Publishing House.

李筱菊 (Li, Xiaoju). (1993). CECL: an acquisition or a learning course?《外国语高教研究》, 2, 1 – 9 页. (*Studies on Higher Foreign Language Education,* 2, pp. 1 – 9. Guangzhou: Guangzhou University of Foreign Languages).

桂诗春, 杨惠中 (Gui, Shichun & Yang, Huizhong). (2003).《中国学习者英语语料库》. 上海：上海外语教育出版社. (*Chinese Learner English Corpus.* Shanghai: Shanghai Foreign Languages Education Publishing House.)

文秋芳 (Wen, Qiufang). (1995). 英语成功者与不成功者在学习方法上的差异，《外语教学与研究》(3), 61 – 66 页. (An investigation of the differences of successful and unsuccessful learners' learning strategies. *Foreign Language Teaching and Research, 3, pp. 61 – 66.)*

吴一安, 刘润清, Jeffrey, P. (Wu, Yi'an, Liu, Runqing and Jeffrey, P.). (1993). 中国英语本科学生素质调查报告，《外语教学与研究》(1), 36 – 46 页. (Learner factors and language learning achievement: a survey. *Foreign*

Language Teaching and Research, 1, pp. 36 – 46.)

吴旭东（Wu, Xudong）. (1994). English Language Development in P. R. China: A Study of the Impact of Some Learner-internal and Learner-external Factors. *Unpublished Ph. D Dissertation*. The University of Tasmania.

吴旭东（Wu, Xudong）. (1999). 外语课堂环境下的口语非语言方面的发展.《现代外语》,（1）, 1 – 33 页. (Non-linguistic development of oral ability in the FL classroom setting. *Modern Foreign Languages, 1, pp. 1 – 33.*)

吴旭东（Wu, Xudong）. (2006).《第二语言习得研究 –方法与实践》. 上海：上海外语教育出版社.（*Second Language Acquisition*: Methods and Practice. Shanghai: Shanghai Foreign Languages Education Publishing House.)

王初明（Wang, Chuming）. (1997). 第二语言习得中的语义重构.《外语教学与研究》,（3）, 59 – 65 页.（Semantic restructuring in second language acquisition. *Foreign Language Teaching and Research, 3, pp. 59 – 65.*)

王　蔷（Wang, Qiang）. (2002).《英语教师行动研究》. 北京：外语教学与研究出版社.（*Action Research for English Teachers.* Beijing: Foreign Language Teaching and Research Press.)

Appendix 1 Relevant Materials in the Experiment

1.1 The Writing Tasks

Notes: To spare space, the writing tasks will be presented in condensed form. The space left for writing will be omitted here.

UI. 书面表达:

【说明】: 上海出版一份“学生英文报”, 对象是我国的中学生。请用英语为该报写一简短人物介绍, 介绍世界篮球名将乔丹(Michael Jordan)。

关于乔丹的情况介绍如下:

乔　丹　简　况		
性别: 男	国籍: 美国人	出生年份: 1963 年
时　　间	大学期间	离大学后 (继续打球)
比赛项目	篮球	篮球
成　　绩	在许多比赛中获胜	夺得两枚奥运会金牌
其它情况	1993 年 10 月 6 日宣布不再参加篮球比赛, 想多和家人在一起; 1993 年 7 月, 父亲被暗杀; 被称为“巨星”; 当今世界上最伟大的篮球运动员	

〖注〗: 巨星: superstar
(球类) 运动员: player
奥运会的: Olympic (形容词)

【要求】: 1. 要有标题。 2. 短文必须包括上表中所有内容。
3. 拼写正确, 句子完整, 意义连惯, 表达准确、得体。
4. 字数: 90—130。

UII. 书面表达

【说明】: 假定你是广州市第一中学的学生, 叫李明, 平时很喜欢集邮。你有一个同学叫黄华, 是你的好朋友。有一天, 黄华提到他有一个美国笔友, 叫 Peter Smith, 也很喜欢集邮, 并且明年夏天可能随父母来中国旅游。你听后很感兴趣。现在你用英语给 Peter 写封信, 说明原由, 并寄给 Peter 几张中国邮票, 希望他也能给你寄些邮票, 表示欢迎他来广州玩玩, 并希望他来时带些邮票来和你交换。

【要求】: 1. 字数: 90—120 字。
2. 必须有恰当的开头和结尾。
3. 拼写正确, 句子完整, 意义连贯, 表达准确, 得体。

〖注〗: 集邮: to collect stamps
交换: exchange (动词: 可做及物动词、不及物动词; 也可做名词; to exchange v.t. 常和介词 with 搭配, 如: to exchange something with somebody)

1.2 The Minimally Passable Versions of the WT

(Notes: the Grammatical forms and lexical items elicited from these two versions are used as the reference points in the KT and the WT)

For Task One: (94 words)

Michael Jordan—a Superstar

Michael Jordan, an American basketball player, was born in 1963. He is called a "superstar". When he was a university student, he with his team won a lot of basketball matches. After he left university, he continued playing and won two Olympic gold medals for basketball. In July, 1993, his father was murdered. Three months later, on October 6, 1993, he announced that he would not play in basketball matches any more and would spend more time with his family. He is the greatest basketball player in the world today.

Ideas expressed:

1. Jordan is an American.
2. Jordan is a basketball player.
3. Jordan was born in 1963.
4. Jordan is called a "superstar".
5. Jordan with his team won a lot of basketball matches during his university days.
6. After he left university, Jordan continued playing (basketball).
7. After he left university, he won two Olympic gold medals for basketball.
8. Jordan's father was murdered in July, 1993.
9. On October 6, 1993, Jordan announced that he would not play in basketball matches any more.
10. Jordan wants to spend more time with his family.
11. Jordan is the greatest basketball player in the world today.

Listed Possible Structures and Phrases: (for analyzing and scoring)

Idea 1 + Idea 2 + Idea 3: nationality, profession and date of birth:

1. Michael Jordan, an American basketball player, was born in 1963.
2. Michael Jordan is an American basketball player. He was born in 1963.
3. Michael Jordan, who was born in 1963, is an American basketball player.
4. Michael Jordan is an American basketball player and he was born in 1963.

Idea 4. Jordan is called a "superstar".

1. He is called a "superstar".
2. He is regarded as a "superstar".
3. He is named a "superstar".
4. People call him a "superstar".

Idea 5. Jordan with his team won a lot of basketball matches during his university days.

1. When he was a university (college) student, he with his

team won a lot of basketball matches.

2. During his university (college) years (days) he and his teammates won a lot of basketball matches.

Idea 6. After he left university, he continued playing...

1. After he left university, he went on playing...
2. After graduation, he kept on playing...
3. After he left university, he continued playing...

Idea 7. ...and he won two Olympic gold medals for basketball.

1. ...and he got two Olympic gold medals for basketball.

Idea 8. Jordan's father was murdered in July, 1993.

1. In July, 1993, his father was murdered.
2. In July, 1993, his father was killed.
3. His father was killed in July, 1993.

Idea 9. On October 6, 1993, he announced that he would not play in basketball matches any more.

1. On October 6, 1993, he told the public that he would give up playing basketball.
2. On October 6, 1993, he announced that he would not take part in basketball matches any more.

Idea 10. Jordan wants to spend more time with his family.

1. He wants to give more time to his family.
2. He wants to spend more time staying with his family.

Idea 11. Jordan is the greatest basketball player in the world today.

1. Jordan is the greatest basketball player in the world.

(In this sentence, the present tense implies the time.)

2. Jordan is the greatest living player in the world.

For Task Two: (86 words)

Dear Peter,

I am (Li Ming,) a friend of Huang Hua. He told me that you liked collecting stamps very much. I like collecting stamps, too. Now I am sending you several of my Chinese stamps. Will you please send me some of your stamps? Huang Hua also told me that you would visit China next summer. I'll be very glad if you'll visit Guangzhou and bring some stamps with you. Then we can exchange stamps with each other.

Best Wishes !

Yours sincerely,
Li Ming.

Ideas expressed:

1. Introduce yourself
2. Explain how you have got to know that Peter likes collecting stamps
3. Tell Peter you also like collecting stamps.
4. Tell Peter you're sending him some stamps
5. Ask Peter to send you some stamps
6. Explain that you know Peter will visit China next summer
7. Express hope that Peter will visit Guangzhou
8. Ask Peter to bring some stamps with him for exchange when he comes

Listed possible structures and phrases: (for analyzing and scoring)

Idea 1: Introduce yourself:

(1). **state your name or your identity**

1. I am Li Ming. 2. My name is Li Ming.

3. I am a middle school student in China/Guangzhou.

(2) **your relationship with Huang Hua**

1. I am Huang Hua's classmate.
2. I am a friend of Huang Hua.
3. I am Huang Hua's classmate and his good friend.
4. I am a friend of Huang Hua — your pen friend in China.

(1) + (2) = **idea 1:**

1. I am Li Ming — a friend of Huang Hua.
2. I am a friend of Huang Hua.
3. I am a middle school student in Guangzhou. I am Huang Hua's classmate.
4. I am a schoolboy in China and I am a friend of Huang Hua.
5. Do you remember Huang Hua — your pen friend in China? I am his classmate and good friend. I am Li Ming.

6. I am Li Ming, a friend of Huang Hua.

7. I am a friend of Huang Hua — your pen friend in China. My name is Li Ming.

Idea 2: Explain how you have got to know that Peter likes collecting stamps:

(1) **explain how you have got to know the information:**

1. Huang Hua told me that...
2. Huang Hua mentioned that...
3. From Huang Hua I have heard of (about) ....
4. Huang Hua said that...

(2) **tell what information you have got:**

1. ...you liked collecting stamps very much.
2. ...you were very interested in collecting stamps.
3. ...your interest in collecting stamps

(1) + (2) = **idea 2**

1. Huang Hua told me that you liked collecting stamps very much.
2. He told me that you were very interested in collecting stamps.
3. Huang Hua mentioned that you liked collecting stamps.
4. From Huang Hua I have heard of (about) your interest in collecting stamps.

("From Huang Hua" is put at the beginning to avoid ambiguity.)

5. Huang Hua said that you liked collecting stamps.

Idea 3: Tell Peter you also like collecting stamps:

(1) **tell Peter about your hobby:**

1. I like collecting stamps, ...
2. I am interested in collecting stamps, ...
3. I am very fond of collecting stamps, ...
4. I am keen on collecting stamps, ...
5. I have the ... interest ....
6. I ... like collecting stamps.

(2). **tell the relation between Peter's hobby and yours:**

1. ..., too.
2. ... also ....
3. ...same...as you do.

(1) + (2) = **idea 3**:

1. I like collecting stamps, too.
2. I also like collecting stamps.
3. I am interested in collecting stamps, too.
4. I am very fond of collecting stamps, too.
5. I am keen on collecting stamps, too.
6. I have the same interest as you do.

Idea 4: Tell Peter you're sending him some stamps:

(1) **tell Peter you are sending him stamps:**

1. Now I am sending you ... of my Chinese stamps.
2. Now I am posting ... of my Chinese stamps to you.
3. Now I'll send (post to) you ...of my Chinese stamps.
4. Now I am sending ... of my Chinese stamps to you.
5. Here are... of my Chinese stamps.
6. Here are ... Chinese stamps for you in this envelope.
7. Now I will give you ... of my Chinese stamps.

(2) **tell how many stamps you'll send to Peter:**

1. ... some...
2. ... a few ...
3. ... several...

(1) + (2) = **idea 4**

1. Now I am sending you several of my Chinese stamps (by post).
2. Now I'll send (post to) you a few of my Chinese stamps.
3. Here are some of my Chinese stamps.
4. Here are some Chinese stamps for you in this envelope.
5. Now I will give you several of my Chinese stamps.
6. Now I am posting to you several of my Chinese stamps.
7. I am posting several of my Chinese stamps to you.
8. I am sending several of my Chinese stamps to you.

Idea 5. Ask Peter to send you some stamps:

(1) **express your request:**

1. Will you please... 2. Would you please...
3. I hope you will... 4. I'll be glad if you could...
5. Could you please... 6. Can you please...
7. Would you mind ...

(2) **tell what you want Peter to do for you:**

1. … send me …your stamps?
2. … post to me … of your stamps?
3. … send …of your stamps to me?
4. … post … of your stamps to me?
5. … giving me … of your stamps?

(3) tell how many stamps you want from Peter:

1. … some… 2. … a few… 3. …several…

(1) + (2) + (3) = idea 5:

1. Will you please give me some of your stamps?
2. Would you please send (post to) me several of your stamps?
3. I hope you will send (post to) me a few of your stamps.
4. I'll be very glad if you could send me some of your stamps.
5. Could you please send me some of your stamps?
6. Can you please send (post to) me a few of your stamps?
7. Would you mind giving me some of your stamps?

Idea 6. Explain that you know Peter will visit China next summer:

(1) explain how you have got the information:

1. Huang Hua also told me that…
2. Huang Hua also mentioned that…
3. Huang Hua also said that…
4. From Huang Hua I have also heard of (about) ….

(2) explain what information you have got from Huang Hua.

1. …you would visit China next summer.
2. …you would come to China next summer.
3. …your plan to visit China next summer.
4. …you would pay a visit to China next summer.

(1) + (2) = idea 6:

1. Huang Hua also told me that you would visit China next summer.
2. Huang Hua also mentioned that you would come to China next summer.
3. From Huang Hua I have also heard of (about) your plan to visit China next summer.
4. Huang Hua also told me that you would pay a visit to China next summer.

Idea 7: Express hope that Peter will visit Guangzhou:

(1) **express hope**: 1. It would be wonderful to...

2. I will be very glad if ...

3. I hope you will ...

4. How wonderful it would be if ...

(2) **express the thing you hope for**:

1. ...meet you in Guangzhou.

2. ...I could meet you in Guangzhou.

3. ...visit (pay a visit to) Guangzhou.

4. ...you'll visit Guangzhou.

(1) + (2) = **idea 7**:

1. It would be wonderful to meet you in Guangzhou.

2. I will be very glad if I could meet you in Guangzhou.

3. I hope you will visit (pay a visit to) Guangzhou.

4. How wonderful it will be if you visit Guangzhou!

Idea 8: Ask Peter to bring some stamps with him for exchange when he comes:

(1) **express your hope**:

1. Please ....

2. Is it possible for you to ... ?

3. Could you please ...?

4. I hope you can ....

(2) **express the thing you hope for**:

1. ...bring some stamps with you when you come and we can exchange stamps with each other

2. ...bring some stamps with you for exchange when you come

(1) + (2) = **idea 8**:

1. Please bring some stamps with you when you come and we can exchange stamps with each other.

2. Is it possible for you to bring some stamps with you when you come and then we can exchange stamps with each other?

3. Could you please bring some stamps with you for exchange when you come?

4. I hope you can bring some stamps with you when you come and then we can exchange stamps with each other.

1.3 Specifications for the Grammar and Lexis Controlled in the KT and the WT

(1) **Major Vocabulary:** (41) (**N.; V.; Adj.; Adv.; Num.**)

Nouns & N. phrases	Verbs	Adjectives	Adverbs	Numerals
university	tell	great	also	two
basketball match	bear	glad	now	
gold medal	call	(several)	too	
July	win		then	
father	leave		not any more	
team	continue			
family	announce			
October	spend			
student	murder			
China	collect			
America	like			
a lot of	send			
in the world	visit			
friend	bring			
Chinese stamp	please			
next summer				

(2) **Morphological forms:**

1. Noun Plurals: -s, -es; (e.g. matches, medals)

2. Verb Conjugation: -s, irregular forms; (e.g. wants, is); -ed, -d; irregular forms; (e. g. called, murdered, continued, played, announced, liked, was, born, won, told, left); -ing, irregular forms; (e.g. sending, playing)

3. Adj. and Adv. degrees: -er, -r; -est, -st; irregular forms; (e.g.later, greatest, more)

(3) **Function Words:**

1. articles: a, an, the; 2. prepositions: in, for, on, of, with, to, at 3. conjunctions: and, that, when, if, after 4. pronouns: he, I, you, me, his, my, your, each other, some, several (also adj.)

(4) **Basic grammatical concepts**:

1. Parts of speech: N., V., Pron., Num., Adv., Adj. Prep., Conj., Art.

2. Sentence patterns:

(1) S +V +P; (2) S +V +O;

(3) S +V +AD;

(4) AD +S +V +Oi +Od or AD +S +V +Od +to +Oi;

(5) Here +V +S;

(6) Adclause +S +V +O +and +V +O +AD;

(7) Will you please +V +Oi +Od ? or Please +V +Oi +Od

(8) AD +S +V +Oclause

3. Negation: ...would not play..

4. Inverted order: simple questions; inverted order as in "Here +V +S", etc.

(5). **Verb forms in sentences**:

1. verb tense:

simple present tense; simple present continuous tense; simple past tense; simple future tense; simple past future tense;

2. verb voice: active voice; passive voice (simple past tense, simple present tense)

3. sentence agreement: subject-verb agreement

4. gerund

1.4 Specifications for the KT

Notes: In order to present the KT in a test format, the KT is designed to include two large sections: (1) Test of Vocabulary and (2) Test of Grammar. The items in each section do not correspond with the five sub-variables. The items that are included into each of the subvariables are presented below.

1. Vocabulary (VOC): Question 1 and 2 (taking 14% in the KT scores)

Question 1: recognize vocabulary by checking spelling

mistakes;

Question 2: recognize words and recall their meanings;

2. Morphological forms (MPH): Questions 5, 6, 7, 8, 9, and 10 (taking 27.5% in the KT scores)

Questions 8, 9 and 10: recognize the morphological forms of N., V., Adj. and Adv.;

Questions 5, 6 and 7: recall the rules of morphological forms of N., V., Adj., and Adv.

3. Function words (FCT): Questions 18, 19, 20, 21 (taking 12% in the KT scores)

Question 18: recall rules concerning articles and judge whether these statements are accurate;

Questions 19 and 20: recognize conjunctions in sentences;

Question 21: recognize prepositions in sentences and recall their meanings.

4. Pronouns (PRON): Question 22 (taking 5.5% in the KT scores)

Question 22: recognize pronouns in sentences and recall their functions.

5. Basic grammatical concepts (CONT): Questions 3, 4, 11, 12, 13, 17 (taking 30.5% in the KT scores)

Questions 3, 4: recognize parts of speeches or words discretely and in sentences;

Questions 11, 12: recognize basic sentence structures and different types of sentences;

Questions 13, 17: recognize inverted sentence and negative sentence;

6. Verb forms in sentences (VFS): Questions 14, 15, 16, 23 (taking 10.5% in the KT scores)

Question 14: recognize passive voice sentence;

Question 15: recognize different tenses in sentences;

Question 16: recognize gerund in sentences;

Question 23: recall rules of concord between subject and predicate, and judge whether the sentences are right or wrong.

For most of the questions in the KT, only recognition and recalling are needed except for questions 18, 22 and 23 which require some judgment and analysis. For comparison, the morphological forms are deliberately devised with corresponding parts, i. e. Questions 8, 9 and 10 are for the recognition of morphological forms, and 5, 6 and 7 are for the recalling of morphological forms.

The questions are arranged mainly from word level to sentence level. To avoid the possibility that some questions might give the learners clues for answering other questions, the questions are arranged in specified order and the pieces of paper in implementation will be distributed in this order, i.e. Question 1 is (the first piece of paper) implemented first, Questions 2, 3, 4 are (the second piece of paper) implemented after Question 1 has been finished and collected, Questions 5, 6, 7 are (the third piece of paper) implemented after the second piece of paper has been collected, and the following questions will be implemented together. The time required by each part is printed on each piece of paper. The KT is required to be finished within one hour.

1.5 The Knowledge Task

Notes: To spare space, the presentation will be in condensed form. Notes will be added to the part that is special in arrangement.

KNOWLEDGE TEST

(1994. 4.)

年级____________; 班级________________; 姓名______________

I. Test of Vocabulary

1. 请在下列单词中找出有拼写错误的单词, 并在拼错单词前面的小框内用“×”号标出, 没有拼错的不标: (2 分钟后交上)

☐ university	☐ student
☐ basktball	☐ freind
☐ madel	☐ graet
☐ July	☐ glad
☐ world	☐ also
☐ Octuber	☐ annonce

☐ leave　　　　　　　☐ contineu

(Notes: Question 1 is distributed separately from other questions, i.e. on one piece of paper. p1)

姓名________________________

2. 请辨认下列英语单词或词组并快速写出它们的汉语意义: (5 分钟)

university __________	too ____________________
then ________________	basketball match ________
tell ________________	gold medal ______________
July ________________	bear (动词的意义) _______
team ________________	call ____________________
time ________________	win _____________________
family ______________	leave ___________________
continue ____________	in the world ____________
October _____________	announce ________________
student _____________	Chinese stamp ___________
friend ______________	murder __________________
collect _____________	spend ___________________
great _______________	like ____________________
glad ________________	send ____________________
also ________________	visit ___________________
now _________________	bring ___________________
please ______________	next summer _____________
two _________________	America _________________
play ________________	a lot of ________________
father ______________	China ___________________
ot any more __________	

3. 请仔细辨认下列单词看它们属于什么词类, 并用汉语在每

个单词后面写出它们的词类名称：(2 分钟)

如：sister __名词__

stamp ____________ and ____________

win ____________ an ____________

time ____________ from ____________

collect ____________ your ____________

two ____________ too ____________

glad ____________

4. 请辨认下列句子画线部分英语单词的词类，用汉语在箭头后面写出各词的词类名称：(3 分钟)

(1) When he was __a__ university student, he __won__ a lot of __basketball__ matches.

A. he ⟶ B. a ⟶

C. won ⟶ D. basketball ⟶

(2) Three months __later__ , __on__ __October__ 6, 1993, he __announced__ __that__ he __would__ not play __in__ basketball matches any __more__ __and__ would spend more time with __his__ family.

E. Three ⟶ F. later ⟶

G. on ⟶ H. October ⟶

I. announced ⟶ J. that ⟶

K. would ⟶ L. in ⟶

M. and ⟶ N. more ⟶

O. his ⟶

(Notes: Questions 2, 3 and 4 are on Page 2, and distributed separately from other pages.)

姓名________________

(8 分钟后交上)

II. Test of Grammar

5. 请写出下列名词的复数形式: (1 分钟) (注: 只需把词尾变化的部分写出即可)

university ________________ match ________________

medal ______________________ month ________________

stamp ______________________

6. 请根据要求写出下列动词的各种变化形式: (5 分钟) (注: 只需把词尾变化的部分写出即可)

	现在时第三人称单数形式	进行时形式	过去时形式	过去分词形式
bear	________	________	________	________
spend	________	________	________	________
announce	________	________	________	________
win	________	________	________	________
leave	________	________	________	________
tell	________	________	________	________
collect	________	________	________	________
send	________	________	________	________
come	________	________	________	________
bring	________	________	________	________

7. 请写出下列形容词的比较级和最高级变化形式: (2 分钟)

	比较级形式	最高级形式
great	____________	____________
many	____________	____________
good	____________	____________
glad	____________	____________
wonderful	____________	____________
late	____________	____________

(Notes: Questions 5, 6 and 7 are on Page3 and this piece of

paper is distributed separately from others.)

姓名______________________________

(以下试卷在 50 分钟后交上, 若提前做完可提前交上)

8. 请仔细辨认下列名词的不同形式, 并用"×"号在单词后面的小框内标出哪些是复数形式的单词, 不是复数形式的单词不标出: (1 分钟)

例如: workers ☒

复数形式的单词 (用"×"号表示)		复数形式的单词 (用"×"号表示)		复数形式的单词 (用"×"号表示)	
players	☐	worlds	☐	gold	☐
universities	☐	time	☐	friends	☐
matches	☐	superstars	☐		
student	☐	stamps	☐		
medals	☐	family	☐		
months	☐	basketballs	☐		

9. 请判断下列动词形式, 并在每个动词后面用所给的缩写形式标出每个动词的所属形式。(3 分钟)

【注】: 请用下列缩写形式:

inf. (不定式)　　3PS. (单数第三人称现在时)

P. (过去时形式)　PP. (过去分词形式)

-ING (现在分词或动名词形式)

(如果一些词的过去时形式和过去分词形式相同, 你可以在一个词后标出 p., pp, 例如: exchanged P., PP)

to play ____________	told ____________	left ____________
born ______________	likes ___________	murdered _______
called ____________	collecting _______	continued ______
spend ____________	sent _____________	came ____________

announces ______	posts __________	exchanges _____
wins ___________	visits _________	brought _______

10. 请在相应直行下划"√",以指出各形容词是原级形式,是比较级变化形式,还是最高级变化形式。(2 分钟)

	原级形式	比较级形式	最高级形式
例如: happy	√		
more	______	______	______
greatest	______	______	______
better	______	______	______
glad	______	______	______
most wonderful	______	______	______
later	______	______	______

11. 请在右边一列选出和左边句子形式相同的句型,并在英语句子前的横线上写出对应句型的字母:(4 分钟)

____ (1). He was born in 1963.	a. 主语 +谓语动词 +表语 +状语从句
____ (2). Please give me some of your pictures.	b. 状语 +主语 +谓语动词 +间接宾语 +直接宾语 +状语
____ (3). After he left school, he continued studying English and wrote many papers for magazines.	c. 主语 +谓语 +状语
____ (4). I will be very happy if you could come to visit me.	d. 谓语 +间接宾语 +直接宾语
____ (5). At the birthday party, his father gave him a gold pen as a present.	e. 状语从句 +主语 +谓语 +宾语 +连词 +谓语 +宾语 +状语

12. 请按照要求回答下列问题: (3 分钟)

(1) The boy liked playing ping pong very much.

(2) The teacher said that the students must hand in their homework tomorrow.

(3) Will you please help me with this sound?

(4) He is one of the best students in his class.

(5) Please join us in the party in the evening.

(6) I will be very happy if you could come to the party.

〖A〗. 英语句子按照它们的使用目的可分为四类, 现在, 请你在上面6个英语句子中挑出下列三类, 并将它们的号码写在每类句子后面的线上:

a. 陈述句______________ b. 疑问句______________

c. 祈使句______________

〖B〗. 英语句子按照它们的结构可分为三类, 现在, 请你在上面6个英语句子中挑出下列两类, 并将它们的号码写在每类句子的后面:

a. 简单句__________________ b. 复合句______________

13. 请指出下列句子中哪个是正常语序, 哪个是倒装语序? 请在英语句子前面的小框内用"+"或"-"号标出。正常语序用"+"表示, 倒装语序用"-"表示。(1 分钟)

□ (1) When he was a middle school student, he often travelled with his father during the summer vacation.

□ (2) Would you please tell me when the film begins?

14. 请指出下列句子中的动词语态哪个是主动语态, 哪个是被动语态? 请在英语句子前面的小框内用"+"或"-"号标出。主动语态用"+"号, 被动语态用"-"号. (1 分钟)

☐ (1) He asked me to help him with his homework.

☐ (2) His bike was stolen last week.

15. 请指出下列句子中动词的不同时态，请在表明时态的动词下面画线，并在画线下面用汉语写出该动词时态的名称: (2 分钟)

例如: I <u>have studied</u> English for five years.

现在完成时

(1) She is always ready to help others.

(2) Are you staying here till next week?

(3) I was glad to get your letter.

(4) He said he would raise the question at the meeting.

(5) When will he be able to give us an answer?

16. 请辨别下列句子中哪些是含有动名词的句子，并请把动名词圈出。(1 分钟)

(1) He wants to speak more in class.

(2) Mike liked playing table tennis very much.

(3) Having put out the fire, the firemen asked the crowd to leave.

(4) He was doing some sewing when I came to see him.

17. 请指出下列句子中哪个句子含有否定的意义? 请在英语句子前的小框内用“ +”号标出。(半分钟)

☐ (1) His father gave him a notebook as a present for the New Year.

☐ (2) He said that he would not gave up smoking for health.

18. 请指出下列关于冠词的陈述中, 哪些是正确的陈述，哪些是错误的陈述，并请在每个陈述前面的横线上用 R 和 W 标出。(R =正确的陈述; W =错误的陈述): (1 分钟)

______ (1) 不定冠词用来表示“一”这个数量，意思和 one 差不多。

______ (2) 英语有两个冠词，它们是 不定冠词和定冠词。

______ (3) the 必须用在专有名词前。

______ (4) an 经常用在元音开头的名词前。

______ (5) 在形容词最高级前面不要加定冠词。

19. 请在下列句子中的从句下面画线，并请用汉语写出从句的名称：(1 分钟)

(1) He told me that his uncle would fly to Britain next month.

(2) When he was a university student, he won a lot of basketball matches.

(3) I will be very glad if I could meet you in Beijing.

20. 请在下列句子中指出哪些是连词，并请把这些连词圈出：(2 分钟)

(1) After he turned off the light, he left the classroom.

(2) The Arab said that he had never seen such a camel.

(3) When I got home, my aunt was watching TV.

(4) If he made better use of his time, he would be more likely to finish his research.

(5) The sky was cloudless and the sun was shining.

21. 请在下列句子中指出哪些是介词，请把这些介词圈出，并在这些介词下面写出每个介词的汉语意义：(3 分钟)

(1) He told us about his visit to the United States.

(2) It happened to be very windy on the morning of the

bicycle race.

(3) They were invited to an important ball for the first time in their lives.

(4) They worked from 8 a. m. to 6 p. m., with an hour for lunch.

22. 请在下列句子中指出哪些是代词, 请把这些代词圈上, 并在这些代词下面写出每个代词在句中的作用 (即句子成分): (5 分钟)

(1) There are only several of the tickets left.

(2) Some of the books are very useful.

(3) Wang Hong and Li Ping are good friends, but they don't often see each other.

(4) I'll go to see him tomorrow morning.

(5) The moon is shining brightly tonight. It is like a round silvery plate.

(6) Have you a ruler in your pencil-box?

(7) I've lost my interest in physics.

23. 请判断下列句子中哪些句子主语和谓语不一致 (因此句子是错的), 哪些是一致的。请在英语句子前面的横线上用 R 或 W 标出。R 表示主谓语一致的句子, W 表示主谓语不一致的句子。(2 分钟)。

____ (1) Few people study Latin now.

____ (2) Maths are an important subject at school.

____ (3) I likes studying English.

____ (4) His sister was sent to the school when she was ten years old.

____ (5) He often go to school on foot.

____ (6) Mary comes to see me last night.

1.6 Instructions for the Experiment

监考教师指令说明

Ⅰ. 考试顺序及时间安排:

1. 写作部分: 先考写作, 共1小时; 每篇作文30分钟, 请按时收回。

2. 知识部分: 写作部分收回后再考知识部分。共1小时。请按下列步骤分发试卷:

(1) 先发第1、2页, 2分钟后收回。

(2) 发第3、4页, 10分钟后收回。

(3) 发第5、6页, 8分钟后收回。

(4) 发第7、8、9、10、11、12页, 35分钟后可收回, 若学生做不完, 可再给5分钟。

★注意: 为节省时间, 分卷和收卷时可让同一排的学生互传, 以最短时间内收回, 以免时间不够。各位老师可按你认为最快的办法来收卷。

★写作 +知识部分共需时间是: 2小时。请老师们掌握好时间, 以让每个学生都做完为最好。

Ⅱ. 问卷:

1. 学生问卷:

■ 考试前, 请各位老师告诉学生考完后暂不要离开。

■ 考试后, 请各位老师把所带问卷发给参加考试的每位学生，让学生在一星期内填完后交给自己的英语老师并再次强调：问卷对个人无任何不良影响，请学生根据实际情况和实际想法填写即可。

2. 教师问卷：

■ 考试后，请各位老师把所带教师问卷发给所在学校已联系好的负责老师，请他（或她）负责把问卷发给所在学校的所有英语老师填写，并请其把教师问卷和学生问卷在一星期内收回，我们以后再去取回。

Ⅲ. 监考过程：

■ 请各监考教师注意学生的写作过程，如有无打草稿、写大纲、反复修改等现象，若有，请在下面记录下来，并注明学校、班级。

■ 请监考教师转告学生，他们考试的结果会以最快速度反馈给他们。

谢谢各位老师的帮助！

监考记录：____

____

Notes: The "Test Papers" in implementation are printed in the form of a large piece of stencil paper which consists of two pages. Thus, Question 1 in the KT is printed on one piece of paper with two pages. Questions 2, 3 and 4 are on the second piece of paper which is in fact "Pages 3 and 4". Thus the instruction sheet follows the page number on the "Test Papers".

Appendix 2 The QL and the QT and Specifications for Them

2.1 The QL:

英语教学与学习调查表
（学生问卷）

【注】：1. 选择方法：请在你要选的数字前的小框内打一小勾。
▲▲▲▲▲▲▲

2. 凡是没加说明的，都只能选一项，例如：②性别：☑1 男 □2 女

3. 凡是题后加说明的，请按说明选择。

例如：5. 如果在学校正式开设英语课之前你学过英语，是怎样学的？

(如没学过，此项不填)

□1 跟父母学　　□2 请家教正式上课

□3 参加社会上的一些英语班　□4 跟电视少儿英语节目学

5 其他（请自填）____________________

谢　谢　合　作　！

★ 您的姓名？________________

一、学生个人基本情况（此大题请自填）：

1. 性别：________________

2. 出生年月：19 ______年 ______月

3. 现在几班：____________班

二、英语学习经历：

4. 什么时候开始学英语？

□1 小学前 □2 小学一至四年级 □3 小学五至六年级

□4 初中 □5 高中

5. 如果在学校正式开设英语课之前你学过英语，你是怎样学的？(如没学过，此项不填)

□1 跟父母学　□2 请家教正式上课

□3 参加社会上的一些英语班　□4 跟电视、广播英语节目学

5 其它（请自填）________________

6. 你的父母经常给你辅导英语吗？

□1 经常辅导　□2 有时辅导过　□3 从没辅导过

三、个人对英语学习的看法和做法：

●下列几种理由是学生学习英语的常见理由，你对哪一项完全同意而认为是你自己学英语的理由？对哪一项完全不同意而认为根本不是你自己的理由？请在各项选择你同意的程度：

	完全同意	基本同意	半同意	基本不同意	完全不同意
7. 我认为学英语可以帮助我找到好工作	□5	□4	□3	□2	□1
8. 学英语可以帮助我更好了解其它国家的人民和他们的生活	□5	□4	□3	□2	□1
9. 了解一门外语可提高社会地位	□5	□4	□3	□2	□1
10. 学英语可使我接触到不同的人并能和他们交谈	□5	□4	□3	□2	□1
11. 学好英语可帮助我考上大学					

□5　□4　□3　□2　□1

12. 学英语可使我能够象其它国家的人那样做事和考虑问题　□5　□4　□3　□2　□1

●请对下列几种说法选择你的赞成程度:

	完全同意	基本同意	半同意	基本不同意	完全不同意
13. 我从没期望过我能把英语说的非常好	□1	□2	□3	□4	□5
14. 我不喜欢学英语	□1	□2	□3	□4	□5
15. 上英语课前我从不准备, 除非我事先知道老师要检查作业	□1	□2	□3	□4	□5

●请根据你的实际感受选择下列问题:

16. 英语课堂上当老师要提问时, 你常常:

□1 非常害怕被提问　□2 无所谓是否被提问

□3 很主动地回答

17. 在课堂上回答英语老师的问题时, 你总是:

□1 非常害怕, 常常忘了想说的话或担心说错被同学笑话

□2 不能肯定自己的回答是否正确

□3 很自信并对自己的回答有把握

18. 你认为自己的英语下列哪方面能力较强? (可选多项)

□1 都不行　□2 发音　□3 词汇量

□4 语法规则熟记程度　□5 句子成分分析

□6 口语会话　□7 阅读理解　□8 写作

四、课外学习情况:

19. 你经常通过看电视英语节目或听广播英语节目来学习英语吗?

□1 从不　□2 很少　□3 有时　4 经常　5 总是

20. 如果看或听过, 它们多是哪些英语节目? (请自填) (如没看或听过, 此处可不填)

____

21. 你课外经常阅读用英文写的材料吗?

□1 从不 □2 很少 □3 有时 4 经常 5 总是

22. 若读过, 你经常读下列哪些? (如果没读过, 此处可不填)(可选多项)

□1 杂志 □2 报纸 □3 英语小读物 □4 高考习题集

23. 你课外经常说英语吗?

□1 从不 □2 很少 □3 有时 4 经常 5 总是

24. 若说过, 你经常和下列哪些人说? (如果没说过, 此处可不填) (可选多项)

□1 父母 □2 兄弟姐妹 □3 老师 □4 亲戚朋友

□5 同学

25. 你课外经常用英语写东西吗?

□1 从没 □2 很少 □3 有时 4 经常 5 总是

26. 若写过, 你经常写些什么? (如果没写过, 此处可不填) (可选多项)

□1 用英语投稿 □2 书信 □3 命题作文 □4 日记

5 其它 (请自填) ___________

27. 你的英语教师经常给你布置什么样的课外作业? (可选多项)

□1 记单词 □2 复习熟记语法规则

□3 语法填空或多项选择练习 □4 背诵课文

□5 背诵句型并造句 □6 反复朗读课文

□7 英汉互译练习 □8 补充阅读材料

□9 组织会话 □10 用英语写命题作文或日记

五、英语学习方法选取

	从不如此	很少如此	有时如此	经常如此	总是如此
28. 你在记英语单词时经常把单词的语音和拼写联系起来吗?	□1	□2	□3	□4	□5

29. 你经常把你已学的东西和新学的东西联系起来吗?

□1　□2　□3　□4　□5

30. 你经常把你听到或读到的英语材料总结一下吗?

□1　□2　□3　□4　□5

31. 你经常试着不要一字一字的翻译而去直接理解英语吗?

□1　□2　□3　□4　□5

32. 在用英语谈话时, 如果想不起来某个英语单词时, 你经常用手势代替吗?　□1　□2　□3　□4　□5

33. 在阅读英语文章时碰到一些不熟悉的单词, 你经常猜它们的意思吗?　□1　□2　□3　□4　□5

34. 你经常制定计划以能有更多的时间学习英语吗?

□1　□2　□3　□4　□5

35. 你经常关注着你的英语有无进步吗?

□1　□2　□3　□4　□5

36. 你经常和别人谈你学英语的感受吗?

□1　□2　□3　□4　□5

37. 尽管你很害怕说错, 但你仍经常鼓励自己说英语?

□1　□2　□3　□4　□5

38. 你经常和其他同学练习说英语吗?

□1　□2　□3　□4　□5

39. 课堂上你经常试着用英语回答问题吗?

□1　□2　□3　□4　□5

40. 你在课外经常通过下列哪种方法巩固所学英语? (可选多项)

□1 学语法、记单词　□2 反复朗读课文

□3 做练习题　□4 复习课堂笔记

□5 听英语磁带　□6 写日记或其它写作练习

□7 和同学说英语

六、英语学习中的重点:

41. 对于英语学习, 你认为下列哪个更重要?

□1 牢记语法规则、词汇

□2 能用英语进行简单生活会话和写作

42. “课堂上不学习语法规则和词汇，心里感到不踏实。”你同意这种说法吗？

□1 同意 □2 有点同意 □3 不太同意

□4 不同意 □5 不知道

七、英语课堂上英语学习情况及看法：

43. 课堂上你们经常进行下列哪方面的活动？(可选多项)

□1 朗读单词、课文 □2 句型替换操练 □3 背诵课文或句型

□4 背诵语法规则 □5 做多项选择练习题

□6 听写单词或短文 □7 英汉互译练习

□8 小组或两人模拟生活会话 □9 听英语磁带回答问题

□10 限定时间和题目写作文

44. 你喜欢第43题中的哪种练习方法？(可选多项)

□1 □2 □3 □4 □5 □6

□7 □8 □9 □10

45. 在课堂上，你的教师经常按下列哪种方法讲课？

□1 大多时间讲授语法知识

□2 讲的较少而让学生练的较多

46. 你觉得你的教师在课堂上对下列哪方面强调较多？(可选多项)

□1 发音准确 □2 熟记词汇 □3 熟记语法规则

□4 听力 □5 阅读理解能力

□6 口头表达能力 □7 写作能力

47. 在英语课堂上，你和老师或和同学用英语交流看法的机会多吗？

□1 从没有 □2 很少有 □3 有时有

□4 有一些 □5 很多

48. 课堂上当你发言出错时，你的老师经常怎样处理？

□1 马上让你停下来给你纠正

□2 等你发言完后再给你指出，不纠正

□3 不正面指出，而是老师自己说出正确答案让你自己纠正

□4 有的给指出了并帮助改正，有的没指出

□5 老师不指出，你以后自己发现后慢慢改正了

49. 如果你交的作业出了错误，你的老师经常怎样给你批改？

□1 指出错误并给出答案

□2 指出错误而不给答案

□3 没有评语，只给出正确答案

□4 有的给指出了并帮助改正，有的没指出

□5 老师没指出，你以后自己发现后改正了

50. 英语课上，你的老师经常用什么语言给你们讲课？

□1 汉语 □2 用英语后再翻译成汉语

□3 有时用英语，有时用汉语 □4 英语

51. 在英语课堂上，你经常用什么语言问问题？

□1 汉语 □2 有时用英语，有时用汉语 □3 英语

52. 在阅读或听英语时，你是否经常在心中把句子译成汉语后理解？

□1 总是如此 □2 经常如此 □3 有时如此

□4 很少如此 □5 从不如此

53. 在说或写英语时，你是否先在心中想出汉语然后再译成英语？

□1 总是如此 □2 经常如此 □3 有时如此

□4 很少如此 □5 从不如此

54. 经过中学的英语学习，你觉得下列哪种教学方式能更好地帮助你学好英语？

□1 教师在课堂上逐句分析讲解课文的语法知识和词汇，然后进行必要的句型操练，因为只要学会了这些语法知识和词汇就能把课文学好

□2 教师每节课适当讲解一些语法知识和词汇，然后组织一些摸拟实际交际的语言活动，因为这样才能既牢记所学知识，又能学着使用这些知识

八、学习条件

55. 你认为你们学校适宜你们的英语读物、报纸、杂志多吗?

□1 不知道 □2 基本没有 □3 很少

□4 有一些 □5 有很多

56. 如果你们学校有一些关于英语方面的图书, 它们是下列哪类? (可选多项)

□1 不太了解 □2 高考练习题

□3 结合教材的复习题 □4 英语报刊 □5 英语小读物

57. 你们学校有供你们使用的听音室吗?

□1 没有 □2 有

58. 如果你们学校有, 你经常使用来训练你的听力吗?

□1 从不用 □2 很少用 □3 有时用

□4 经常用 □5 总是用

谢 谢 合 作!

2.2 The QT:

英语教学与学习调查

(教师问卷)

【注】: 1. 选择方法: 请在你要选的数字前的小框内打一小勾。

▲▲▲▲▲▲▲

2. 凡是没加说明的, 都只能选一项, 如: ② 性别: ☑1 男 □2 女

3. 凡是题后加说明的, 请按说明选择, 如: 一、教师个人基本情况 (此大题请自填):

谢 谢 合 作 !

一、教师个人基本情况 (此大题请自填):

1. 性别：____ 2. 出生年月：19 ____年 ____月
3. 从事教师职业的时间：________________年
4. 现在所教 年级 和 班级：__________年级____________班
5. 现在学历 (此题请打勾选择)
□1 无 □2 中学 □3 中专 □4 大专
□5 大学本科 □6 研究生

二、关于教学理论与方法：

6. 你听说过下列任一教学理论吗 (可以选多项)？
□ 1 Grammar-Translation Method
□ 2 Audio-lingual Method
□ 3 The Cognitive Approach
□ 4 The Natural Approach
□ 5 The Total Physical Response Method
□ 6 Suggestopedia
□ 7 The Immersion Approach
□ 8 The Communicative Approach

7. 如果你听说过以上的教学理论，相对来说你对其中哪一种理论最熟悉？
□1 □2 □3 □4 □5
□6 □7 □8

三、基本看法

8. 你现在的教学目标是 (此题可多选)：
□1 训练学生做题的能力，帮助学生考上大学
□2 帮助学生牢记大纲规定的全部语法知识
□3 训练学生怎样用所学英语完成一些实际生活中的简单任务

9. 作为英语教师，你认为下列哪方面能力对学生最重要？(可选多项)
□1 发音准确 □2 熟记词汇 □3 熟记语法规则

□4 听力 □5 阅读理解能力

□6 口头表达能力 □7 写作能力

10. 你认为中学生学好英语是指：(可选多项)

□1 熟记或知道全部所学语法规则、词汇、发音规则

□2 在平时及期终考试语法知识测验中经常取得好成绩

□3 句子分析总是很准确

□4 虽然英语说的不流利，发音却很准确，考试中也很少语法错误

□5 虽然意义不太恰当，讲的句子语法都正确

□6 高考笔试中取得好成绩

□7 不必能讲出语言规则，但能用英语完成一些简单的任务，如生活对话、阅读、写作等

11. 在平时考试中，你认为测试重点应放在下列哪些方面？

□1 词汇意义、句子成分、音素辨别、单句理解和写作

□2 理解的程度、快慢，语言运用的得体性、灵活性

四、教学过程

12. 课堂上你经常给学生安排下列哪方面的活动？(可选多项)

□1 朗读单词、课文 □2 句型替换操练

□3 背诵课文或句型 □4 背诵语法规则

□5 做多项选择练习题 □6 听写单词或短文

□7 英汉互译练习 □8 小组或两人模拟生活会话

□9 听英语磁带回答问题 □10 限定时间和题目写作文

13. 对待学生作业中的的错误，你经常怎样处理：

□1 认真指出来并帮他改正

□2 指出错误让学生自己去找原因

□3 给出正确答案，让学生自己慢慢发现自己的错误

□4 根据具体情况决定是否指出并帮他改正

□5 不必指出，认为是学习过程中不可避免的

14. 在学生回答问题时，对于学生的错误你怎样处理？

□1 发现后立即给学生指出并及时纠正

□2 等学生发言完后再指出

□3 不及时指出，而是等给学生正确答案时让学生自己发现错误

□4 根据具体情况决定是否指出并帮他改正

□5 不打断学生，也不纠正，而是随着学生水平的提高让学生自动改正

15. 一般来说，你在课堂上大约花多少时间讲授？

□1 全部课堂时间 □2 一节课的三分之二

□3 一节课的二分之一 □4 一节课的三分之一

□5 很少讲授

16. 你经常用什么语言给学生讲课？

□1 汉语 □2 用英语后再翻译成汉语

□3 有时用英语，有时用汉语 □4 英语

17. 你的学生经常用什么语言问问题？

□1 汉语 □2 有时用英语，有时用汉语 □3 英语

18. 你经常和学生或组织活动让学生自己用英语交流思想吗？

□1 从不 □2 很少 □3 有时

□4 经常 □5 总是

19. 你经常给学生讲一些英语使用的文化背景知识吗？

□1 从不 □2 很少 □3 有时

□4 经常 □5 总是

20. 你认为有必要给学生讲在各种场合下英语的不同用法吗？

□1 没必要 □2 有时有必要

□3 比较有必要 □4 很有必要

21. 你经常给学生布置下列哪种作业？(可选多项)

□1 记单词 □2 熟记语法规则

□3 语法填空或多项选择练习 □4 背诵课文

□5 背诵句型并造句 □6 反复朗读课文

□7 英汉互译练习 □8 阅读补充材料

□9 出题让学生课后练习会话

□10 用英语写命题作文或日记

22. 在平时的成绩测验中，你经常使用下列哪些题型（可选多项）？

□1 多项选择题　□2 真假判断题（True or False）

□3 句型转换 □4 句子分析

□5 默写单词并翻译　□6 背默语法条文

□7 划线提问　□8 改错　□9 问答题

□10 配对选择题（matching）　□11 复述（retelling）

□12 改写（rewriting）　□13 句子翻译

□14 完成句子　□15 用所给词或句型造句

□16 成段翻译　□17 听写

□18 阅读后回答问题　□19 完形填空

□20 读后写摘要　□21 控制性会话（controlled speaking）

□22 控制性写作　□23 快速阅读理解

□24 命题作文　□25 校对阅读（proofreading）

26. 其它（请自填）：________、________、________、________、________

五、自我评估：

23. 你认为自己目前的英语水平足够教学使用了吗？

□1 相差很远　□2 不太够　□3 刚够

□4 高些　□5 绰绰有余

24. 你对自己采用的教学方法满意程度如何？

□1 不满意　□2 不太满意　□3 一般

□4 比较满意　□5 很满意

25. 你认为你的学生下列哪方面能力较强？（可选多项）

□1 都不行　□2 发音　□3 词汇量

□4 语法规则熟记程度　□5 句子成分分析

□6 口语会话　□7 阅读理解　□8 写作

六、教学条件：

26. 根据你的了解，你所在学校的图书馆有没有关于英语教学理论方面的书籍?

□1 基本没有 □2 很少 □3 有一些

□4 比较多 □5 非常多

27. 如果你们学校有一些关于英语方面的资料, 它们大多是下列哪类? (可选多项)

□1 高考练习题 □2 结合教材的复习题

□3 英语小读物 □4 英语报刊

28. 你们学校有为英语课准备的听音、放影设备吗?

□1 什么也没有 □2 有收录机 □3 有听音室

□4 有放影室 □5 有全套设备

29. 如果你们学校有一些英语电教设备, 你经常利用它们来教学吗?

□1 从没用过 □2 很少用 □3 有时用

□4 经常用 □5 总是用

谢 谢 合 作!

2.3 Specifications for the QL and QT

1. The Aim of the Questionnaires:

The questionnaires are written to investigate the secondary school EFL learning and teaching processes. The major factors under consideration include *motivations, attitudes, outside class language exposure, learning strategies, classroom instruction, teachers' knowledge of the prevailing teaching approaches, and the teaching practices in the selected schools.* Three broad aspects were included in the devising of the questionnaires, viz. *the learners, the EFL teachers,* and *the EFL learning conditions.*

Two questionnaires were finally produced: the one for the students (QL) and the one for the teachers (QT). The questionnaires are presented in Chinese to avoid misunderstandings of the instructions and the questions.

2. Outline of the QL:

QL contains eight sections: (Ⅰ) Background information, (Ⅱ) Learning experiences, (Ⅲ) Motivations and attitudes, (Ⅳ) Outside class language exposure, (Ⅴ) Learning strategies, (Ⅵ) Focus of attention in learning, (Ⅶ) Reports of teachers' classroom instruction methods, (Ⅷ) Reports of learners' learning conditions.

3. Specifications for the questions in the QL

(Ⅰ) **Background information**

This section asks for information pertaining to the gender, age and class of the respondent (Questions 1, 2, 3).

(Ⅱ) **Learning experiences**

This section asks for information concerning the initial EFL learning experience of the learner (Questions 4, 5), and the possible help they obtained from their parents (Question 6).

(Ⅲ) **Learners' motivations and attitudes**

The questions in this section are to investigate the learners' motivations in EFL learning and their attitudes towards EFL learning. Questions 7, 9 and 11 reflect the motivations of an instrumental orientation, while Questions 8, 10 and 12 reflect the motivations of an integrative orientation. Questions 13 to 15 measure the learners' attitudes towards EFL learning. The writing of these items are based on Chandrasegaran's questionnaire (1981) with some modifications in this research. Values are assigned to responses to the questions about motivations and attitudes. For the questions concerning motivations, the values are: Strongly agree =5, Basically agree =4, Half agree =3, Basically disagree =2, Strongly disagree =1. This scale yields for each student a total score ranging from 6 to a maximum of 30 to indicate his intensity of motivation. On the basis of the score, three categories of motivational intensity are distinguished:

Strong motivation	Score 30 – 24
Moderate motivation	23 – 14
Weak motivation	13 – 6

For the questions concerning attitudes, the values assigned to the items are just in reverse order, i.e. strong disagreement scores

5. The same categories of attitudinal intensity are also distinguished on the basis of the total score:

Very favorable	Score	15 - 12
Moderately favorable		11 - 7
Unfavorable		6 - 3

Questions 16 and 17 are to investigate the learners' attitudes towards their teachers' questions. The learners' responses to these questions help us understand their psychological barriers in EFL learning. The learners' responses to Question 19 help us infer the relationship between the learners' ability and the classroom instruction methods.

(IV). Learners' outside class language exposure

The questions in this section are to measure the amount of exposure to English the learner experiences after class. The four questions (Questions 19, 21, 23 and 25) are scored according to the following scale: Never =1, Seldom =2, Sometimes =3, Often =4, and Always =5. The sum of scores over all the four questions, ranging from 4 to 20, is used as the measure of the degree of exposure to English after class. Thus, three categories are distinguished as follows:

High exposure	Score	20 - 16
Moderate exposure		15 - 9
Low exposure		8 - 4

Questions 20, 22, 24 and 26 are for reference, not for analysis. Question 27 aims to investigate the instruction method by means of asking for information pertaining to the learners' homework types. The learners' responses are presented in frequency form.

(V) Learners' learning strategies and techniques

The questions in this section are devised to obtain information about Chinese secondary school EFL learners' employment of learning strategies and techniques. These questions are selected from the SILL (Oxford 1990, pp. 283 - 291).

Questions 28 and 29 ask for information about two learning techniques related to the strategy of memorizing vocabulary. Question 28 asks for information as to whether the learner often associates the sound of the word and the spelling of the word. Question 29 asks for information as to whether the learner often creates associations between new words and familiar words.

Questions 30 and 31 seek for information about the strategy of using mental processes in reading and understanding, i. e. cognitive learning strategies.

Questions 32 and 34 cover the strategy of compensating for missing knowledge in speaking and reading.

Questions 35 and 36 ask for information concerning the metacognitive strategies which focus on the organization and evaluation of EFL learning.

Questions 37 and 38 investigate the affective strategies, i.e. the learners' management of their emotions in learning.

Questions 39 and 40 explore the social strategies, i.e. learning with others.

Responses to these questions are coded from 1 to 5 in the direction of increasing frequency. The average over any of the above pairs of scores is used to represent how often the learner employs that strategy, i. e. one of the six types of strategies (Memory, Cognitive, Compensation, Metacognitive, Affective and Social).

In order to see whether each type of strategies is definitely used or not, the average of each pair of scores also serves as the basis of assigning the subjects to one of the following three categories:

Definitely use (one type of the strategies) $3.5 < \text{average} \leq 5$
Probably use (one type of the strategies) $2 < \text{average} \leq 3.5$
Not use (one type of the strategies) $0 \leq \text{average} \leq 2$

The distribution of the participants in the employment of the six types of strategies is displayed according to the three categories.

Question 40 is different from all the above questions. It aims to ask how the classroom instruction method influences the learner's choice of learning methods after class. It can be considered as a kind of supplement to the questions concerning learning strategies. This question helps us understand the nature of the learner's learning process.

(Ⅵ) Learners' focus of attention in EFL learning

This section consists of two questions: questions 41 and

42. They ask for information as to how learners' attitudes of language competence are influenced by their teachers' focus in classroom instruction.

(Ⅶ) Learners' reports on their teachers' classroom instruction methods

This section is devised to obtain information concerning the EFL teachers' classroom instruction methods. The questions cover the factors of *classroom activities, teachers' focus in teaching, learners' opportunities for interaction in class, teachers' attitudes towards learners' errors*, and *the use of Chinese in class.* These questions are also considered together with Questions 27, 40, 41, and 42.

Questions 43 and 44 are devised to investigate the activities employed by the teachers in EFL classes and the learners' attitudes to them. The frequency tables for these questions are obtained.

Question 45 seeks for information about the teachers' arrangement of time for rules explanation and the learners' practice.

Question 46 is to investigate the teachers' focus in teaching in class.

Question 47 aims to obtain information about the frequency of interaction between teachers and learners in class.

Questions 48 and 49 aim to obtain information as to how teachers handle the learners' errors in class and in homework.

Questions 50 and 51 are meant to elicit information about the language usually used by the teachers and the learners in class.

Questions 52 and 53 ask for information about the frequency of the use of Chinese in EFL learning by the learners. Question 54 aims to investigate the learners' general attitudes towards different ways of classroom instruction.

(Ⅷ) Learners' reports on their learning conditions.

Four questions are devised to obtain information about the learning conditions in these schools (Questions 55, 56, 57, and 58). They are concerned with the aspects of English materials for reading and equipment for EFL learning. This kind of information is also considered as background information.

4. Outline of the Questionnaire for the Teachers (QT)

The QT is composed of six sections: (Ⅰ). Background Information, (ii). Knowledge of Teaching Approaches, (Ⅲ). Teachers' Views of Language Competence, (Ⅳ). Teaching Processes, (Ⅴ). Teachers' Self-evaluation, and (Ⅵ). Teaching Conditions.

5. Specifications for the questions in the QT

(Ⅰ) **Background Information**: This section asks for information about the teachers' sex, age and education.

(Ⅱ) **Knowledge of Teaching Approaches**: This section asks for information about the teachers' knowledge of eight popular teaching approaches.

(Ⅲ) **Teachers' Views of Language Competence**: This section is to investigate the teachers' goal in teaching, their views of competence, and their views of a good learner.

(Ⅳ) **Teaching Processes**: This section is mainly concerned with *the activities the teachers usually employ in class, the types of homework these teachers usually assign to their students, the teachers' attitudes towards their students' errors, the time the teachers usually use in class, the language used by these teachers and their students in class, the teachers' introduction of culture in EFL teaching, the opportunities for interaction in class the teachers give to their students, and the test forms the teachers usually employ in small-scale classroom testing.*

(Ⅴ) **Teachers' Self-evaluation**: This section requests the teachers to evaluate their English level, their teaching effect, and their students' EFL competence.

(Ⅵ) **Teaching Conditions**: The final section asks for information about the materials and equipment for teaching in these schools.

Appendix 3
Data Collecting Procedure

3.1 Specifications for the Scoring Procedure in the WT

The scoring procedure in the WT refers to the scoring of the WT from a holistic view, i.e. the WT is scored on the basis of whether the subjects convey the meaning accurately and appropriately from a communicative point of view. Two kinds of scoring methods are employed: the impression method and the analytic method. The procedure goes as follows:

1. The decision on the factors to be considered in the scoring. Five factors are chosen to be considered. They are *message*, *organization*, *accuracy*, *appropriacy* and *mechanics*.

2. The distribution of scores to each aspect. Message is the most important aspect in accomplishing communicative tasks. However, for the guided writing tasks, since the ideas have been given in Chinese, what learners need to do is to convey these ideas accurately and appropriately. Therefore, Accuracy plays an important role in the accomplishment of these tasks. In addition, the writing tasks here are communicative tasks. To accomplish such kind of tasks requires the employment of other kinds of competence like discourse competence and sociolinguistic competence. But comparatively speaking, appropriate expressions will certainly have more influence on the final conveyance of the exact message than appropriate organization does. The distribution of scores to each criterion is based on the above thinking. (see Table 6 – 5 for reference)

3. The aspects that are not considered in scoring the WT: (1) In Task Two in the WT, the subjects' expressions of the " inside address ", the " date ", the " salutation " and the

"signature" are not considered in the scoring, but the appropriate use of punctuation is a piece of evidence to indicate the learners' ability, thus it will be taken into consideration. (2) The names like "Jordan", "Huang Hua", "Guangzhou" are not considered in the scoring. (3) The words that are given below each task are not considered in the scoring. But if they are used in wrong forms, they will be recorded. (4) If the subjects conveyed more ideas in addition to the essential ones, and these ideas accord with the essential ideas, these ideas will not be considered in the scoring. Extra expressions will not be considered, either, whether they are correct or wrong. (5) The words like "1963", "1993" will not be considered in the scoring for they can be copied from the introduction.

4. Two raters are engaged in the scoring. Both raters have been trained in applied linguistics and testing.

5. Each rater starts first from the employment of the impression method, i.e. to read through the papers and have a general impression, and mark the mistakes, then the analytic method is employed, i.e. to score the papers according to the five aspects, and then read the papers again to check or adjust the scores already marked.

6. The final holistic score for each subject in the WT is the average of the scores given by the two raters. The difference between the two raters' scores can be seen from Table VI-11.

7. Each writing task takes 50% of the total 100 scale. The percentages distributed to each aspect in each writing task are: Message: 10%; Organization: 6%; Accuracy: 18%; Appropriacy: 10%; Mechanics: 6%.

8. Deduction of the scores: the deduction of scores in respect of the message is based on the portion each essential idea takes in each writing task. For Task One (about Jordan), the distribution of scores among the ideas is:

(1) Jordan is an American. (0.5%);

(2) Jordan is a basketball player. (0.5%)

(3) Jordan was born in 1963. (0.5%);

(4) Jordan is called a " superstar". (0.5%)

(5) Jordan won a lot of basketball matches during his

university days. (1%)

(6) After he left university, Jordan continued playing (basketball). (1%)

(7) After he left university, he won two Olympic gold medals for basketball. (1%)

(8) Jordan's father was murdered in July, 1993. (1%)

(9) On October 6, 1993, Jordan announced that he would not play in basketball matches any more. (2%)

(10) Jordan wants to spend more time with his family. (1%)

(11) Jordan is the greatest basketball player in the world today. (1%)

For Task Two, the distribution of scores among the ideas is:

(1) Introduce yourself (1%)

(2) Explain how you have got to know that Peter likes collecting stamps (1%)

(3) Tell Peter you also like collecting stamps. (1%)

(4) Tell Peter you're sending him some stamps (1%)

(5) Ask Peter to send you some stamps (1%)

(6) Explain that you know Peter will visit China next summer (2%)

(7) Express hope that Peter will visit Guangzhou (1%)

(8) Ask Peter to bring some stamps with him for exchange when he comes (2%)

When any one of the above ideas is not conveyed, the score for that one will be lost. If the ideas are not clearly expressed, half of the scores will be lost. The deduction of scores for other aspects can be seen from the following:

(1). spelling mistake: −0.5% (for one);

(2). Punctuation: −0.5% (for one)

(3). grammar mistake: −1% (for one, for local), −2% (for one, for global)

(4). appropriacy mistake: Vocabulary. str.: −2% (for one)

(5). Organization: not logical, not fluent: −1; no title: −3%; style not proper: −1; transition: −1

The analytical method is carried out by means of the following table:

Category / Name	Message		Organiz.		Accuracy		Appropriacy		Mechanics		Total	
	P1	P2	P1	P2	P1	P2	P1	P2	P1	P2	P1	P2

Notes: P1 = Passage One; P2 = Passage Two

3.2 Specifications for the Grammatical forms and Lexical Items Used as Criteria for the Counting of Errors in the WT

1. Vocabulary (VOC): 41 words: the same as listed in Appendix I.

2. Morphological forms (MPH): 17 points:

(1) N. -plurals: -s (a. medals; b. stamps);

(2) N. -plurals: -es (matches)

(3) is (a. is +N. or adj.; b. is +pp.) ——3rd person singular in simple present tense

(4) was (a. was +pp; b. was +N. or adj.) ——simple past form of "be"

(5) born (past form of "bear");

(6) won (past form of "win")

(7) left (past form of "leave");

(8) -ed (a. called; b. murdered;)

(9) -d (a. continued; b. announced or declared; c. liked)

(10) -ing (a. playing; b. collecting; c. sending)

(11) would (a. would play; b. would spend; c. would visit)

(12) told (past form of "tell")

(13) verb original form: (a. like; b. (can) bring or (please) bring; c. (would) spend)

(14) will +V (a. will send; b. will be; c. will visit)

(15) Adjective degree forms: more +N. (more time)

(16) Adjective degree forms: greatest

(17) Adverb degree forms: (not) any more or (not) any longer

3. Function words (FCT): 13 points

(1) a (a. a student; b. a player; c. a superstar; d. a friend);

(2) an (an American ... player)
(3) the (a. the greatest...; b. the world;);
(4) in (a. in +place; b. in +time; c. in ... matches)
(5) with (a. with +sb. or sth.; b. exchange ... with...);
(6) for (for basketball)
(7) on (on October 6);
(8) of (a. several of...; b. some of ...;)
(9) when (10) after (11) and (12) that (13) if

4. Pronouns (PRON): 11 points
(1) I (2) he (3) you (subjective)
(4) me (5) you (objective) (6) his
(7) my (8) your (9) some
(10) several or a few (11) each other

5. Basic Grammatical Concepts (CONT): 23 points
(1) N. (2) V. (3) Adj. (4) Adv. (5) Pron. (6) Prep.
(7) Conj. (8) Art. (9) Num. (10) S +V +P;
(11) S +V +Oclause; (12) S +V +P +ADclause; (13) S +V +ADphrase;
(14) ADclause +S +ADphrase +V +O
(15) ADclause +S +V +O +and +V +O +Adphrase
(16) ADphrase +S +V; (17) ADphrase +S +V +Oclause
(18) S +V +O +ADphrase;
(19) Adphrase +S +V +Oi +Od; or Adphrase +S +V +Od +to +Oi or Here +V +S
(20) Will you please +V +Oi +Od? (e. g. Will you please send me some of your stamps?);
(21) and +V +O +AD or Please +V +O +Adphrase or S +V +O +Adphrase (or S +V +Oclause)
(22) Negative sentence: ...would not play...
(23) Inverted order in questions or in Pattern "Here are...".

6. Verb Forms in Sentences (VFS): 9 points
(1) simple present tense (a. verb original form; b. is +pp)
(2) simple past tense (a. simple active voice past form; b. was +pp)
(3) simple future tense (will +v.)
(4) simple present continuous tense (I am sending...)
(5) past future tense (would +v)

(6) active voice
(7) passive voice
(8) gerund (a. continue playing; b. like collecting)
(9) S-V agreement (a. I am...; b. He is...; c. I like...; d. I hope ... etc.)

3.3 The Procedure of the Counting of Errors and the Obtaining of the Number of the Correct Expressions the Learners Have Generated in the WT

The counting of errors is carried out after the analysis of each subject's two pieces of writing. The analysis is by means of a table with the above listed linguistic forms and the possible linguistic forms which the subjects might use to express the ideas contained in the WT. Each subject, thus, has two tables. Their production of each required form is marked with a tick "√" or a cross " × " symbols according to the above standard forms.

1. If learners generated expressions other than the listed ones and use them correctly and the ideas contained in the WT are conveyed accurately, these expressions will also be considered as correct.

2. If one linguistic form has been used in several places, and if the number of wrong uses adds up to more than half of the total, this form will be considered to be used wrongly.

3. As for the grammatical form that includes several variant forms, one variant form takes one portion of the total form.

4. If the expected forms are not used, and the essential ideas are not expressed, all the lost forms will be considered as errors.

5. The linguistic forms appeared in the two writing tasks are considered together.

By means of this procedure, the number of the learners' errors in each variable is obtained, i.e. the number of errors in vocabulary, morphological forms, function words, basic grammatical concepts and verb forms in sentences. Then a simple subtraction procedure is carried out to get the number of the correct linguistic forms the learners have generated. The scores the subjects obtain about their linguistic production in the WT are then obtained by a simple transformation process which is shown in Table 6 – 5.

3.4 The Sample Table for Analyzing the Learners' Production in the WT

Analysis Table For Task One (about Jordan)

School No.: **Class:** **Student Name:**

No	Id	Vocabulary			Morphological Forms			Function Words			Pron.	Basic Gr. Concepts		V.forms in sent.			
		N.	V.+pttrns	Adj&Adv	Np.&('s)	V.forms	Aj&Ad	Art	Prep	Conj		Patterns	PS	Tns	Vce	Grd	Agr
1		Michael Jordan, (America),(man)	(be)	American		(is(3ps))		an (a)			(he)	(S+V+P) Nprase	N.Adj. (V.) (Pp.)	(Pr.)	(Av.)		
2		basketball player, (Jordan)	(be)			is(3ps)		(a)			(he)	Nphrase (S+V+P)	N.(Pn.) (V.) Art.	(Pr.)	(Av.)		
3		(Jordan)	bear			was born(pp)			in		he	S+V(=be +pp)	Pn.V.Pp. N.	Pa.	Pv.		
4		(Jordan), superstar	call, (name)			is(3ps) called(pp)		a			he	S+V(=be +pp)	Pn.V. N.Art.	Pr.	Pv.		
5		basketball match, team, university student, a lot of	be, win, (study, obtain, gain), V+O		matches, (days, years)	was, won(p) (studied) (other p.)		a (the)	of, (in) with (dur-ing)	when	he his	ADc+S+ AD+V+O, (AD+S+ AD+V+O)	Pn.V.Art. N.Cj.	Pa.	Av.		
6		university, (graduation), basketball (college)	leave, continue, play V+Oving (graduate) (go on., etc)			left, (went on) continued(p), playing(g), (kept on)		(the)	(after)	after	he	ADc+S+ V+O, (AD+S+ V+O)	Cj.V.Pn. N.	Pa.	Av.	Grd	
7		gold medal, (Game), (team) basketball,	win, (get, obtain gain) V+O	Olympic	medals, (Games, Olympics)	p=won, (got, obtained, gained)		(the)	for (in) (with)	and	(he)	&+V+O+ AD, (S+V+ O+AD)	Pn.V.Num. Adj.N.Pp.	Pa.	Av.		
8		father, July, (Jordan), 1993	murder, (kill)		(Jordan's)	was(p), murdered(pp) (killed(pp)			in		his	AD+S+V(= be+pp)	Pa.N.V. Pp.	Pa.	Pv.		
9		basketball match, October 6, 1993 month, (public),	announce, V+Ocl. play (tell V+O), (declare), will, (join)	later not	matches	p=announced, (declared, told), would, play(I)	any more (longer)	(the)	on, in	that	he	(AD+)S+V+ Ocl(=S+V+ O+AD), Ocl=neg. sent.	Pn.V.Cj. Adv.N.Pp.	Pa. Pf.	Av.		
10		time, family, (Jordan)	will, spend, (want, have), V+O+prep. phrase	(together)		would(p), spend(I), (wants(3ps)) (stay, have(I))	more +N (time)		with, (in, at)	and	(he) his	and+V+O+ AD, (S+V+ O+AD)	Cj.Pn.V. Adj.N.Pp.	Pf. (Pr.)	Av.		
11		basketball player, today, (Jordan) world	be	(now) great		is (3ps)	great-est	the	in of		he	S+V+P +AD	Pn.V.Art. Adj.N. Pp.	Pr.	Av.		
Oth		Numerals: two															

Notes: p=past forms; pp=past participle forms; I=infinitives; Pr=present tense; Pa.=past tense; Pf.=past future tense; Av.=Active voice; Pv.=passive voice; 3ps=the third person singular; Grd.=gerund; sent.=sentence; Id=ideas experssed, Tse=tense, Vce=voice, Agr=sentence agreement.

Appendix 3 *Data Collecting Procedure*

Analysis Table For Task Two (about the letter)

School No.: **Class:** **Student Name:**

No	Id	Vocabulary			Morphological Forms		Function Words			Pron.	Bas.Gr.Concepts		V.Forms in Sent.			
		N.	V.	Adj&Adv	Np&'s	V.forms	Art.	Prep.	Conj.		Patterns	PS	Tns.	Voc	Grd.	Agr
1		Li Ming, name Huang Hua, friend (student),(school) (Guangzhou), (city),(pen friend),	be, (study)		(Huang Hua's)	am, (study)	a	(in) of	(and)	I, (he) (his)	S+V+P (S+V+AD)	Pn. Art. Pp. V. N.	Pr.	Av.		
2		(Huang Hua), stamp,(one day), (stamp collector)	tell (V+Ocl) (hear V+O) like(V+O) collect (V+O) (love),(be keen on,be fond of)	very much	stamps	told(p), liked(p) collect- ing(g), (heard, loved,were)	(a)	(from) (of) (on)	that	he me you	S+V+Ocl OCL=S+V +Oving+O+AD; (Ocl=S+be+adj. +prep.+Ving+O +AD)	N.V. Cj.Pn. Adv. (Art) Adj. (Pp.)	Pn.	Av.	Grd.	
3		stamp, (stamp collector)	like,collect V+O	too (also)	stamps	like(I), collecting(g)	(a)			I	S+V+Oving+AD	Pn.V. Adv. N.(Art)	Pr.	Av.	Grd.	
4		Chinese stamp, (letter, envelope)	send, (post), (give,mail),(be) (will); V+Oi+Od	now, Chinese, (here)	stamps	am,(send), sending(ing) (are) (will)	(the)	(to),(in) (for) of (with)		I,you, several my (some, a few)	AD+S+V+Oi+Od (AD+S+V+Od+to +Oi) (AD+V+S+AD)	Adv. V.N. Pn. Pp.	Ft. or Prc.	Av. or Pv.		
5		stamp	please,send (hope),will,	too, (American)	stamps	please,will send(I)		of (to)	(that)	you,me some, your (a few)	Will+S+please+V +Oi+Od? Please+V+Oi+Od (...V+Od+to+Oi)	V.N. Pp. Pn. (Adj)	Ft. or Pr.	Av.		
6		Huang Hua, China, (visit) (travel) (parent) next summer	tell, (hear), visit,(travel), (come to) will	also		told,would visit(I), (heard), (travel,etc(I))		(to) (from) (in) (with)	that (and)	me you (your)	S+V+Ocl, Ocl=S+V+O+AD (AD+S+V+Ocl)	N.V. Cj.Pn. Adv. Pp.	Pn. Pf.	AV.		
7		Guangzhou, (visit, China) (parent) (house)	be, (hope),visit, will	also glad (welcome)		will be, will visit, (hope),(are) (could)		(to) (at) (with)	(that) if	I,you (your) (our)	S+V+P+Adcl ADcl=S+V+O, (S+V+P)	Pn.V. Cj.Adj. (Pp. N.)	Ft. or Pr. (Pf.)	Av.		
8		stamp (exchange)	(hope,will) bring, exchange (come)	then (thus) some	stamps	bring(I) exchange(I) can,(come)		with (for) (to) of	and (when) (if)	your each other (I,you)	and+V+O+AD, AD+S+V+O+AD (S+V+Ocl) (Ocl=S+V+O+AD)	V.Pn. Pp. N. Cj.	Pr. Ft.	AV.		
Oth																

Notes:Pn=pron.,Pp.=prep.,Cj.=conj.,Ft=future tense, Pf.=past future tense, Prc.=present continuous tense, PS.=parts of speech

Appendix 4 Statistical Results of the Experiment and the Investigation

(1) Descriptive Statistics for the Low, Average and Top Level Groups in the KT and the WT

A. Descriptive Statistics for the KT Variables in Original Scores for Groups A, B and C.

Variables	Means	SD	Mini.	Maxi.	ValidN
Group A.					
KTVOC	12. 33	. 96	9. 5	14. 0	58
KTMPH	22. 28	2. 82	12. 5	26. 5	58
KTFCT	7. 96	1. 42	3. 8	11. 8	58
KTPRON	2. 82	. 91	. 5	5. 0	58
KTCONT	24. 57	2. 63	16. 0	28. 0	58
KTVFS	7. 07	1. 58	1. 0	10. 0	58
KTTOTL	77. 03	6. 33	49. 75	87. 00	58
Group B.					
KTVOC	13. 07	. 64	11. 0	14. 0	115
KTMPH	24. 80	1. 36	20. 0	27. 0	115
KTFCT	8. 27	1. 48	4. 3	11. 5	115
KTPRON	3. 26	. 93	. 5	5. 3	115
KTCONT	26. 46	2. 16	19. 5	30. 5	115
KTVFS	7. 80	1. 35	3. 0	10. 0	115
KTTOTL	83. 66	4. 55	68. 75	93. 00	115

Continued

Variables	Means	SD	Mini.	Maxi.	ValidN
Group C.					
KTVOC	13. 57	. 49	11. 8	14. 0	58
KTMPH	25. 99	. 94	24. 0	27. 5	58
KTFCT	9. 50	1. 19	7. 0	11. 5	58
KTPRON	3. 90	. 82	2. 3	5. 5	58
KTCONT	27. 79	1. 69	23. 0	30. 5	58
KTVFS	8. 35	. 86	6. 5	10. 0	58
KTTOTL	89. 11	3. 20	79. 75	95. 75	58

B. The KT Variables in Percentage Form for Groups A, B and C

Variables	Means	SD	Mini.	Maxi.	ValidN
Group A.					
KTVOCP	88. 08	6. 83	67. 86	100. 00	58
KTMPHP	81. 00	10. 25	45. 45	96. 36	58
KTFCTP	66. 31	11. 82	31. 25	97. 92	58
KTPRONP	51. 25	16. 46	9. 09	90. 91	58
KTCONTP	80. 57	8. 61	52. 46	91. 80	58
KTVFSP	67. 32	15. 04	9. 52	95. 24	58
KTTOTLP	434. 54	40. 50	277. 49	507. 10	58
Group B.					
KTVOCP	93. 34	4. 57	78. 57	100. 00	115
KTMPHP	90. 20	4. 95	72. 73	98. 18	115
KTFCTP	68. 89	12. 29	35. 42	95. 83	115
KTPRONP	59. 21	16. 97	9. 09	95. 45	115
KTCONTP	86. 75	7. 08	63. 93	100. 00	115
KTVFSP	74. 31	12. 82	28. 57	95. 24	115
KTTOTLP	472. 70	35. 78	362. 59	540. 38	115

Continued

Variables	Means	SD	Mini.	Maxi.	ValidN
Group C					
KTVOCP	96. 95	3. 48	83. 93	100. 00	58
KTMPHP	94. 51	3. 43	87. 27	100. 00	58
KTFCTP	79. 17	9. 88	58. 33	95. 83	58
KTPRONP	70. 92	14. 87	40. 91	100. 00	58
KTCONTP	91. 12	5. 53	75. 41	100. 00	58
KTVFSP	79. 56	8. 16	61. 90	95. 24	58
KTTOTLP	512. 24	24. 93	444. 14	561. 44	58

C. Descriptive Statistics for the WTK Variables for Groups A, B and C (Scores Matching the KT Variables)

Variables	Means	SD	Mini.	Maxi.	ValidN
Group A.					
WTKVOC	6. 86	1. 26	4. 44	9. 90	58
WTKMPH	5. 01	3. 38	. 81	13. 75	58
WTKFCT	6. 25	1. 42	3. 23	9. 23	58
WTKPRON	3. 89	. 82	1. 00	5. 00	58
WTKCONT	16. 80	3. 21	9. 28	23. 87	58
WTKVFS	2. 78	1. 04	1. 17	5. 83	58
WTKTOTL	41. 59	7. 24	23. 31	58. 99	58
Group B.					
WTKVOC	8. 61	1. 16	5. 80	11. 61	115
WTKMPH	9. 31	3. 80	1. 62	17. 79	115
WTKFCT	7. 00	1. 45	2. 77	10. 15	115
WTKPRON	4. 28	. 54	3. 00	5. 00	115
WTKCONT	21. 03	2. 59	13. 26	26. 52	115
WTKVFS	4. 36	1. 36	2. 33	8. 17	115
WTKTOTL	54. 59	6. 92	39. 52	71. 03	115

Continued

Variables	Means	SD	Mini.	Maxi.	ValidN
Group C.					
WTKVOC	10. 22	1. 19	7. 85	12. 63	58
WTKMPH	13. 51	4. 41	4. 04	22. 65	58
WTKFCT	7. 97	1. 24	5. 08	11. 08	58
WTKPRON	4. 40	. 57	2. 50	5. 50	58
WTKCONT	23. 05	2. 68	17. 24	27. 85	58
WTKVFS	6. 05	1. 51	2. 33	9. 33	58
WTKTOTL	65. 21	8. 56	48. 85	85. 27	58

D. Descriptive Statistics for the WTK Variables for Groups A, B and C in Percentage Form

Variables	Means	SD	Mini.	Maxi.	ValidN
Group A.					
WTKVOCP	49. 03	8. 97	31. 71	70. 73	58
WTKMPHP	18. 20	12. 30	2. 94	50. 00	58
WTKFCTP	52. 06	11. 86	26. 92	76. 92	58
WTKPRONP	70. 69	14. 85	18. 18	90. 91	58
WTKCONTP	55. 10	10. 54	30. 43	78. 26	58
WTKVFSP	26. 44	9. 94	11. 11	55. 56	58
WTKTLP	271. 52	41. 05	155. 10	386. 03	58
Group B.					
WTKVOCP	61. 48	8. 29	41. 46	82. 93	115
WTKMPHP	33. 86	13. 81	5. 88	64. 71	115
WTKFCTP	58. 33	12. 11	23. 08	84. 62	115
WTKPRONP	77. 75	9. 88	54. 55	90. 91	115
WTKCONTP	68. 96	8. 50	43. 48	86. 96	115
WTKVFSP	41. 50	12. 96	22. 22	77. 78	115
WTKTLP	341. 88	38. 21	247. 93	445. 21	115

Continued

Variables	Means	SD	Mini.	Maxi.	ValidN
Group C.					
WTKVOCP	73.00	8.53	56.10	90.24	58
WTKMPHP	49.14	16.03	14.71	82.35	58
WTKFCTP	66.45	10.36	42.31	92.31	58
WTKPRONP	80.02	10.36	45.45	100.00	58
WTKCONTP	75.56	8.80	56.52	91.30	58
WTKVFSP	57.66	14.34	22.22	88.89	58
WTKTLP	401.83	45.34	327.73	503.84	58

E. Descriptive Statistics for WTTOTL for Groups A, B and C.

Group A.					
Variables	Mean	SD	Mini.	Maxi.	ValidN
WTCXP	42.83	6.87	26.00	55.50	58
WTYAO	42.00	10.01	22.00	64.00	58
WTTOTL	42.41	7.19	25.75	52.50	58
Group B.					
WTCXP	60.06	5.77	46.00	72.50	115
WTYAO	62.16	5.80	47.50	73.00	115
WTTOTL	61.11	4.33	53.00	68.25	115
Group C.					
WTCXP	73.97	4.85	65.00	85.00	58
WTYAO	73.87	4.42	65.50	83.50	58
WTTOTL	73.92	3.66	68.25	83.25	58

F. Descriptive Statistics for the Number of the Learners' Correct Expressions in the WT — the WTK Variables for Groups A, B and C

Variables	Means	SD	Mini.	Maxi.	ValidN
Group A.					
WKCVOC	20. 10	3. 68	13. 0	29. 0	58
WKCMPH	3. 09	2. 09	. 5	8. 5	58
WKCFCT	6. 77	1. 54	3. 5	10. 0	58
WKCPRON	7. 78	1. 63	2. 0	10. 0	58
WKCCONT	12. 67	2. 42	7. 0	18. 0	58
WKCVFS	2. 38	. 89	1. 0	5. 0	58
WKCTOTL	52. 79	7. 96	32. 50	74. 00	58
Group B.					
WKCVOC	25. 21	3. 40	17. 0	34. 0	115
WKCMPH	5. 76	2. 35	1. 0	11. 0	115
WKCFCT	7. 58	1. 57	3. 0	11. 0	115
WKCPRON	8. 55	1. 09	6. 0	10. 0	115
WKCCONT	15. 86	1. 96	10. 0	20. 0	115
WKCVFS	3. 73	1. 17	2. 0	7. 0	115
WKCTOTL	66. 70	7. 27	50. 00	87. 00	115
Group C.					
WKCVOC	29. 93	3. 50	23. 0	37. 0	58
WKCMPH	8. 35	2. 73	2. 5	14. 0	58
WKCFCT	8. 64	1. 35	5. 5	12. 0	58
WKCPRON	8. 80	1. 14	5. 0	11. 0	58
WKCCONT	17. 38	2. 02	13. 0	21. 0	58
WKCVFS	5. 19	1. 29	2. 0	8. 0	58
WKCTOTL	78. 29	8. 50	64. 00	98. 00	58

(2) Correlation matrix between the KT Variables and the WT Variables (for 231 cases)

Correlation Coefficients Matrix Between the KT Varaibles and the WT Variables

Variables	KTTOTL	WTKTOTL	WTTOTL	KTVOC	KTMPH	KTFCT	KTPRON	KTCONT
KTTOTL	1.0000	.6408**	.7260**	.5287**	.7751**	.6356**	.5834**	.7554**
WTKTOTL	.6408**	1.0000	.8036**	.5104**	.5505**	.3576**	.3559**	.4043**
WTTOTL	.7260**	.8036**	1.0000	.5978**	.6446**	.3749**	.4160**	.5193**
KTVOC	.5287**	.5104**	.5978**	1.0000	.4698**	.2106**	.2160**	.3036**
KTMPH	.7751**	.5505**	.6446**	.4698**	1.0000	.4019**	.3011**	.4069**
KTFCT	.6356**	.3576**	.3749**	.2106**	.4019**	1.0000	.3269**	.2575**
KTPRON	.5834**	.3559**	.4160**	.2160**	.3011**	.3269**	1.0000	.3845**
KTCONT	.7554**	.4043**	.5193**	.3036**	.4069**	.2575**	.3845**	1.0000
KTVFS	.6296**	.4229**	.3482**	.1774**	.3322**	.3977**	.3485**	.3392**
WTKVOC	.6414**	.8569**	.7661**	.5111**	.5674**	.3527**	.3223**	.4192**
WTKMPH	.5146**	.8825**	.6540**	.4903**	.4581**	.2540**	.2651**	.3138**
WTKFCT	.3748**	.5689**	.4485**	.1978**	.2890**	.2108**	.1735**	.2965**
WTKPRON	.1838**	.3666**	.3390**	.1689*	.2176**	.1809**	.0504	.0548
WTKCONT	.5381**	.8278**	.6706**	.3552**	.4586**	.3079**	.3503**	.3306**
WTKVFS	.5455**	.7762**	.6828**	.4388**	.4221**	.3554**	.3368**	.3495**

Variables	KTVFS	WTKVOC	WTKMPH	WTKFCT	WTKPRON	WTKCONT	WTKVFS
KTTOTL	.6296**	.6414**	.5146**	.3748**	.1838**	.5381**	.5455**
WTKTOTL	.4229**	.8569**	.8825**	.5689**	.3666**	.8278**	.7762**
WTTOTL	.3482**	.7661**	.6540**	.4485**	.3390**	.6706**	.6828**
KTVOC	.1774**	.5111**	.4903**	.1978**	.1689*	.3552**	.4388**
KTMPH	.3322**	.5674**	.4581**	.2890**	.2176**	.4586**	.4221**
KTFCT	.3977**	.3527**	.2540**	.2108**	.1809**	.3079**	.3554**
KTPRON	.3485**	.3223**	.2651**	.1735**	.0504	.3503**	.3368**
KTCONT	.3392**	.4192**	.3138**	.2965**	.0548	.3306**	.3495**
KTVFS	1.0000	.4004**	.3358**	.2765**	.0711	.3761**	.3432**
WTKVOC	.4004**	1.0000	.7217**	.4292**	.3210**	.6683**	.6386**
WTKMPH	.3358**	.7217**	1.0000	.3504**	.2215**	.5500**	.6409**
WTKFCT	.2765**	.4292**	.3504**	1.0000	.3220**	.4581**	.3188**
WTKPRON	.0711	.3210**	.2215**	.3220**	1.0000	.2421**	.2663**
WTKCONT	.3761**	.6683**	.5500**	.4581**	.2421**	1.0000	.5754**
WTKVFS	.3432**	.6386**	.6409**	.3188**	.2663**	.5754**	1.0000

* $p < .05$ ** $p < .01$ (2-tailed)

(3) F-values and R squares in Multiple Regression Analyses for the KT variables on the WT variables (231 cases)

	F-Value	Sig. F	Rsquare	AjstRsquare
(1) KTTOTL on WTKTOTL	159.58683	.0000	.41069	.40811
(2) KTTOTL on WTTOTL:	255.14921	.0000	.52701	.52494
(3) KT subvariables on WTKTOTL:	32.68817	.0000	.46683	.45255
(4) KT subvariables on WTTOTL:	58.02238	.0000	.60848	.59800
(5) KTVOC on WTKVOC:	80.99273	.0000	.26127	.25805
(6) KTMPH on WTKMPH:	60.80943	.0000	.20983	.20638
(7) KTFCT on WTKFCT:	10.64574	.0013	.04442	.04025
(8) KTPRON on WTKPRON:	.58416	.4455	.00254	-.00181
(9) KTCONT on WTKCONT:	28.09735	.0000	.10929	.10540
(10) KTVFS on WTKVFS:	30.57895	.0000	.11780	.11395

(4) Intensity of Motivations and Attitudes by Sex and Schools

A. Distribution of the Intensity of Motivations and Attitudes of the Subjects by Sex

Female			Male		
Intensity of Motivations	N	%	Intensity of Motivations	N	%
Strong	82	62.60	Strong	61	61.00
Moderate	48	36.64	Moderate	39	39.00
Weak	1	0.76	Weak	0	0.00
Total	131	100.00	Total	100	100.00
Intensity of Attitudes	N	%	Intensity of attitudes	N	%
Very Fav.	89	67.94	Very Fav.	55	55.00
Mod. Fav.	39	29.77	Mod. Fav.	39	39.00
Unfavorable	3	2.29	Unfavorable	6	6.00
Total	131	100.00	Total	100	100.00

Note: Chi square for Intensity of Motivation by Sex with 2 d.f. = 0.870454, n.s.; Chi square for Intensity of Attitudes by Sex with 2 d.f. = 4.956875, n.s..

B. Distribution of the Intensity of Motivations and Attitudes of the Subjects by Schools

School No.	No. 2		No. 28		No. 11	
Intensityof motivations	N	%	N	%	N	%
Strong	37	64. 91	50	59. 52	56	62. 22
Moderate	20	35. 09	33	39. 29	34	37. 78
Weak	0	0. 00	1	1. 19	0	0. 00
Total	57	100. 00	84	100. 00	90	100. 00
Intensityof Attitudes	N	%	N	%	N	%
Very Fav.	42	73. 68	53	63. 10	49	54. 44
Mod. Fav.	15	26. 32	27	32. 14	36	40. 00
Unfav.	0	0. 00	4	4. 76	5	5. 56
Total	57	100. 00	84	100. 00	90	100. 00

Note: Chi square (for the Intensity of Motivations by Schools) with 4 d. f. = 2. 071091, n. s. ; Chi square (for the Intensity of Attitudes by Schools) with 4 d. f. = 7. 141315, n. s. .

(5) Intensity of Outside Class Language Exposure by Sex and Schools

	Female		Male	
Intensity of Exposure	N	%	N	%
High	0	0. 00	0	0. 00
Moderate	84	64. 12	66	66. 00
Low	47	35. 88	34	34. 00
Total	131	100. 00	100	100. 00

Continued

	Female				Male	
School No.	No. 2		No. 28		No. 11	
Intensity of Exposure	N	%	N	%	N	%
Strong	0	0. 00	0	0. 00	0	0. 00
Moderate	42	73. 68	58	69. 05	50	55. 56
Low	15	26. 32	26	30. 95	40	44. 44
Total	57	100. 00	84	100. 00	90	100. 00

Note: Chi square (for the intensity of exposure by sex) with 1 d. f. = 0. 087828, n. s. ; Chi square (for the intensity of exposure by schools) with 2 d. f. = 6. 017574, p. <. 05.

(6) Frequency Distribution of the Learning strategies (for all subjects and for subjects in the three groups)

A. Frequency distribution of the learning strategies for all subjects (231) when all choices are considered

Strategies	Never		Seldom		Sometimes		Often		Always		Chi-test	
		N	%	N	%	N	%	N	%	N	%	
Mem1	5	2. 2	21	9. 1	45	19. 5	73	31. 6	87	37. 7	4 d. f.	**
Mem2	4	1. 7	40	17. 3	106	45. 9	59	25. 5	22	9. 5	4 d. f.	**
Cogn1	45	19. 5	89	38. 5	82	35. 5	14	6. 1	1	0. 4	4 d. f.	**
Cogn2	7	3. 0	35	15. 2	86	37. 2	86	37. 2	17	7. 4	4 d. f.	**
Compst1	50	21. 6	68	29. 4	59	25. 5	40	17. 3	14	6. 1	4 d. f.	**
Compst2	2	0. 9	7	3. 0	55	23. 8	112	48. 5	55	23. 8	4 d. f.	**
Metacog1	28	12. 1	82	35. 5	89	38. 5	27	11. 7	5	2. 2	4 d. f.	**
Metacog2	2	0. 9	20	8. 7	57	24. 7	97	42. 0	55	23. 8	4 d. f.	**
Affect1	31	13. 4	99	42. 9	82	35. 5	17	7. 4	2	0. 9	4 d. f.	**
Affect2	18	7. 8	44	19. 0	84	36. 4	52	22. 5	33	14. 3	4 d. f.	**
Social1	38	16. 5	123	53. 2	65	28. 1	4	1. 7	1	0. 4	4 d. f.	**
Social2	16	6. 9	57	24. 7	86	37. 2	51	22. 1	21	9. 1	4 d. f.	**

Notes: For each variable, the total number is 231, and the percentage is 100. ** p <. 01

B. Frequency distribution of learning strategies by 3 groups when all choices are considered

Mem1							Mem2					
	GroupA		GroupB		GroupC		GroupA		GroupB		GroupC	
	N	%	N	%	N	%	N	%	N	%		
Never	0	0.0	3	2.6	2	3.4	2	3.4	1	0.9	1	1.7
Seldom	13	22.4	4	3.5	4	6.9	21	36.2	14	12.2	5	8.6
Sometimes	14	24.1	27	23.5	4	6.9	26	44.8	57	49.6	23	39.7
Often	22	37.9	32	27.8	19	32.8	8	13.8	30	26.1	21	36.2
Always	9	15.5	49	42.6	29	50.0	1	1.7	13	11.3	8	13.8
Chi-test	8 d.f. **						8 d.f. **					

Cogn1							Cogn2					
	GroupA		GroupB		GroupC		GroupA		GroupB		GroupC	
	N	%	N	%	N	%	N	%	N	%	N	%
Never	19	32.8	18	15.7	8	13.8	3	5.2	4	3.5	0	0.0
Seldom	23	39.7	44	38.3	22	37.9	19	32.8	13	11.3	3	5.2
Sometimes	14	24.1	44	38.3	24	41.4	23	39.7	45	39.1	18	31.0
Often	2	3.4	8	7.0	4	6.9	12	20.7	45	39.1	29	50.0
Always	0	0.0	1	0.9	0	0.0	1	1.7	8	7.0	8	13.8
Chi-test	8 d.f. **						8 d.f. **					

Compst1							Compst2					
	GroupA		GroupB		GroupC		GroupA		GroupB		GroupC	
	N	%	N	%	N	%	N	%	N	%	N	%
Never	17	29.3	27	23.5	6	10.3	1	1.7	1	0.9	0	0.0
Seldom	13	22.4	41	35.7	14	24.1	0	0.0	6	5.2	1	1.7
Sometimes	11	19.0	24	20.9	24	41.4	11	19.0	32	27.8	12	20.7
Often	10	17.2	16	13.9	14	24.1	35	60.3	41	35.7	36	62.1
Always	7	12.1	7	6.1	0	0.0	11	19.0	35	30.4	9	15.5
Chi-test	8 d.f. **						8 d.f. **					

Continued

Metacog1							Metacog2					
	GroupA		GroupB		GroupC		GroupA		GroupB		GroupC	
	N	%	N	%	N	%	N	%	N	%	N	%
Never	9	15. 5	13	11. 3	6	10. 3	0	0. 0	1	0. 9	1	1. 7
Seldom	18	31. 0	47	40. 9	17	29. 3	9	15. 5	5	4. 3	6	10. 3
Sometimes	24	41. 4	43	37. 4	22	37. 9	16	27. 6	29	25. 2	12	20. 7
Often	6	10. 3	10	8. 7	11	19. 0	20	34. 5	55	47. 8	22	37. 9
Always	1	1. 7	2	1. 7	2	3. 4	13	22. 4	25	21. 7	17	29. 3
Chi-test	8 d. f. N. S.						8 d. f. N. S.					
Affect1							Affect2					
	GroupA		GroupB		GroupC		GroupA		GroupB		GroupC	
N	%	N	%	N	%	N	%	N	%	N	%	
Never	10	17. 2	14	12. 2	7	12. 1	8	13. 8	6	5. 2	4	6. 9
Seldom	30	51. 7	50	43. 5	19	32. 8	15	25. 9	23	20. 0	6	10. 3
Sometimes	13	22. 4	42	36. 5	27	46. 6	18	31. 0	43	37. 4	23	39. 7
Often	5	8. 6	9	7. 8	3	5. 2	14	24. 1	24	20. 9	14	24. 1
Always	0	0. 0	0	0. 0	2	3. 4	3	5. 2	19	16. 5	11	19. 0
Chi-test	8 d. f. N. S.						8 d. f. N. S.					
Social1							Social2					
	GroupA		GroupB		GroupC		GroupA		GroupB		GroupC	
	N	%	N	%	N	%	N	%	N	%	N	%
Never	17	29. 3	16	13. 9	5	8. 6	6	10. 3	8	7. 0	2	3. 4
Seldom	32	55. 2	61	50. 0	30	51. 7	25	43. 1	23	20. 0	9	15. 5
Sometimes	8	13. 8	35	30. 4	22	37. 9	19	32. 8	47	40. 9	20	34. 5
Often	1	1. 7	2	1. 7	1	1. 7	5	8. 6	29	25. 2	17	29. 3
Always	0	0. 0	1	0. 9	0	0. 0	3	5. 2	8	7. 0	10	17. 2
Chi-test	8 d. f. *						8 d. f. **					

Note: * $p < .05$; ** $p < .01$; N. S. = non-significant;
The total number for Group A is 58; for Group B, 115; for Group C, 58.

(7) Distribution of Subjects for the Use of the Six Types of Strategies by Sex and Schools

By sex

Strategies	Memory				Cognitive				Compensation			
	Female		Male		Female		Male		Female		Male	
	N	%	N	%	N	%	N	%	N	%	N	%
Definitely used	69	52.7	32	32.0	8	6.1	6	6.0	31	23.7	21	21.00
Probably used	52	39.7	59	59.0	98	74.8	71	71.0	89	67.9	74	74.0
Not used	10	7.6	9	9.0	25	19.1	23	23.0	11	8.4	5	5.0
Total	131	100.0	100	100.0	131	100.0	100	100.0	131	100.0	100	100.0
Chi-test	2 d.f. **				2 d.f. N.S.				2 d.f. N.S.			

	Metacognitive				Affective				Social			
	Female		Male		Female		Male		Female		Male	
	N	%	N	%	N	%	N	%	N	%	N	%
Defintely used	28	21.4	21	21.0	9	6.9	13	13.0	5	3.8	5	5.0
Probably used	87	66.4	67	67.0	96	73.3	57	57.0	94	71.8	49	49.0
Not used	16	12.2	12	12.0	26	19.9	30	30.0	32	24.4	46	46.0
Total	131	100.0	100	100.0	131	100.0	100	100.0	131	100.0	100	100.0
Chi-test	2 d.f. N.S.				2 d.f. *				2 d.f. **			

Note: * $p < .05$; ** $P < .01$; N.S. = non-significant.

By schools

	Memory						Cognitive					
	No. 2		No. 28		No. 11		No. 2		No. 28		No. 11	
	N	%	N	%	N	%	N	%	N	%	N	%
Defintely used	38	66.8	37	40.1	26	28.9	3	5.3	7	8.3	4	4.4
Probably used	17	29.8	42	50.0	52	57.8	49	86.0	63	75.0	57	63.3
Not used	2	3.5	5	6.0	12	13.3	5	8.8	14	16.7	29	32.2
Total	57	100.0	84	100.0	90	100.0	57	100.0	84	100.0	90	100.0
Chi-test	4 d.f. **						4 d.f. **					

Continued

	Compensation						Metacognitive					
	No. 2		No. 28		No. 11		No. 2		No. 28		No. 11	
	N	%	N	%	N	%	N	%	N	%	N	%
Defintely used	13	22. 8	26	31. 0	13	14. 4	21	36. 9	17	20. 2	11	12. 2
Probably used	42	73. 7	53	63. 1	68	75. 6	30	52. 6	62	73. 8	62	68. 9
Not used	2	3. 5	5	6. 0	9	10. 0	6	10. 5	5	6. 0	17	18. 9
Total	57	100. 0	84	100. 0	90	100. 0	57	100. 0	84	100. 0	90	100. 0
Chi-test	4 d. f. N. S.						4 d. f. **					
	Affective						Social					
	No. 2		No. 28		No. 11		No. 2		No. 28		No. 11	
	N	%	N	%	N	%	N	%	N	%	N	%
Defintely used	8	14. 0	6	7. 14	8	8. 9	5	8. 8	4	4. 8	1	1. 1
Probably used	42	73. 9	59	70. 2	52	57. 8	41	71. 9	55	65. 5	47	52. 2
Not used	7	12. 3	19	22. 6	30	33. 3	11	19. 3	25	29. 8	40	44. 4
Total	57	100. 0	84	100. 0	90	100. 0	57	100. 0	84	100. 0	90	100. 0
Chi-test	4 d. f. *						4 d. f. **					

Note: * p <. 05; * * p <. 01; N. S. = non-significant.

(8) Correlation Analyses of the Learners' Motivations with Their Use of the Learning Strategies (for the three groups)

Correlation Analysis of Motivations with Learning Strategies for Group A (58 cases) (the low level group)

Variables	MOTL	MINST1	MINST2	MINST3	MINTG1	MINTG2	MINTG3	MINSTRTL	MINTGTL
MEM1	. 0089	. 1473	. 1500	. 0415	. 0581	. 1925	-. 3780 **	. 1675	-. 1309
MEM2	. 2514	. 1873	. 2940 *	. 3326 *	. 3303 *	. 1806	-. 2425	. 3840 **	. 0604
COGN1	. 0711	-. 0799	. 1473	. 1749	. 1935	-. 1139	-. 0698	. 1368	-. 0073
COGN2	. 1185	. 0586	-. 0120	. 1473	. 2127	. 1740	-. 0456	. 0643	. 1293
COMPST1	. 1529	. 2107	. 1049	-. 0329	. 0310	-. 0586	. 2214	. 1312	. 1251
COMPST2	-. 2815 *	. 0334	-. 1560	-. 0509	-. 1987	-. 0516	-. 3887 **	-. 1140	-. 3407 **

Continued

Variables	MOTL	MINST1	MINST2	MINST3	MINTG1	MINTG2	MINTG3	MINSTRTL	MINTGTL
METCOG1	.2352	.0720	.1199	.0844	.2178	.1583	.1565	.1368	.2489
METCOG2	.2396	.1428	.1610	.1662	.1532	.0905	.1405	.2181	.1854
AFFECT1	-.0538	-.1042	-.0517	.0336	.0021	.0211	-.0694	-.0586	-.0332
AFFECT2	.2611*	.0977	.1660	.2854*	.2766*	.0632	.0853	.2490	.1921
SOCIAL1	.1090	.0140	.0103	.0664	.2148	.0232	.0669	.0355	.1394
SOCIAL2	.0325	-.2000	.3037*	-.2498	-.0648	.1570	-.0474	.0515	.0061
MEMORY	.1345	.1906	.2470	.1970	.2065	.2162	-.3671**	.3043*	-.0532
COGNITIVE	.1183	-.0112	.0817	.1995	.2523	.0414	-.0712	.1237	.0777
COMPST	.0034	.2081	.0203	-.0546	-.0677	-.0783	.0141	.0645	-.0505
METACOG	.2832*	.1294	.1682	.1510	.2200	.1470	.1768	.2131	.2577
AFFECT	.1538	.0135	.0886	.2166	.1939	.0551	.0231	.1429	.1165
SOCIAL	.0861	-.1474	.2414	-.1568	.0697	.1348	.0006	.0598	.0826

* $p < .05$ ** $p < .01$ (2-tailed)

Correlation Analysis of Motivations with Learning Strategies for Group B (115 cases) (the average group)

Variables	MOTL	MINST1	MINST2	MINST3	MINTG1	MINTG2	MINTG3	MINSTRTL	MINTGTL
MEM1	.1128	.1137	.0082	.0593	.1557	.1562	.0070	.0677	.1210
MEM2	.1731	.1039	.0256	.1685	.2121*	.0686	.1122	.1165	.1737
COGN1	.2055*	.1247	.0937	.0260	.0873	.2230*	.1955*	.1078	.2352*
COGN2	-.0539	.0502	-.1362	-.1367	.0258	.0600	-.0212	-.1136	.0191
COMPST1	.0482	.0640	.0601	-.1456	-.0187	.0757	.0938	.0007	.0784
COMPST2	.1890*	.1116	.2141*	.0070	.1610	.1996*	.0312	.1650	.1538
METCOG1	.1025	.0171	-.0242	.0403	.0123	.0733	.2113*	.0077	.1609
METCOG2	.1138	.0734	.0086	.0610	.0903	.1016	.1040	.0544	.1353
AFFECT1	.0818	.1261	.0154	-.0372	.0195	.0226	.1339	.0388	.0976
AFFECT2	.2246*	-.0124	.1832*	.0722	.1599	.1532	.2119*	.1289	.2465**
SOCIAL1	.3183**	.0788	.2360*	.0582	.3096**	.2733**	.2098*	.1859*	.3462**
SOCIAL2	.0332	-.0142	.0517	-.0495	.0887	.0263	.0101	.0056	.0493
MEMORY	.1730	.1351	.0198	.1342	.2239*	.1442	.0674	.1109	.1790
COGNITIVE	.0920	.1097	-.0306	-.0727	.0707	.1768	.1070	-.0072	.1577
COMPST	.1495	.1150	.1735	-.1053	.0824	.1766	.0892	.0994	.1512
METACOG	.1334	.0547	-.0104	.0622	.0617	.1074	.1971*	.0373	.1836*
AFFECT	.2085*	.0579	.1428	.0333	.1279	.1245	.2268*	.1153	.2329*
SOCIAL	.1816	.0293	.1535	-.0055	.2159*	.1543	.1114	.0964	.2066*

* $p < .05$ ** $p < .01$ (2-tailed)

Correlation Analysis of Motivations with Learning Strategies for Group C (58 cases) (the top level group)

Variables	MOTL	MINST1	MINST2	MINST3	MINTG1	MINTG2	MINTG3	MINSTRTL	MINTGTL
MEM1	−.0246	−.0426	−.1618	−.0289	.2025	.1832	−.1078	−.1349	.0907
MEM2	.0995	.0000	−.0523	.1538	.2438	.2491	−.1097	.0205	.1334
COGN1	.1110	−.0342	.0127	−.0625	.1471	.1429	.1321	−.0265	.1958
COGN2	.1024	.1304	.0170	.0778	.1311	.2134	−.1110	.0870	.0746
COMPST1	.3050*	.0899	.1237	.1924	.3040*	.3491**	.0460	.1856	.2920*
COMPST2	.0996	−.1072	−.0355	−.0970	.3288*	.2684*	.0115	−.0980	.2463
METCOG1	.0804	−.0438	−.0182	.0318	.1561	.0966	.0649	−.0166	.1393
METCOG2	.2803*	.2172	.2105	.1997	.2090	.2490	−.0568	.2930*	.1517
AFFECT1	.1945	.1239	−.0069	.1209	.2248	.2227	.0642	.0841	.2188
AFFECT2	.2399	.1245	.1472	.0809	.3271*	.3068*	−.0868	.1736	.2033
SOCIAL1	.2175	.1007	.1434	−.0494	.1379	.1229	.2002	.1152	.2246
SOCIAL2	.1922	−.0527	.0524	.0837	.1374	.1740	.2083	.0465	.2510
MEMORY	.0408	−.0260	−.1280	.0685	.2602*	.2514	−.1272	−.0708	.1300
COGNITIVE	.1449	.0604	.0200	.0063	.1890	.2394	.0214	.0376	.1868
COMPST	.3133*	.0125	.0827	.1043	.4464**	.4488**	.0452	.0980	.3881**
METACOG	.2203	.1096	.1202	.1423	.2198	.2103	.0022	.1723	.1745
AFFECT	.2706*	.1530	.0967	.1216	.3467**	.3318*	−.0241	.1647	.2589*
SOCIAL	.2676*	.0105	.1169	.0411	.1821	.2035	.2714*	.0975	.3183*

* $p < .05$　** $p < .01$　(2-tailed)

Appendix 5
Related Results

5.1 List of sample sentences with errors in the WT

Task One (a report about Jordan)

1. He is an America and was born in 1963.
2. I think everybody was know who is Jordan.
3. He joined in a basketball team and take the No. 1 in many baskeball match.
4. at then, he was became a famous player of the basketball.
5. He liked to play basketball very much.
6. Jordan is not more than a good player, he is also a warm-hearted people.
7. ...and he played the basketball since in his childhood.
8. He was like playing basketball very much.
9. He was so fond of basketball match that he won in many matches.
10. It is known that he is borned in American in 1963.
11. In his childhood, he was very liked to play basketball.
12. Here, I produce a great basketball player to you.
13. He was born in negro family.
14. He started to play basketball during university.
15. He like playing basketball and is good at it also.
16. Still in college, he has played basketball and won many matches.
17. He played basketball during he was in university and leaving the university.
18. He started playing basketball during the study course of university.

19. During he study at the university, he was good at play basketball.

20. When he in the university, he play basketball very good.

Task Two (**writing a letter**)

1. So I am very anxious to make a friend with you.
2. Because I can learn many knowledge from you.
3. Do you remember Li Ming, a writing friend of yours in China?
4. Because I like collecting stamps very much, too, I want to make a friend with you.
5. I often hear the talk about you.
6. I studied at No. I middle school.
7. One day Huang Hua talks about you, so I want to make friends with you.
8. He often talks about you.
9. One day, Huang Hua tell me you are his pen friend and live in the United States.
10. One day Wang hua said you was his friend and was fond of collecting stamps.
11. I hear that you are interested in it, aren't you?
12. I've heard that you liked to collecting stamps. So it is with me.
13. The hopeness of a stamps collector is like that.
14. We have the same interesting.
15. One day he refered to you.
16. Let I introduce myself.
17. Hearing there, How glad I were !
18. Huang Hua has ever told me that you was interested in collecting stamps.
19. That will be very interested.
20. I will very happy.

5.2 Results of the Case Analysis

Data from the Experiment for the Three Sampled Subjects

Variables	Mean*	Stubent No. 1	Stubent No. 2	Stubent No. 3
KTTOTL	83. 36	82. 00	85. 00	86. 25
WTKTOTL	53. 99	35. 04	52. 40	62. 89
WTTOTL	59. 63	36. 25	55. 00	71. 25
KTVOCP	92. 93	78. 57	85. 71	98. 21
KTMPHP	88. 97	89. 09	92. 73	94. 55
KTFCTP	70. 82	70. 83	83. 33	75. 00
KTPRONP	60. 15	36. 36	63. 64	45. 45
KTCONTP	86. 30	90. 16	83. 61	86. 89
KTVFSP	73. 87	80. 95	80. 95	80. 95
WTKVOCP	61. 25	53. 66	60. 98	73. 17
WTKMPHP	33. 77	14. 71	38. 24	58. 82
WTKFCTP	58. 79	61. 54	53. 85	57. 69
WTKPRONP	76. 54	54. 55	63. 64	45. 45
WTKCONTP	67. 14	39. 13	65. 22	69. 57
WTKVFSP	41. 77	11. 11	33. 33	55. 56

* The "Mean" refers to the mean scores of the listed variables when all subjects are considered.

Descriptions Based on the Three Students' Responses to the QL

Items	Stubent No. 1	Stubent No. 2	Stubent No. 3
背景	A 组，28 中，男，小学开始学英语，此前从没学过，父母没辅导过	B 组，28 中，男，初中开始学英语，此前从没学过，父母没辅导过	C 组，11 中，女，小学前开始学英语，入学前跟父母学，上学后父母有时辅导
动机	学习动机强烈	学习动机强烈	学习动机强烈
态度	态度非常积极	态度一般	态度非常积极
课外接触英语机会	很少	有一些接触	有一些接触
课外巩固学习方法	记单词、学语法朗读课文，做练习复习课堂笔记，听录音带	记单词、学语法、做练习	记单词、学语法、朗读课文，做练习复习课堂笔记，写日记、作文
学习技巧选用	经常用 "metacognitive strategies" 其它几种偶而用	经常用 "memory" 有时用 "Cognitive", "Metacognitive", "Affect", "Social"	经常用 "memory", "cognitive", "compensation", "metacognitive", "affective" 有时用 "social"
自我评估	什么都不行	语音，词汇，语法，阅读理解	词汇，语法，阅读理解
喜欢的课堂活动	命题写作，听录音	学语法规则，做多项选择题	模拟实际的交际活动，听录音，写作
汉语使用情况	课堂上试着用英语问问题，听说读写时经常借用汉语	课堂上有时用英语，有时用汉语，听说读写时经常借用汉语	课堂上有时用英语，有时用汉语，听、读时很少借助汉语，说、写时经常借助汉语